Capital Mobility and Dis Conflict in Chile, South and Turkey

Why did many emerging countries pursue risky financial opening policies in a reckless manner, even after the painful example of the Latin American debt crisis? Unlike trade liberalization, which has mostly been beneficial in emerging countries, the removal of capital controls has led to boom-bust patterns in many countries. It is not simply driven by class or sectoral interests, nor is it just a result of ideational changes in policy-making circles, or international pressure. Gemici argues that to fully understand the motivation for these policies, we need to take into account distributional struggles prior to their enactment.

In this book, Gemici shows that conflictual distribution relations significantly increase the likelihood of capital account liberalization. Through in-depth comparative case studies, he also demonstrates that countries which liberalize in the most comprehensive manner tend to be the countries characterized by a high degree of distributional conflict. The case studies—Argentina, Chile, South Korea, and Turkey—have been chosen to maximize variation in distribution relations and to escape regional clustering, showing quite different trajectories of capital account liberalization.

This will be of great interest to readers in sociology, international political economy and heterodox economics, as well as specialists on the countries examined.

Kurtuluş Gemici is One Hundred Talent Associate Professor of Sociology at Zhejiang University, China.

Routledge Studies in Development Economics

147 **Unlocking SME Finance in Asia**
Roles of Credit Rating and Credit Guarantee Schemes
Edited by Naoyuki Yoshino and Farhad Taghizadeh-Hesary

148 **Full and Productive Employment in Developing Economies**
Towards the Sustainable Development Goals
Rizwanul Islam

149 **Information and Communication Technologies for Development Evaluation**
Edited by Oscar A. García and Prashanth Kotturi

150 **Rent Seeking and Development**
The Political Economy of Industrialization in Vietnam
Authored by Christine Ngoc Ngo

151 **Capital Mobility and Distributional Conflict in Chile, South Korea, and Turkey**
Kurtuluş Gemici

152 **Cooperation Networks and Economic Development**
Cuba's High-Tech Potential
Andrés Cárdenas O'Farrill

153 **Undernutrition, Agriculture and Public Provisioning**
The Impact on Women and Children in India
Edited by Swarna Sadasivam Vepa and Brinda Viswanathan

154 **Gender, Poverty and Access to Justice**
Policy Implementation in Sub-Saharan Africa
Edited by David Lawson, Adam Dubin and Lea Mwambene

For more information about this series, please visit www.routledge.com/series/SE0266

Capital Mobility and Distributional Conflict in Chile, South Korea, and Turkey

Kurtuluş Gemici

Routledge
Taylor & Francis Group
LONDON AND NEW YORK

First published 2020 by Routledge

2 Park Square, Milton Park, Abingdon, Oxon OX14 4RN
605 Third Avenue, New York, NY 10017

Routledge is an imprint of the Taylor & Francis Group, an informa business

First issued in paperback 2022

Publisher's Note

The publisher has gone to great lengths to ensure the quality of this reprint but points out that some imperfections in the original copies may be apparent.

British Library Cataloguing-in-Publication Data
A catalogue record for this book is available from the British Library

Library of Congress Cataloging-in-Publication Data
Names: Gemici, Kurtuluş, author.
Title: Capital mobility and distributional conflict in Chile, South Korea, and Turkey / Kurtuluş Gemici.
Description: First Edition. | New York : Routledge, 2020. | Series: Routledge studies in development economics | Includes bibliographical references and index.
Identifiers: LCCN 2019056446 (print) | LCCN 2019056447 (ebook) | ISBN 9781138386488 (hardback) | ISBN 9780429426803 (ebook)
Subjects: LCSH: Capital movements–Chile. | Capital movements–Korea (South). | Capital movements–Turkey. | Free trade. | Distribution (Economic theory) | Chile–Economic conditions–1988- Classification: LCC HG3891 .G466 2020 (print) | LCC HG3891 (ebook) | DDC 332/.0424–dc23
LC record available at https://lccn.loc.gov/2019056446
LC ebook record available at https://lccn.loc.gov/2019056447

ISBN: 978-1-138-38648-8 (hbk)
ISBN: 978-1-03-233624-4 (pbk)
DOI: 10.4324/9780429426803

Typeset in Galliard
by codeMantra

Sevgili annem ve babama...

Contents

Figures

Tables

Preface

Coming of age in the 1980s and 1990s of Turkey meant growing up with market reforms, a vague yet incessant ideological propaganda on how the country was changing for the better, and rising inequality in the midst of all the abundance that a market economy offers. A massive economic crisis in 1994 made the contradictions of economic liberalization and market economy much more poignant for me. When another, and even harsher, economic crisis occurred in 2001, I made my mind up that understanding the why of these repeated crises and of the unmistakable transformations that shaped my childhood and teenage years was more pressing than other pursuits. Since then I have been writing about the market economy, inequality, and structural transformations. But, perhaps because the topic at hand required a much closer look at the crucial decades of the 1970s, 1980s, and 1990s, this book gave me the best opportunity to go back to the initial curiosities that shaped my intellectual pursuits. Hence, this is simultaneously an academic and a personal book. It is academic in the sense that it is a systematic and rigorous (one hopes!) comparative-historical examination of the origins of international capital mobility in emerging economies. It is personal in that the causal narratives I offer in this book make me grasp my personal history by situating it on the canvas of much broader structural transformations.

A book that covers many countries and decades does not write itself. Nor can it be entirely the work of a single individual. Over the years, I have benefited from the generosity of countless mentors and friends. In particular, I am deeply grateful to the following people for making this book possible: Michael Mann, Bill Roy, David Lopez, Greta Krippner, Bob Brenner, Perry Anderson, Fred Block, Didem Buner, Belma Aral, Enrique Accorsi Opazo, Matías Folatre, Gabrielle Raley, Robert Jansen, Rahul Mukherji, Qiushi Feng, Manjusha Nair, Claire Lee, Barış Büyükokutan, Şevket Pamuk, Charmelia Sugianto, and Georgios Piliouras. I have also benefited from the feedback on parts of this book that have been presented at various talks at UCLA, Koç University, Sabancı University, London School of Economics, University of Wisconsin Madison, National University of Singapore, Zhejiang University, and Max Planck Institute for the Study of Societies. Needless to say, the usual disclaimer applies.

A shorter version of Chapter 4 was published in *New Perspectives on Turkey* ("Rushing toward Currency Convertibility," 2012, vol. 47, pp. 33–55), and some of the data and arguments in Chapter 3 have been used in my contribution to *A Tale of Two Crises*, edited by Seetharam Kallidaikurichi ("Social Origins of Financial Crises," 2012, pp. 25–42). I thank Cambridge University Press and Taylor & Francis for the permission to use this material.

My parents have supported the writing of this book in countless ways. In particular, the logistics of my research while in Turkey would have been quite difficult without their help. In addition, both my parents have encouraged me to write this book—I can hear them saying "it's a crucial issue!"—and listened to my arguments patiently. My sister, Ahu Gemici, answered all my questions on statistics, data sources, and economics with the wisdom of a veteran labor economist and a master econometrician. She also endured the rather unenviable task of reading the early drafts of this book. Nina read countless drafts of this book with the sharp eye of a lawyer. I am grateful for their unwavering support, which was crucial in finishing a research project that involved many countries and many years.

1 Introduction

Distribution relations and capital mobility

On December 18, 2006, the recently installed military government in Thailand announced its plan to implement controls on capital inflows, effective the next day.[1] An unpleasant chain of events followed the Thai government's announcement of capital controls. Within one day, Bangkok's SET index dropped by 15 percent, and the Thai markets showed signs of financial crisis. The Thai administration revoked capital controls on December 19, in a move the *Financial Times* called "an astonishing retreat" and "a new record in short-lived economic strategies."[2] Within two days, the Thai government learned the bitter lesson that hot money can leave almost as easily as it comes and that the economic consequences of its mass flight are perilous.

Perhaps, the Thai authorities were "intent on committing financial hara-kiri," as suggested by a financial expert on the Asia-Pacific markets.[3] The real reason was the fact that the *baht* rose to levels unseen since the Asian financial crisis.[4] Such appreciation hurt Thai exports and was a major source of economic concern for the Thai government.[5] The objective of the government was made clear by the Thai finance minister, Pridiyathorn Devakula, who called the controls "a historic effort to counter speculative pressure on the baht."[6]

In hindsight, it is easy to recognize how hazardous the Thai authorities' intervention into financial markets was. At the time, it was estimated that foreign investors owned 30 percent of the Thai stock market, in stocks worth $50bn.[7] The amount of foreign investment that entered Thailand until December 2006 was estimated to be around $13bn.[8] Obviously, under such circumstances, any macroeconomic decision that prompts foreign investors to leave is a dangerous bargain.

1 "Thailand acts to aid its currency," *The International Herald Tribune*, December 19, 2006. The control was a 30 percent unrenumerated reserve requirement on new foreign currency deposits, similar to the Chilean *encaje* of the early 1990s.
2 "Thailand retreats on investment controls," December 20, 2006.
3 "Thailand retreats on investment controls," *Financial Times*, December 20, 2006.
4 "Baht will hurt export targets," *The Nation (Thailand)*, December 18, 2006.
5 "A Government haunted by 1997 panicked into protecting the baht," *The Times (London)*, December 20, 2006.
6 "Thais put baht under tight capital controls," *Financial Times*, December 19, 2006.
7 "Thailand retreats on investment controls," *Financial Times*, December 20, 2006.
8 "Thai U-turn amid fears of meltdown in Asia," *The Guardian*, December 20, 2006.

Yet, in virtually all emerging economies, hot money—money that can come and go with ease, money that is fluid and dynamic—reached record amounts in the 1990s and 2000s. Hence, it is no wonder that, in the days following the Thai debacle, the Korean deputy Finance Minister Kim Sung-jin preventively announced that "Seoul has unlimited resources to bring currency stability." Similarly, Rhee Yeung-kyun, the Assistant Governor of the Central Bank of Korea, announced that "The Bank of Korea won't take any 'artificial' measures such as capital controls to help curb appreciation in the won."[9] With $234bn in foreign currency reserves, the Korean economy was much sounder and stronger than the Thai economy, but there was no point in stirring up trouble.[10]

Thailand's botched attempt to introduce capital controls underlines the severe constraints and risks imposed by the free mobility of capital across national borders. In this book, I examine how international capital mobility was deregulated in emerging economies. I argue that distribution relations played a fundamental role in bringing about the free flow of capital across the borders of emerging economies. Freedom of capital mobility was most perilous when portfolio and debt flows, which often amounted to funds that are oriented toward short-term gains, were among the types of capital flows that got liberalized. This book shows that such a liberalization trajectory ended up being disastrous for emerging economies and that conflictual distribution relations paved the way for this type of risky liberalization.

Which type of capital mobility?

A globalized international financial system with high degree of capital mobility embodied a momentous sea change in the international economy. To understand why, we need to briefly delve into the history of capital flows since the end of the nineteenth century.

Orthodox liberalism characterized the world economy between 1870s and 1914. Its two economic pillars were the gold standard and the self-regulating market (Polanyi, 2001 [1944]). Under the gold standard, the value of a national currency was fixed to a certain amount of gold: economic actors could convert their currency assets into gold at a fixed, predetermined rate as long as the gold reserves of the monetary authority were sufficient. The rates of exchange among national currencies were fixed, and the flow of gold among nations served as the adjustment mechanism if a currency became over- or under-appreciated.

The interwar world economic order stood in stark opposition to the international economic cooperation of the nineteenth century. After the First World War, for a brief period of time, exchange rates floated with no gold convertibility and no controls on international capital flows (Eichengreen, 1996). This resulted in grave economic consequences: capital flows—largely of speculative

9 "Seoul has 'unlimited' resources to bring currency stability," *The Korea Herald*, December 23, 2006.

10 "Disarray in Thailand as stocks and baht fall; Government tries to win back markets," *The International Herald Tribune*, December 22, 2006.

nature—exacerbated the existing imbalances rather than acting as an adjustment mechanism (Bernanke, 1993; Nurkse, 1944). Partially as a response to the failing Gold Standard, the international monetary system was reestablished in the second half of the 1920s in a hybrid form, the Gold-Exchange Standard, where countries held their reserves both in gold and foreign exchanges that could be converted into gold (e.g., sterling). The Gold-Exchange Standard lacked the international cooperation necessary for its smooth functioning and was plagued by inherent instabilities (Eichengreen, 1996). It collapsed with the Great Depression, which led to national autarky and protectionism in the world economy.

The postwar economic order established at the Bretton-Woods conference reflected the painful experiences of the interwar period and opted for "embedded liberalism," a compromise between market forces, international economic cooperation, regulation, and interventionism in economic governance (Ruggie, 1983, 209). The architects of the Bretton-Woods system viewed the free flow of capital across nations as dangerous and undesirable (as opposed to the Gold Standard, which, in theory, treated capital flows as an adjustment mechanism); they rejected capital account convertibility and allowed controls on capital flows (Block, 1977; Helleiner, 1994). Exchange rates were fixed to the U.S. dollar, the reserve currency, which was convertible to gold at a fixed rate. The International Monetary Fund (IMF) was established to provide international liquidity and oversee balance of payments problems (Hirschman, 1980). The Bretton-Woods system embraced economic interventionism. In advanced industrialized countries, this took the form of the state assuming the role of Keynesian demand management, active involvement in areas where markets failed, and provision of social welfare services. In developing countries, disbelief in market forces led to import substitution industrialization (ISI) enabled by protectionist trade measures (Toye, 2003).

The Bretton-Woods system was a success in terms of international stability (Mann, 2012, 136–41), but it faced tensions arising from increasing international competition, mounting U.S. deficits, and the rise of Eurodollar markets (Block, 1977; Helleiner, 1994; Wandschneider, 2008; Germann, 2013). These increasing pressures led to its collapse and to the emergence of a new international financial system where exchange rates of major countries floated against each other. The collapse of the Bretton-Woods system marked a turning point; the last three decades of the twentieth century saw the rise of neoliberalism, a series of significant transformations in the social and economic structure of developed and developing countries, where the pendulum—once again—swung toward market rationality and a curtailed role of the state in economic life (Harvey, 2005; Fourcade-Gourinchas and Babb, 2002).

The painful experiences of the past were forgotten in the 1980s and 1990s (Abdelal, 2007). Thus, capital account liberalization and the mobility of capital became the new norm and accepted wisdom. (Capital account liberalization—financial opening—is the removal of restrictions on the movement of liquid capital assets into and out of a country. Full capital account liberalization, i.e., capital account convertibility, implies no restrictions on the purchase of capital assets

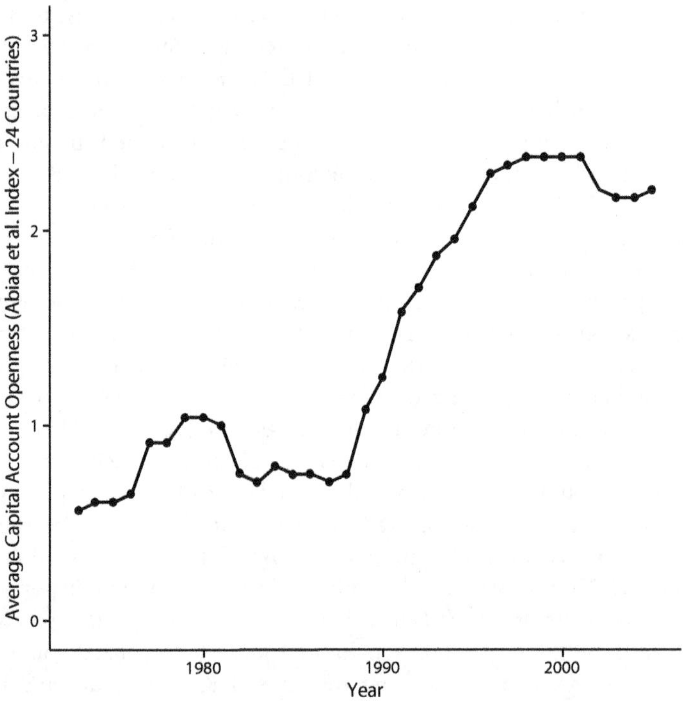

Figure 1.1 Average Capital Account Openness in 24 Emerging Countries, 1973–2005.
Source: Abiad et al. (2010).

abroad by residents of the country and on the purchase of domestic capital assets by foreign nationals. As such, it leads to the financial integration of a country with the rest of the world.) In most developing and emerging countries, controls on international capital transactions were effective until the second half of the 1980s (some minor partial liberalization measures notwithstanding). After this date, one country after another began the removal of capital controls that culminated in a substantial level of financial openness and integration with the world by the end of the 1990s (Kaminsky and Schmukler, 2003; Miniane, 2004; Williamson and Mahar, 1998). As can be seen in Figure 1.1, by the end of the 1990s, a substantial majority of emerging countries took a long and difficult series of reforms culminating in open financial markets (Abiad et al., 2010; Miniane, 2004; Williamson and Mahar, 1998).[11]

11 Calculations for this set of countries are based on the capital account liberalization measures developed by Abiad et al. (2010). Higher values indicate greater capital account openness. See Appendix D for a discussion of measuring capital account openness and a comparison between available measures. Countries in this set are: Argentina, Brazil, Chile, China, Colombia, Egypt, India, Indonesia, Israel, Jordan, Malaysia, Mexico, Morocco, Pakistan, Peru, Philippines, South Africa, South Korea, Sri Lanka, Taiwan, Thailand, Turkey, Venezuela, and Zimbabwe.

However, the steady march toward capital account liberalization evident in the overall trend hides that there is significant variation in the timing and type of capital account liberalization emerging countries pursued. Figure 1.2 presents the trajectory and scope of capital account liberalization in 24 emerging countries between 1973 and 2005. As can be seen in this figure, while the majority of these 24 countries moved toward greater financial openness over time, the timing of the reforms varied considerably. Furthermore, while some countries like Argentina and Turkey liberalized both capital inflows and outflows at a rapid pace in the early 1990s, this is far from the norm among emerging countries. For instance, Brazil, Chile, India, and Taiwan were gradual in their approach to capital account liberalization. These countries eschewed rapid opening of their capital account and were selective in the type of capital movements that they allowed.

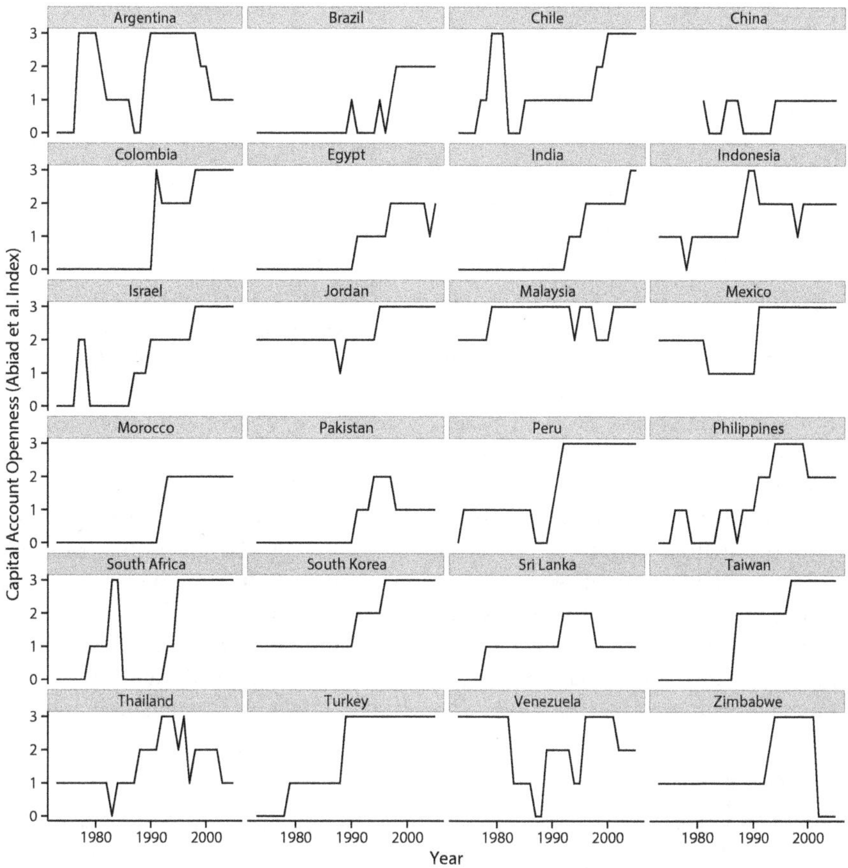

Figure 1.2 Trajectory of Capital Account Liberalization in 24 Emerging Countries, 1973–2005.
Source: Abiad et al. (2010).

Both the timing and the type of capital account liberalization are crucial in understanding the effects of financial opening on emerging countries (Kaminsky and Schmukler, 2008). Financial opening pursued when the global financial markets are awash in liquid capital is much more likely to lead to greater financial integration with the rest of the world compared to financial opening at a period of scarce liquidity.[12] The type of capital account liberalization that an emerging country pursues might be even more consequential than its timing. Studies show that foreign direct investment, debt flows, and portfolio investment have vastly different impacts on emerging countries (Bosworth et al., 1999; Köse et al., 2009). In particular, only foreign direct investment is associated with welfare-enhancing productivity gains, whereas portfolio investment and debt flows such as syndicated bank loans have a tendency to boost consumption rather than production (Grabel, 1996). Such use of funds borrowed from the rest of the world often makes developing and emerging countries more indebted. Furthermore, there is compelling evidence that relying on debt flows leads to financial fragility (Angkinand et al., 2010; Kaminsky and Schmukler, 2008; Bosworth et al., 1999; Prasad et al., 2007).

While there is a voluminous literature on capital account liberalization, the majority of existing studies on the politics of capital account liberalization do not differentiate between different styles of financial opening. As a result, there are relatively few studies that explicitly aim to explain the timing and the type of capital account liberalization (Lukauskas and Minushkin, 2000; Brooks, 2004; Brooks and Kurtz, 2012; Shambaugh, 2004). In this book, I aim to explain how and why policies concerning hot and cold money are adopted in emerging economies. I focus on emerging economies because these countries have been the largest recipients of capital from the rest of the world since the 1990s. Unlike trade liberalization, which has been beneficial to many emerging countries, financial opening has been a classic case of over-promise and under-delivery for this set of countries. International financial institutions and the mainstream economic thinking promoted capital account liberalization as a crucial component of neoliberal development based on the promise that channeling funds from the mature capitalist economies to developing and emerging countries would result in more efficient use of capital (Abdelal, 2007; Chwieroth, 2007; Williamson, ed, 1994). In contrast to such promise, there is overwhelming evidence that financial opening has led to boom-bust patterns in many emerging countries (Bussiere and Fratzscher, 2008; Kaminsky and Reinhart, 1999; Kaminsky and Schmukler, 2008; Köse et al., 2009).[13] The financial fragility

12 Global liquidity can be measured with reference to the money supply of key advanced economies (Forbes and Warnock, 2012).

13 There is a large literature on the relationship between financial opening and economic growth. Most of the studies in this literature rely on panel data analysis by using *de jure* and *de facto* measures of financial liberalization. These studies face several limitations arising from the nature of cross-country data and severe endogeneity problems (Obstfeld, 2009; Rodrik and Subramanian, 2009). (See Appendix D for a discussion of different measures of financial liberalization and their limitations.) Even if one takes the findings arising from this literature seriously, the results reported are either inconclusive or quite weak, as the meta-analysis conducted by Bumann et al. (2013) shows.

that followed capital account liberalization was closely related to the type of capital inflows a country received in the aftermath of financial opening. Many emerging countries that liberalized debt and portfolio inflows in the 1980s and the 1990s have experienced financial instability, if not currency or banking crises (Obstfeld, 2009; Rodrik and Subramanian, 2009). What was surprising is that the wave of financial opening came after the painful experience of the Latin American debt crisis and a history of capital movements that clearly indicated the significant risks capital account liberalization carried. That is the conundrum I aim to address in this book; my goal is to understand why many emerging countries pursued risky financial opening policies in a reckless manner and exposed their economies to the worst vagaries of international financial markets.

In contradistinction to the existing studies on the topic, I suggest that capital account liberalization—and, in particular the timing, depth, and scope of reforms affecting capital mobility—can be explained only by taking into account distributional struggles prior to enactment of reforms. Capital account liberalization is not simply driven by class or sectoral interests. Nor is it just a result of ideational changes in policy-making circles. Furthermore, reforms on capital mobility cannot be understood solely with reference to international pressures and diffusion of ideas. All of these factors, repeatedly stressed in the existing literature, play a role in capital account liberalization in emerging economies. However, they are not sufficient in understanding the significant variation in the timing and scope of capital account liberalization in emerging economies. That is because these explanations ignore the distribution relations that fundamentally shape the capital account liberalization process. In this book, I start from a theoretical framework that conceptualizes every economic relation and macroeconomic variable—from wage-labor to interest rates—as distribution-laden. Such an assumption has far-reaching implications for understanding institutional change. In particular, I argue that conflictual distribution relations significantly increase the likelihood of capital account liberalization in emerging countries. Furthermore, countries that liberalize in the most reckless and comprehensive manner are also likely to be the countries characterized by a high degree of distributional conflict. That is not an accident. Conflictual distribution relations erode institutions and alter the balance of power that reinforce existing institutional arrangements. In addition, distributional conflict provides strong incentives to social groups and power-holders to refashion the existing institutions pertaining to capital account. Given that "importing" capital from the rest of the world can significantly alter the growth patterns in an emerging economy, such pressures and incentives are often consequential. In what follows, I develop these arguments through a critique of the existing approaches to capital account liberalization.

In contrast to such inconclusive results, the relationship between financial opening and financial fragility is robust (Köse et al., 2009; Rodrik and Subramanian, 2009).

Explaining capital account liberalization

Studies aiming to explain capital account liberalization fall into three broad approaches.[14] The first approach consists of works emphasizing domestic preferences as the most important causal determinant of capital account liberalization. The second approach comprises studies concerned with ideas, norms, and values that shape the capital account liberalization process. The third approach involves analyses of how capital account liberalization policies spread around the world through social construction, learning, coercion, and competition. As can be seen, the analytical motivation of these three approaches are somewhat different. While the first two approaches are concerned primarily with which social factors cause policy change, the third approach focuses also on whether the source of institutional change lies in the domestic or international political economy.

Studies that emphasize domestic preferences portray the policy-making process as shaped by the interests of various groups in society, which are assumed to be sensitive to the distributional implications of capital account liberalization (Frieden, 1991b; Rogowski, 1989). While these studies unite in investigating capital account policies based on social actors' expected gains and losses (Frieden, 1991b, 426), there is diversity in the conceptualization of external liberalization's distributional implications. Such diversity follows from the sensitivity of the analysis to the underlying economic model. Simply put, one can reach quite different implications depending on the economic model used to theorize different actors' gains and losses from capital account liberalization. For instance, studies adhering to a class-analytical framework focus largely on how different segments of the capitalist class are affected by the external liberalization process. Quite distinct from such an analysis, most political scientists follow Frieden's specific-factors model, where the analytical emphasis is on sectoral interests (1991b).[15] In recent years, political scientists embraced a new version of this line of thought inspired by the Mundell-Fleming model—open economy politics (Fleming, 1962; Lake, 2009; Mundell, 1960, 1962, 1963; Frenkel and Razin, 1987). Open economy politics, while economically more sophisticated, share the same drawbacks with the earlier approaches (Chwieroth and Sinclair, 2013; Oatley, 2011).

As opposed to studies that take preferences as given, the second approach rests on the recognition that preferences are themselves constructed through ideas, beliefs, and norms. Building on a voluminous literature on the relationship

14 Chwieroth and Sinclair (2013) offer a more comprehensive typology of different schools of thought on international capital mobility. They distinguish between explanations that rely on class antagonism, position in the world economy, market forces, technological change, open economy politics, power, policy diffusion, ideas, structural constructivism, and agent-centered social facts. While such a typology is useful in deciphering the vast scholarly literature on international capital mobility, it offers less analytical value on understanding policy reform and thus the origins of capital account liberalization in emerging economies. For instance, it is hard to find convincing explanations of policy reform that emphasize market forces, technological change, or position in the world economy. Such explanations offer, at best, very partial accounts of the origins of financial opening in developing and emerging countries. For this reason, I rely on a three-pronged classification of the existing literature.

15 See Appendix B for a detailed discussion of these models and the framework I employ to examine class and sectoral interests.

between ideas and economic policy (Berman, 1998; Blyth, 2007, 2002; Campbell, 1998, 2002; Abdelal, 2007; Chwieroth, 2010a,b, 2008, 2007; Haas, 1992; Hall, 1989; Weir and Skocpol, 1985; Rueschemeyer and Skocpol, eds, 1996), such a recognition leads to a research program that focuses on "the endogenous construction of new intersubjective beliefs that necessitate change" (Chwieroth, 2010b, 496). The causal mechanism highlighted by the constructivist approach is the role of ideational carriers who deploy their ideas as "blueprints for new institutions" (Blyth, 2002, 11).[16] In the context of capital account liberalization, the constructivist perspective highlights how the options that policy-makers perceive as appropriate are sensitive to their interpretations of international capital mobility and the effectiveness of capital controls (Chwieroth and Sinclair, 2013, 474–76).

The third approach does not necessarily commit to an objectivist or ideational causal analysis. Rather, it stresses that capital account policies are conditioned by transformations that occur outside the national boundaries of the country under investigation. Instead of locating the source of policy change in the domestic political economy, these studies emphasize the diffusion of policies across countries. Several factors play a role in the diffusion of policies across countries. Dobbin et al. (2007) distinguish four families of causal mechanisms: social construction, learning, coercion, and competition. Social construction perspectives in diffusion studies have much in common with the constructivist approach discussed above. However, diffusion studies inspired by constructivism are analytically distinct. That is because the central claim in these studies is that ideas, norms, and ideational carriers that shape policy change are closely linked to external actors and organizations (Kogut and Macpherson, 2011; Quinn and Toyoda, 2007; Chwieroth, 2007). Learning, as a causal mechanism, also highlights the role of ideas, but here the focus is on how policy-makers update their beliefs based on new evidence emerging from the experiences of their peers and competitors. This mechanism of diffusion rests on the idea that spread of policies is driven by rational actors evaluating and adjusting their policies by observing the experiences of other countries with capital account liberalization. Modeling policy diffusion as a learning process—which occurs both at the level of how to achieve certain objectives and which objectives to pursue at the first place—has a distinguished history in political science (Dobbin et al., 2007; Hall, 1993). The best studies in this literature offer rigorous accounts of financial liberalization without exaggerating the analytical power of this particular mechanism (Meseguer, 2009; Meseguer and Gilardi, 2009; Meseguer, 2005; Weyland, 2007). Coercion, in contrast to the deliberate process of learning, emphasizes power asymmetries shaping the spread of external liberalization policies.[17] Some commonly cited

16 As argued persuasively by many scholars, the causal weight of this mechanism is high in particular during times of rapid change and crises (Blyth, 2002; Chwieroth, 2010a; Widmaier et al., 2007).

17 Coercion is an unfortunate name for this mechanism, as it connotes the use of brute force or negative sanctions to override the will of another actor (Weber, 1978, 53–54).

causes of such power asymmetries are the IMF (International Monetary Fund) conditionality, the OECD (Organisation for Economic Co-operation and Development) pressure, and the hegemonic influence of the United States over developing countries (Moschella, 2012; Mukherjee and Singer, 2010; Howarth and Sadeh, 2011; Chorev and Babb, 2009; Babb, 2013; Simmons et al., 2006). Competition portrays the spread of liberalization policies as an outcome of developing and emerging countries aiming to attract financial funds from the global pool of capital (Bartolini and Drazen, 1997). A good illustration of this causal mechanism of diffusion is Simmons and Elkins's explanation of the spread of capital account liberalization policies (2004). Their key insight is that the market for foreign funds among emerging economies is competitive. The adoption of liberalization reforms by one country reduces the foreign funds available to other countries, because capital account liberalization reduces the cost of investing in a country.

These three families of explanations on capital account liberalization are not mutually exclusive, despite some acrimonious debates in the literature. While the open economy politics school is strong in delineating how international capital mobility is related to domestic interests, the heavy reliance on orthodox economic theory to predict how social groups act makes it vulnerable to various criticisms leveled against methodological individualism. In addition, the predictions derived from such models are highly sensitive to assumptions and parameterization employed in constructing the models. Constructivists, by showing how interests and policies emerge from ideas and norms, provide a welcome correction to the open economy politics perspective. However, constructivists have a tendency to miss the path-dependence and inertia of existing policy frameworks. This danger is particularly pronounced in the case of a strong constructivist program such as the one suggested by Chwieroth and Sinclair (2013). Constructivism has a valid emphasis on how every institution is, ultimately, a social construction. But such an emphasis is blind to the fact that both social structures and institutions are often "hard" social facts, constraining social action and limiting the choices available to institutional carriers. Policy diffusion studies, compared to the open economy politics models and constructivism, are strong in escaping methodological nationalism. However, here the danger lies in exaggerating the impact of international diffusion. Diffusion explanations, while strong in explaining a trend common to many cases, have to rely on *ad hoc* variables in accounting for variation in capital account policies across cases.

These weaknesses in the existing literature are not accidental. To the contrary, it can be shown that the blind spots of the existing literature on capital account liberalization are closely related to a view of institutional change that has little recognition of power dynamics and conflict between social actors. This omission is particularly noteworthy in the light of a recent and compelling body of literature in political sociology and historical institutionalism in political science, which shows that liberal reforms and neoliberalism as an ideology have their roots in distributional struggles (Fourcade-Gourinchas and Babb, 2002; Thelen, 2012; Streeck and Thelen, 2005; Alderson and Nielsen, 2002; Chorev, 2010; Gemici,

2016; Kristal, 2010; Hung and Thompson, 2016; Prasad, 2006, 2012; Krippner, 2011).[18] This growing body of scholarly research shows that distributional struggles over the welfare state, social security, taxation, and housing fundamentally shaped both the timing and nature of neoliberal reforms. For instance, in an influential article on the trajectory of neoliberal reforms in Britain, Chile, France, and Mexico, Fourcade-Gourinchas and Babb (2002, 539) argue that "differences in the ability to mediate distributional conflicts and control inflation affected not only the *timing* of neoliberal transitions, but also their *qualitative* nature" [original emphasis]. Hence, if one agrees with the findings of this emerging literature, we should expect distributional struggles to structure the timing and nature of capital account liberalization reforms as well.

Below, I will illustrate the strengths and weaknesses of the existing approaches vis-à-vis an explanatory framework that focuses on distributional struggles through a telegraphic account of economic reforms in Argentina during the early 1990s. The examination of the Argentinian case shall provide practical pointers for improving on the existing explanations of capital account liberalization.

Currency convertibility in Argentina

In April 1991, Domingo Cavallo, the freshly appointed minister of the economy, announced a novel plan to combat hyperinflation in Argentina. Cavallo's plan abandoned the ill-fated *austral* as legal tender and went back to *peso* (Lewis, 2002; Romero, 2002). This plan, implemented through the Convertibility Law, fixed the *peso* "on par to the U.S. dollar" (Brown, 2010, 266). After several failed monetary stabilization attempts in the 1980s, Cavallo's plan was radical because it reduced the Central Bank to a currency board that had little control over the money supply (Hedges, 2011, 254). It was drastic because, as Veigel (2009, 179) notes, the Convertibility Law had the effect of "eliminating independent monetary policy" in Argentina. To put it simply, all domestic currency had to be "fully backed by foreign exchange reserves" under the new system (Veigel, 2009, 179). The law also implied, by definition, a virtually complete capital account liberalization, as reflected in Figure 1.2 (Armijo and Faucher, 2002; Starr, 1997).

There can be, and has been, explanations of Argentine capital account liberalization that adhere fairly closely to the three schools of thought outlined in the previous section. The existing studies remark that the Argentine turn to neoliberalism and policies of openness started under the military regime after the 1976 coup. Furthermore, the gradual reforms continued under the Alfonsín presidency during the 1980s and received impetus from the exigencies of the debt crisis. However, the real turning point came in 1991, two years into the Menem presidency, with the Convertibility Law.

One common explanation of the Cavallo plan and the ensuing financial internationalization combines an interest-based approach focusing on policy preferences

18 See also Rodrik (1996) for an early formulation on the link between distributional struggles and policy reform.

of particular social groups with a framework attentive to political power. Such a perspective puts a heavy emphasis on the role of *grupos económicos*–the large, oligarchic, and international segment of the Argentine capitalist class (Teubal, 2004; O'Donnell, 1978; Frieden, 1991a). There are three reasons for taking this perspective seriously. First, starting in the late 1950s and intensifying under the military regime in the late 1970s, *grupos económicos* with substantial connections to international capital and finance increased their weight in the Argentine economy (Romero, 2002, 221). Second, as O'Donnell (1978) observes in a classic article on the Argentine political economy, this segment of the capitalist class had the means for and a history of benefiting from openness to international capital. Third, there is sufficient evidence to show that the politicians and technocrats who implemented the policies under question had tangible connections to *grupos económicos* and other actors in the capitalist class with an international orientation. This is all too apparent for José Alfredo Martínez de Hoz, the minister of the economy under the military regime, who came from a landed family and was "the president of the largest private steel company" prior to his role in the brutal military rule in the late 1970s (Lewis, 2002, 149). Likewise, Carlos Menem chose his first two ministers of the economy from the executives of *Bunge y Born*, an iconic representative of big business in Argentina (Carranza, 2005, 67). Menem's fourth minister of the economy, Cavallo—an economist with a Ph.D. from Harvard—had started his career in the think tank *Fundación Mediterránea*, which was financed by a group of capitalists from Córdoba (Teichman, 1997, 35).

That being said, it would be a mistake to ignore the role of ideas and economic doctrines in the Argentine currency convertibility episode. First of all, the convertibility plan was the brainchild of Domingo Cavallo—a technocrat with impeccable neoliberal and monetarist credentials—who was clearly inspired by an idealized conceptualization of the gold standard—a historical episode that continues to inspire orthodox economic thinking (Lewis, 2002, 162).[19] Second, Cavallo was surrounded by a cohesive, like-minded, and similarly trained group of technocrats, who virtually monopolized economic policy-making between 1991 and 1996 in Argentina (Teichman, 1997; Huneeus, 1998; Williams, 2002). Third, as documented by Teichman (1997), the Argentine hyperinflation and economic chaos in the late 1980s and the early 1990s led Menem to desperately seek for new ideas to fix the economy. Such extreme uncertainty and search for policy solutions are hallmarks of constructivist explanations and strong predictors of ideational change in the policy sphere (Hall, 1989; Blyth, 2002).

Although explanations emphasizing diffusion are relatively scarce in the literature on the Argentine case, several students of the Argentine political economy have highlighted the role of the IMF, the U.S. Treasury, and the spread of ideas from the U.S. universities to Argentine policy circles (Teubal, 2004; Teichman, 1997; Veigel, 2009). For instance, by using archival sources,

19 The Gold Standard in the monetarist imagination and in reality are fairly different economic systems. See Polanyi (2001 [1944]), Eichengreen and Flandreau (1996), De Cecco (1996), and Flandreau and Jobst (2005) for extended analyses.

Veigel (2009, 149–71) documents how debt negotiations and the necessity to secure the support of the IMF and the U.S. Treasury shaped the gradual turn to neoliberalism in Argentina. Furthermore, the ground for such a conversion was partially laid during the military regime, a period in which many future politicians and technocrats escaped the repressive rule by pursuing postgraduate education in the United States (Teichman, 1997). As Teichman (1997, 36) argues, "many of these people returned with graduate degrees and with new ideas about the necessity of economic reform."

Despite various merits, all of these explanations of the Argentine case are partial; they can be misleading if given too much causal weight. They glaringly omit the defining characteristic of the Argentine political economy since the 1930s: the cycles of distributional conflict with varying intensity. As admirably analyzed by O'Donnell (1978), recurring distributional conflicts in Argentina had their root cause in the distinct integration of Argentina into the world economy. In Argentina, a highly productive and export-oriented agrarian sector—owned and operated by a domestic agrarian bourgeoisie—produced wealth and urbanization that were much more advanced than comparable cases in Latin America. However, the fact that crucial wage-goods such as beef and cereal were also the main export items of the Argentine economy led to complex alliances between the different segments of the capitalist class and the popular classes. Given that the private and public workers in Argentina were well-organized and that various social groups could easily penetrate the state intensified the distributional conflict over the prices of wage-goods, protection of the domestic market, inflation rate, wages, and profits. These structural and political constraints led to recurring episodes of high inflation and balance of payments crises in the period after World War II (Lewis, 2002, 147).

What was distinctive in the Argentine case is that no stable alliance or hegemonic political project could overcome occasionally sharp distributional conflicts for an extended period of time. This was partly a result of the shifting loyalties of the large capitalists, who allied with the agrarian bourgeoisie when balance of payment problems intensified but gave their support to urban bourgeoisie when recessionary policies were implemented (O'Donnell, 1978). Furthermore, the Argentine military, through multiple coups, repeatedly became a party to the economic and political conflicts. Although the military was sympathetic to large business interests, it also contained branches and officers with strong statist orientation. However, the intense distributional conflicts in the 1970s, increasing political violence, and the weak presidency of Isabel Perón strengthened the leading officers who were ready to embrace drastic changes in economic and social policies. As Hedges (2011, 215) argues, "with the intention of making a permanent change in the country's culture and economic structure, the regime was characterized by repression and a penetration in the national life without precedent." The appointment of José Alfredo Martínez de Hoz as minister of the economy, which initiated the neoliberal turn, should be understood in this historical context shaped by a remarkable degree of distributional conflict.

The importance of distributional struggles in understanding the Argentine neoliberal turn becomes much more apparent once we focus on the Menem presidency and the Convertibility Law. As outlined above, a cohesive team of technocrats implemented the neoliberal policies under Menem and these policies had the backing of *grupos económicos*. Hence, both the constructivist and interest-based explanations are corroborated by the Argentine case. However, several shortcomings in these explanations emerge upon closer scrutiny. First of all, the constructivists explanations ignore a fundamental puzzle: why did Carlos Menem, a Peronist populist who campaigned by explicitly opposing many of the liberal policies implemented during the Alfonsín presidency, wholeheartedly embrace neoliberal solutions? After all, Menem "promised a huge salary increase (*salariazo*) and a 'revolution in production' in the classic populist political style of the Peronists" during his electoral campaign (Romero, 2002, 287). A genuine ideological conversion of Menem himself is out of question, as his ideological flexibility and pragmatism are well-documented (Acuña, 1994; Armijo, 1999; Brown, 2010, 264–74; Lewis, 2002; Romero, 2002, 287–92).[20]

Pointing out the neoliberal convictions of the cohesive technocratic team around Cavallo conveniently ignores another puzzle: how did the technocrats acquire a policy-making monopoly at the expense of bureaucrats with different convictions and at the expense of political opposition from traditional Peronist quarters such as the unions?

Interest-based explanations run into similar problems. First, it is not clear at all how interest-based explanations account for Menem's surprising embrace of the neoliberal agenda. In fact, causality seems to be running in a direction quite different than what these theories predict. Rather than being driven by the interests of big business with international orientation, Menem's appointment of ministers from the conglomerate *Bunge y Born* makes much more sense as a strategic signal to the IMF, the U.S. Treasury Department, and other international creditors that Argentina was willing to embrace market reforms (Bartolini and Drazen, 1997; Smith, 1991, 64). Second, interest-based explanations have little credibility in accounting for the radical nature of the convertibility plan. Néstor Mario Rapanelli—the executive of *Bunge y Born* who became the second minister of the economy in the Menem presidency and who was under immense pressure to solve mounting economic problems—did not even attempt to pass audacious reforms regarding the capital account (Veigel, 2009, 173–76).

The real impetus behind the radical capital account reform of 1991 lay in the chronic distributional struggles that caused Argentina to descend into economic chaos from 1987 onwards. The inflation rate jumped from an already high 137 percent in 1987 to 343 percent in 1988 and an astronomical 3,079

20 Furthermore, as Hedges (2011, 251) remarks,

> ideology played a minimal role in his [Menem's] political make-up: Menem, like Perón himself, had little difficulty in attracting support from people to both the Left and the Right, being totally prepared to include any useful segment within his coalition and being blessed with the ability to make his listener believe that he was in agreement with him.

percent in 1989. In 1990, the year before Cavallo became minister of the economy, inflation rate was 2,314 percent (Lewis, 2002, 266). Monetarism is keen to reduce inflation to a mere monetary phenomenon (Friedman, 1970). However, to the contrary, the existing evidence shows that inflation is "in fact tied closely to the distribution of power between classes" (Hung and Thompson, 2016, 448). The sustained hyperinflation in Argentina during the 1980s led to a zero-sum game where all economic actors aimed to avoid loss of real income by exerting pressures on the state regarding wages, prices of virtually all goods, and interest rates (Smith, 1990, 1991). As a result, by 1989, the Argentine state was in financial collapse. Furthermore, distributional struggles also engendered widespread riots and looting of grocery stores (Walton and Seddon, 1994).

Menem's embrace of neoliberalism and Cavallo's radical convertibility plan can be understood only if we take into account this sobering history of chronic distributional conflict in Argentina. In other words, the driving forces behind adopting a drastic and untested policy such as the convertibility plan were the hyperinflation, food riots, and intensifying distributional struggle in the late 1980s (Corrales, 1998; Carranza, 2005; Treisman, 2004; Walton and Seddon, 1994). Given the remarkable economic chaos of the early years of Menem presidency, continuing capital flight, and high inflation, the policy-makers in Argentina were desperate for quick and effective solutions. Currency convertibility and capital account liberalization offered such a solution (Starr, 1997). To understand why, we need to look into the effects of capital inflows on the growth and distribution trajectories of a country where capital is scarce compared to advanced industrialized countries.

Capital flows, growth, and distribution

In a closed economy with no capital mobility, domestic saving is equal to domestic investment by accounting identity; thus, domestic saving is a binding constraint over investment (Keynes, 1936). The domestic saving constraint over investment decreases as capital mobility increases (Bosworth, 1993). The relaxation of domestic saving constraint implies that domestic investment, consumption, and government deficit can be financed by foreign saving as long as foreign investors are willing to invest in a nation.

Accordingly, financing investment, private consumption, or government consumption through capital flows from the rest of the world has consequences for both income growth and the distribution of income among social groups. Take a hypothetical economy with a typical income distribution, presented in Figure 1.3. In this figure, the horizontal axis represents population distribution. The vertical axis shows the cumulative average income. The curve in Figure 1.3 is the Generalized Lorenz Curve (Shorrocks, 1983), i.e., the plot of the mean income for the corresponding percentage of population. Naturally, the average income increases with the percentage of population. Hence, the end point of the curve is the mean income (Y_1) for the entire country.

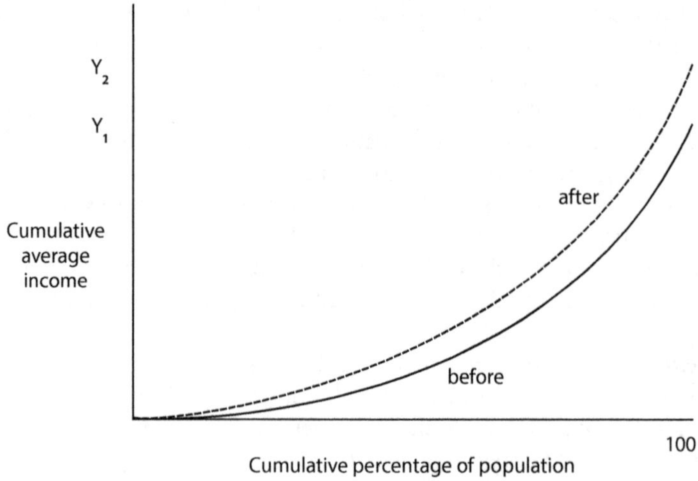

Figure 1.3 Average Income Before and After Financial Opening.

Now, imagine an increase in capital flows from the rest of the world.[21] The effect of such a surge of funds available to economic agents' consumption and investment needs is an increase in the mean income. This is shown by the dotted curve in Figure 1.3, which yields a higher mean income (Y_2) for the entire country.

Thus, capital flows bring forth an increase in domestic disposable income. Yet, that is not the sole positive effect of capital flows from the rest of the world. Equally important is the potential increase in the future domestic output as funds from the rest of the world become available. Consider again the case of an economy that receives inflows of capital from the rest of the world. As depicted in Figure 1.3, such inflows create more disposable income for economic agents. Suppose that the increase in disposable income finances investment, i.e., that it leads to greater capital accumulation. Suppose further that there is a relative abundance of labor, that labor can be allocated between different sectors, and that the outputs of new investment are marketable. Under these assumptions, greater capital accumulation raises potential output of domestic industries. Thus, it leads to an increase in the future potential domestic output.

Figure 1.4 illustrates these ideas. In this figure, the horizontal axis measures consumption. The vertical axis measures investment. The production possibilities frontier is the locus of different combinations of investment and consumption that give the same level of gross domestic output. The curve PPF_1 represents the production possibilities frontier before funds from the rest of the world become available. The curve PPF_2 portrays the increase in domestic potential output as a result of an inflow of capital from the rest of the world.

21 For simplicity, I assume an even distribution of new funds. This is an assumption that is relaxed in Appendix B.

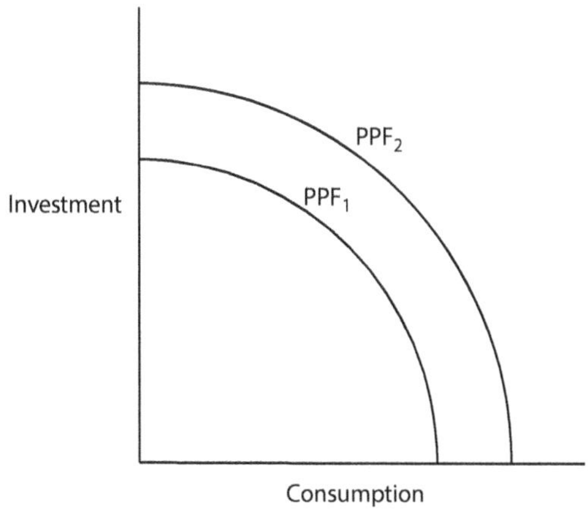

Figure 1.4 Financial Opening and Capital Accumulation.

The opportunity to boost domestic capital formation is much desired in the developing world. This follows from the relative scarcity of capital and abundance of labor in developing countries, a contrast when compared to advanced industrialized countries. Development economists have long stressed the importance of increasing domestic capital stock under such conditions. As Rosenberg (1960) argues, "One need not subscribe to a monocausal theory of development to argue that an increase in the percentage of annual output devoted to investment is an urgent and indispensable prerequisite to a long-term rise in real per capita incomes."[22] Furthermore, the historical record of the late European industrializers show that there was a marked difference between early industrializers and late industrializers in the development of domestic stock of capital. Late industrialization is characterized by a bias toward the production of capital goods and an institutional and organizational environment to assure the rapid growth of capital stock (Gerschenkron, 1962). Thus, as Bartolini and Drazen (1997, 142) emphasize, the issue of capital mobility is inextricably linked with "governments' desire to increase the stock of domestic capital."

In brief, as Eichengreen and Hausmann (2005, 3) note, increases in capital formation and current consumption have been central promises of capital account liberalization. Naturally, the abundance of finance capital—high global liquidity—strengthens the twin promises of financial opening. Since the collapse of the Bretton-Woods system, high global liquidity has been a recurring aspect of global economy. During the 1970s, one of its main causes was the abundance of petrodollars. During the late 1980s and early 1990s, it was low real interest rates in advanced industrialized countries that led to the abundance of finance capital

22 This does not imply that capital accumulation is a *sufficient* condition for long-term economic growth. It is well-known that long-term rise in real per capita incomes is linked to increases in technology and productivity (Barro and Sala-i-Martin, 2004; Hirschman, 1968). However, capital accumulation is clearly a *necessary* condition for such a rise.

seeking higher returns. The drop in the world's most influential interest rate, the Federal Funds rate, was 5 percent in real terms between 1989 and 1993 (Brenner, 2002, 68). In the period after September 11 until the financial crash in 2007–08, it was high corporate savings and global imbalances in trade patterns that were feeding the previously unseen levels of global liquidity. Regardless of its causes, high global liquidity means a considerable decrease in the cost of acquiring capital for emerging market countries.

However, capital mobility is no free lunch. As hinted in the previous sections and analyzed in a detailed fashion in Appendix C, international capital mobility carries significant risks and costs. Capital inflows are often used in unproductive ways in developing and emerging economies, which leads to current account deficit, increasing private and public debt, and balance-sheet mismatch for various economic actors. Capital account liberalization inevitably goes together with a certain loss of monetary and fiscal policy autonomy. Furthermore, for countries where macroeconomic aggregates are not balanced, it is associated with erratic exchange rate behavior. Countries that are heavily dependent on capital inflows face a significant risk of sudden stop and current account reversal, which can easily trigger currency collapse and bank insolvency. Many Asian countries that accumulated large international reserves as a result of capital inflows obtain low returns on these reserves, which is not necessarily the most productive use of financial funds (see Appendix C for a detailed analysis and Figure C.1 for a summary of these risks and adverse consequences).

Thus, capital account liberalization carries grave risks—risks that cannot be easily discounted—in addition to significant promises. Furthermore, as the Argentine case demonstrates, *the history of distributional outcomes and struggles* has a direct impact on the evaluation of these risks and promises, which in turn shapes the timing, scope, and breadth of capital account liberalization. It is particularly on this point—*the impact of the history of distributional outcomes and struggles*—that the existing studies are most lacking. Interest-based explanations are attentive to distribution only to the extent of benefits and costs economic actors face under international capital mobility. Constructivist and diffusion approaches focus on how norms, world-views, and ideas provide *models for* growth and distribution (Geertz, 1973). However, neither the interests, nor the world-views of social classes, economic sectors, and policy-makers are independent from *the history of distributional outcomes and struggles* in a particular country. To illustrate why that is the case, the next two sections provide a brief account of how distributional struggles underlie institutional change.

Theories of institutional change

Institutions arise when practices, social relations, and organizational structures become formalized and acquire persistence through habitualization, objectification, and sedimentation (Zucker, 1977; Tolbert and Zucker, 1996; Zucker, 1988; Giddens, 1984; Berger and Luckmann, 1967; Douglas, 1986). The conduct of capital account in an economy is an institution because it consists of (1) formal rules such as law and regulations pertaining to capital account transactions, (2) practices with varying degree of codification, such as residents holding offshore accounts or foreign institutional investors buying and selling shares in the domestic stock market, and (3) organizational structures (usually the treasury department or the central bank, depending on the country) monitoring capital account transactions and enforcing existing rules on these transactions.

There are four broad perspectives on institutionalization, institutional stability, and institutional change. The first perspective, associated with rational-choice theorists and authors with close affinity to neoclassical economics, portrays institutionalization as a result of increasing returns and positive feedback effects (North, 1990; Goldstein and Keohane, 1993; Schotter, 2008 [1981]). Either institutions may arise as a result of evolutionary processes where the winner institutional practices generate greater increasing returns (Arthur, 1994; Alchian, 1950) or they may be the coordination mechanisms that ensure beneficial and self-reinforcing equilibria among strategic actors (Shepsle, 1989, 137). In this school of thought, the sources of institutionalization are the returns generated by evolutionary dynamics or by the forward-looking actions of strategic actors (Table 1.1). The second, old institutionalism in sociology, explains institutions through normative commitments and substantive importance (Selznick, 1949; Hinings and Greenwood, 2015; Selznick, 1957; Stinchcombe, 1968). Here, the key to institutionalization lies in the rationality embodied in a commitment to a particular value, which imbues certain objectives and techniques with priority (Selznick, 1957, 16–17).[23] The sources of institutionalization are the normative orders and value systems in society. The third perspective, new institutionalism in sociology—the most influential in contemporary sociology and organization theory—emphasizes the role of cognition, culture, and ideas. In this perspective, institutions emerge from practices and relations becoming objective (in the sense that they can be shared and learned) through habitualization and externalization (Berger and Luckmann, 1967; Zucker, 1977; Tolbert and Zucker, 1996). The sources of institutionalization are meaning systems, classification schemas, and beliefs in society (Table 1.1).

The fourth perspective stresses the role of power in the emergence of formal rules and persistent practices. This perspective is not associated with any particular school of thought, although historical institutionalism in political science is one approach that consistently emphasizes the role of power (Streeck and Thelen, 2005; Mahoney and Thelen, 2010). It is rather the case that in each influential approach to institutions, we find authors who draw attention to distribution of power among actors as a crucial source of institutional stability and change. For instance, in rational-choice and historical institutionalism, one finds authors who suggest power as a factor generating increasing returns and thus leading to institutionalization (Mahoney and Thelen, 2010, 9–10). Similarly, in old institutionalism, Stinchcombe (1968, 107–08) argues that "the key to institutionalizing

23 Per Stinchcombe's lucid formulation (1997, 10): "The more ritualized a thing is in an institution, the less it is merely a ritual, because the more substantively important it is."

Table 1.1 Mechanisms and Sources of Institutionalization

	Mechanisms	*Sources*
Rational-choice institutionalism	• Increasing returns	• Self-interest • Mutual coordination
Old institutionalism in sociology	• Normative commitments • Substantive importance	• Normative order • Value system
New institutionalism in sociology	• Habitualization • Externalization • Objectification	• Meaning system • Classification schema • Beliefs
Various schools	• All of the above mechanisms	• Distribution of power

a value is to concentrate power in the hands of those who believe in that value." In new institutionalism, DiMaggio (1988, 14) contends that "new institutions arise when organized actors with sufficient resources (***institutional entrepreneurs***) see in them an opportunity to realize interests that they value highly" [original emphasis]. What is crucial in all of these eclectic formulations is the recognition that power asymmetries created by a particular power distribution affect the very mechanisms of institutionalization under question (Table 1.1).

Thus, institutional stability and change can arise through multiple mechanisms. The next section illustrates how relations of distribution in an economy impact all of the four group of mechanisms discussed earlier.[24]

Distribution and institutional change

The dominant approach to political economy in contemporary social sciences is neoclassical economics. This school of thought—although it portrays itself as the culmination and refinement of ideas found in Smith, Ricardo, and other liberal thinkers of classical political economy—examines economic outcomes in radically different ways than how classical political economists analyze the economy (Roncaglia, 2006, 278–86). Classical political economists conceptualize economic life as a circular process where the distribution of surplus plays a fundamental role in the determination of wages, profits, prices of commodities, interest rates, and asset prices (Bharadwaj, 1986; Garegnani, 1984; Sraffa, 1960). What distinguishes classical political economy is a core idea shared by thinkers

24 Increasing returns explanations, where the causal argument rests on positive feedback loops such as network effects (Pierson, 2000; Arthur, 1994), should be employed extremely cautiously in explaining the emergence, transformation, or stability of political institutions. The reason is that various factors—including the other three broad mechanisms discussed here—can intervene into the feedback loops that are crucial for having rigorous increasing returns explanations. For a discussion of the dangers of loose feedback loop explanations, see Demerath (1996), Mahner and Bunge (2001), and particularly the classic text of Stinchcombe (1968). Explaining institutions and patterns of action through values and norms is equally dangerous. To put it simply, it is a fallacy to assume that there is a direct link between values/norms and particular patterns of action. That is because (1) values are often vague and too general, (2) values conflict with each other, making their impact on action quite ambiguous, and (3) their effect on action is always dependent on the social context (Mann, 1970).

as different as Quesnay, Smith, Ricardo, and Marx—that "the wage, the social product and the technical conditions of production" are taken as determined by historical, institutional, and political conditions (Garegnani, 1984, 294–97). As a result, in classical political economy, the wage rate is taken as determined by exogenous factors and the focus of the analysis is on the distribution of surplus in a given period between different economic actors (Bharadwaj, 1986, 35–36).[25] In particular, Sraffa's (1960) landmark reinterpretation of classical political economy demonstrates—in a logically coherent and mathematically rigorous manner—a key insight shared by all major classical political economists and formulated most famously by Marx (1978, 1993 [1939], 1990 [1876]). Historically transmitted social conditions, accumulated knowledge and techniques of production, and relations of distribution—and not the prices determined through the meeting of supply and demand—shape the trajectory of an economy. At the core of this approach lies (1) the "picture of the system of production and consumption as a circular process" (Sraffa, 1960, 93), (2) the proposition that historically transmitted power relations determine the distribution of surplus produced in this system in any given period, and (3) the idea that such distribution relations set the accumulation and thus growth patterns in an economy.

Neoclassical economics,[26] in contrast, presents

> an approach to value, distribution, and output wherein the theories of distribution and relative prices, output(s) and employment, are treated in terms of the mutual interactions of demands and supplies for commodities and 'factors of production', these supply-and-demand forces being understood to determine simultaneously all the relevant 'prices' and quantities (Aspromourgos, 1986, 265).

In this approach, distribution is epiphenomenal; it plays no role in the simultaneous determination of crucial economic variables through the price-supply-demand mechanism (Garegnani, 1984, 297).[27] The essential idea is that prices

25 It should be noted that Marx's economics is only one perspective in classical political economy; and, in many ways, the deterministic formulations in Marx's economics stands in contrast to the mode of analysis that is sensitive to history, institutions, and politics in classical political economy. Furthermore, Marx's reliance on labor theory of value leads him to questionable conclusions on issues as important as the level of prices and the falling rate of profit (Roncaglia, 2006; Meek, 1956; Blaug, 1997).

26 Neoclassical economics has its roots in the marginalist revolution of Jevons, Menger, and Walras (Aspromourgos, 1986; Lawson, 2013). However, unlike marginalism, contemporary mainstream economics has little theoretical unity (Lawson, 2013). It is rather the case that the unity of contemporary mainstream economics—if it exists at all—arises from its practitioners' insistence on methodological individualism, mathematical modeling, and optimization techniques.

27 Although approaches such as cooperative and non-cooperative game theory are relevant to understanding distributional outcomes and struggles (Moulin, 1991; Osborne and Rubinstein, 1990, 1994), the flatly unrealistic assumptions of neoclassical microeconomics pose formidable barriers to capturing interaction between economic actors and distributional struggles that are context-dependent, historically-structured, and driven by institutionalized patterns of social action. For instance, neoclassical economics takes tastes and preferences as data but it further assumes that these tastes and preferences follow certain formal properties such as transitivity, without which rationality and utility maximization cannot be defined in a rigorous manner. See Becker (1976) for a representative and accessible example of the neoclassical approach to human behavior.

are "indexes of relative scarcity" in the sense that "the equilibrium values for prices and quantities produced are determined through a confrontation between the preferences of economic agents and the scarcity of available resources" (Roncaglia, 2009, 10–11).[28] As a result, neoclassical economics offers a picture of the economy where balance and harmony prevail, as long as markets are in equilibrium (Sabine, 1961, 686–92). That is because the market is self-regulating—the supply and demand mechanism automatically balances the divergent preferences in society with scarce resources through the voluntary decisions of myriad consumers and producers (Polanyi, 2001 [1944]; Gemici, 2015).

Suppose, by following the key idea of a political economic analysis inspired by Smith, Ricardo, Marx, and Sraffa, that the distribution of surplus among different social groups forms the central determinant of all economic activity. Then, the distribution relations among different social groups—take workers and capitalists for the sake of simplicity—are reflected in the level of wages. Furthermore, the level of wages that materializes as a result of particular distribution relations affects the level of profits, prices of commodities, and asset prices. Although there is a causal dependence between distribution and the level of economic variables, this dependence does not necessarily mean that the relations between social groups are zero-sum. In fact, quite the opposite could be the case if the economy is on an expansionary path. Under such conditions, distribution relations may very well be cooperative. Hence, in an expanding economy, the conflictual dimension of distribution relations is likely to remain latent. Furthermore, the distribution relations among social groups could continue being non-conflictual even in stagnating or recessionary economies. That is because the disadvantaged social groups might (1) be "organizationally outflanked" (Mann, 1986, 7), or more importantly (2) lack the consensus and organizational capacity necessary to advance claims against other social groups or political authority (Mann, 1970, 1973; Shorter and Tilly, 1974; Silver, 2003). In fact, as Mann (1970, 437) argues, one of the most fundamental reasons why established political orders have cohesion and continuity in capitalist countries is the lack of consensus among the lower classes regarding their economic and political experiences.

A political economy model that incorporates some of the above insights is found in Bhaduri and Marglin's (1990) influential account of distribution and growth regimes. In line with Sraffa (1960), neoclassical notions such as marginal productivity plays no role in determining the wage rate. Instead, political and institutional factors that these authors take as exogenous determine the wage rate. Their key idea is that the real wage rate has opposing effects. On the one hand, a rise in real wages increases consumption. On the other hand, a rise in real wages depresses profits and investment. Say the real wage rate rises. In the short run, such an increase might be conducive to growth if the increase in consumption

28 The seemingly "obvious" nature of the demand-supply analysis hides several unrealistic assumptions and internal contradictions (Bharadwaj, 1986). Most importantly, the idea of the increasing quantity of supply as a response to increasing price—a cornerstone of neoclassical price and equilibrium theory (Marshall, 2013 [1920], Book IV)—has been shown to be logically flawed and devoid of empirical validity (Sraffa, 1926; Marchionatti, 2001).

is more than the decrease in investment. In particular, if capitalists increase their capacity utilization rate in such a manner that overcomes the decline in investment as a result of decreasing profits, then capitalists and workers have strong incentives to cooperate. However, in the opposite case of investment decrease dominating the increase in capacity utilization rate, capitalists encounter profit loss and the relations between capitalists and workers are likely to be conflictual. Likewise, Bhaduri and Marglin (1990) show that a decrease in real wages might also lead to cooperation if the ensuing rise in investment compensates for the decline in consumption. Bhaduri and Marglin's (1990) model is noteworthy because these authors are keenly aware that a strictly economic analysis can offer predictions only for the short run. In the long run, causality is highly reciprocal. Distribution and growth can set the stage for inter- and intra-class cooperation and conflict. The opposite is also true: inter- and intra-class conflict can have serious effects on the distribution and growth patterns.

It should be observed that a model such as Bhaduri and Marglin (1990) is necessarily narrow in scope. For instance, these authors do not consider monetary factors such as interest rates, inflation, and money-credit supply. Take interest rates. The neoclassical tradition conceptualizes interest rates as determined by productivity and time preference (Smithin, 2006). However, as Smithin (2006, 275) argues, the historical evidence and a formidable corpus of theoretical arguments point out that interest rates, alongside wages and profits, should be seen as a "competing claim" on output and income in an economy. Accordingly, the level of interest rates in an economy is closely related to the balance of power between financial capital, industrial capital, and workers.

Inflation is another crucial factor with profound effects on distribution and growth. The orthodox tradition, embodied in monetarism and quantity theory, views inflation as merely a consequence of an increase in money supply (Friedman, 1970; Friedman and Schwartz, 1963; Hamilton, 1934; Friedman, 1968). As opposed to such orthodoxy, a voluminous record of historical scholarship shows that inflation has deep roots in structural factors, distribution relations, and the power balance between debtors and creditors (Vernengo, 2006; Vilar, 1974). In understanding the important episodes of inflation in history—episodes such as the price revolution of the 1870s, the German hyperinflation in the 1920s, and the inflation of the 1960s and 1970s—the complex interplay between inflation and distribution offers much greater explanatory leverage than orthodox ideas linking inflation simply to money supply increase.

Once economic factors such as inflation are conceptualized as distribution-laden, we should expect economic processes pertinent to distribution-growth dynamics in an economy to affect institutional change. Take the case of stagnation. A stagnating or recessionary economy significantly increases the likelihood of distributional conflict. High levels of inflation and economic crises raise this likelihood even further, and often in dramatic ways. As Argentina in the 1980s illustrates, a crisis—be it a currency crisis, bank run, or balance of payments crisis—combined with high inflation has widespread effects on the income of different social groups. Under such conditions, every macroeconomic variable (e.g., key interest rates, salaries, tax rates) and every economic relation (e.g., business contracts, credit lines, insurance policies) are sites of contestation and struggle. Furthermore, if the economic conditions threaten the survival, taken-for-granted economic rights, and access to basic necessities of certain social groups, then distributional struggles are likely to cause widespread mobilization and conflict—contentious politics that explicitly threaten political authority. The collective mobilization, riots, and looting of grocery stores in major Argentine city centers such as Rosario, Córdoba, and Buenos Aires in 1989 provide a vivid example of how distributional struggles can turn into explicit conflict (Walton and Seddon, 1994).

Thus, if one accepts the proposition that market outcomes and economic aggregates in a capitalist market economy are built on relations of distribution, then the links between distribution, institutional stability, and institutional change follow as direct corollaries.[29] Assume that the existing relations of distribution and growth patterns are such that the majority of social groups experience improvements in their income and lifestyles from one period to the next. Such a state of the economy is likely to sustain and reinforce the existing institutions according to all different approaches to institutionalization. From the perspective of rational-choice institutionalism, relations of distribution that generate positive returns for the majority of social groups in society are likely to be sustained because these groups are the beneficiaries of such institutions. For old institutionalism, such relations of distribution contribute to the persistence of existing institutions because they make it likely that "population at large believes in them" (Stinchcombe, 1968, 112). If we follow new institutionalism, such relations of distribution generate coherence and rich interconnections in society, thus minimizing entropy and institutional erosion that can lead to institutional change (Zucker, 1988, 27–32). Most importantly, such relations of distribution are likely to reinforce the existing balance of power in society, which amplifies the effects of all of the mechanisms discussed above (Thelen and Steinmo, 1992, 14–18).

Institutional change is the reverse image of such mutual reinforcement. Suppose there is a change in the existing distribution relations among social groups.[30] A transformation in distribution relations is likely to cause tensions in the existing political and economic institutions. The most salient cause of such tensions is the changing balance of power among groups as a result of the transformation in distribution relations. For instance, the increasing share of internationally

29 Knight (1992) offers an approach that anticipates some of the arguments I offer here. As he (1992, 40) argues, "Institutions are not created to constrain groups or societies in an effort to avoid suboptimal outcomes but, rather, are the by-product of substantive conflicts over the distributions inherent in social outcomes." Unfortunately, Knight's argument rests on a view of institutional change predicated on social groups acting largely on the basis of their interests. Following the theoretical apparatus of rational choice theory, Knight focuses on strategic action and how institutional change ultimately follows from the distributional effects of institutions. As argued here, such an approach captures only one of the mechanisms through which distributional outcomes affect institutional stability and change.

30 Such a change could arise from both endogenous (e.g., an increase in organizational capacity of a particular group) and exogenous (e.g., terms of trade) factors.

connected conglomerates in the Argentine economy from the late 1950s onwards was the concrete base upon which this segment of the capitalist class attempted to reconstruct existing institutions starting in 1966 (O'Donnell, 1978, 23–25). At a more fundamental level, the transformation of distribution relations leads existing groups to alter their orientations to institutions because such transformations have direct effects on interests, values, and beliefs of these groups. Furthermore, the transformation of distribution relations creates the opportunity space for new actors to convert or displace existing institutions, leading to gradual but transformative institutional change (Streeck and Thelen, 2005). The likelihood of institutional change as a result of changes in distribution relations multiplies in the case of sustained distributional conflict.

The link between distribution and institutional change—summarized in the above paragraphs—becomes particularly relevant for capital account liberalization because capital mobility has direct and foreseeable impact on both distribution and growth in emerging economies. As argued in the previous sections, the prospects of substantial increases in capital formation and consumption provide strong incentives to social groups and power-holders to refashion or radically alter the existing institutions pertaining to capital account. Distributional struggles and conflicts increase the salience of such incentives. Furthermore, distributional struggles and conflicts erode the existing institutions, and thus prepare the ground for ideational change. That happens not only because ideas associated with the previous set of institutions get discredited but also because actors with novel ideas become more powerful in society. Likewise, distributional struggles and conflicts make domestic policy-makers much more susceptible to international diffusion, including coercion from international financial organizations.

The logic of the comparative-historical analysis

In this book, I offer a causal argument on how distribution relations and growth patterns underpin capital account liberalization in emerging economies. To be strict, I do not claim that distribution relations and growth patterns by themselves are sufficient to determine the trajectory and scope of capital account liberalization. To the contrary, intermediate mechanisms such as ideational carriers are necessary for turning the opportunities created by distribution relations into an institutional change pertaining to the capital account. Thus, what matters is the combination of distribution relations and growth patterns with an intermediate mechanism such as political elite's interest in boosting economic growth. In non-technical terms, I suggest that there are multiple pathways to capital account liberalization. In technical terms, I argue that the factors I examine in this book, including conflictual distribution relations, are all INUS causes—"an insufficient but necessary part of a condition which is itself unnecessary but sufficient for the result" (Mackie, 1965, 245). That is a mouthful when expressed in English but the underlying idea is fairly simple. To illustrate it through the causal framework employed in this book, neither ideas nor interests are by themselves sufficient to produce capital account liberalization in emerging economies.

However, they become sufficient when combined with structural factors such as conflictual distribution relations and low growth that create the environment in which particular interests and ideas become effective.

The mode of analysis I adopt is historical because my main objective is to demonstrate how distribution relations unfold over time and lead to particular institutional outcomes (Stinchcombe, 1968, 1978). Such an objective requires "a genetic and sequential mode of explanation" (Mahoney, 2008, 412), where action and event sequences are analyzed to investigate how institutions persist or change. To be more specific, I am interested in the mechanisms—"chains or aggregations of actors confronting problem situations and mobilizing more or less habitual responses" (Gross, 2009, 393)—that are sufficient to maintain or transform institutions. Methodologically, my approach follows process-tracing—"the examination of 'diagnostic' pieces of evidence within a case that contribute to supporting or overturning alternative explanatory hypotheses" (Bennett, 2010, 208). Process-tracing is a must because one needs to link structural conditions (such as distribution relations) to various actors' responses. In making such links, it is possible to use generalizations that rely on social science theories and common patterns of human behavior (Mahoney, 2012). However, what is really required is to examine the posited causal connection vis-à-vis alternative hypotheses, to investigate the "preponderance of evidence" regarding competing theories (Goldstone, 2004, 35). Such an assessment is possible only through extensive analysis of a particular case's historical trajectory.

The analysis in this book is comparative because I posit that the argument I advance has value in explaining capital account liberalization in emerging economies, and not just in Argentina, Chile, South Korea, and Turkey. If the main problem of historical sociology is "how to use general causal theory to account for unique historical outcomes" (Swidler, 1993, xiii), the main problem of comparative-historical sociology is how to generalize from particular causal explanations pertaining to historical individuals to theories applicable to a larger population of cases (Danto, 1966; Smelser, 1976; Geddes, 2003; George and Bennett, 2007; Tilly, 1984). To address this problem, I use "historical trajectories as the units of comparison" (Skocpol, 1979, 35–36)—as instances of evidence of the different causal pathways that an emerging economy might go through in the process of financial integration with the rest of the world. The strength of this methodological approach rests, partially, on the case selection employed to develop the general theoretical argument.

Case selection and data sources

One of the main pitfalls in selecting cases for explaining capital account liberalization lies in the possibility of regional clustering in the timing and type of reforms. Figure 1.5 presents, based on the UNIDO (United Nations Industrial Development Organization) classification of developing and emerging economies, the trajectory of capital account liberalization in different world regions between 1973 and 2005. All the regions exhibit a liberalization trajectory

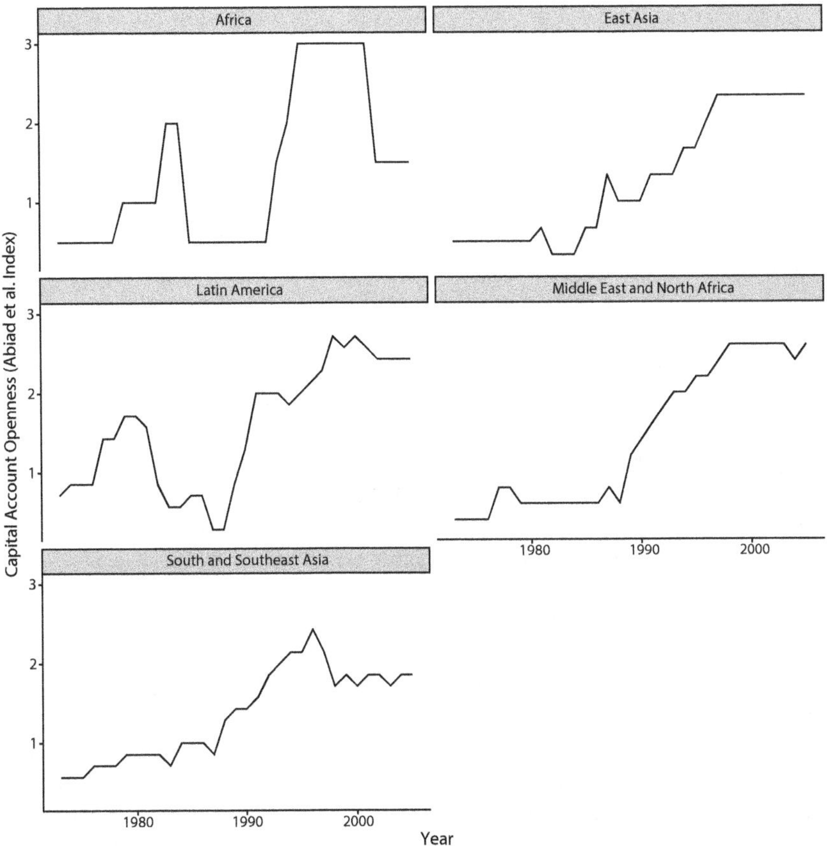

Figure 1.5 Trajectory of Capital Account Liberalization by Region, 1973–2005.
Source: Abiad et al. (2010).

that accelerates by either the late 1980s or early 1990s. However, there are significant differences among regions. For instance, Latin America stands out as an early liberalizer, driven by the liberalization experiences of countries such as Argentina and Chile as well as the existing permissive regimes of Mexico, Peru, and Venezuela (Figure 1.2). In contrast, countries in East Asia are late liberalizers, with very limited capital mobility until the 1990s. South Korea and Taiwan adopted a high degree of capital mobility only after the Asian Crisis, whereas China has been restricting capital mobility all along. In the Middle East and North Africa, most countries (except Jordan and a brief openness episode in Israel) featured shielded capital accounts until the mid-1990s. Turkey stands out as an early liberalizer, but even the Turkish liberalization was relatively late compared to Latin America (Figure 1.2).

These patterns might be the result of several factors. On the one hand, regional clustering might reflect structural factors such as distribution and technological capability shared by many countries in a particular region. On the other hand, such regional clustering might be the outcome of the diffusion of ideas and emulation bolstered by geographical proximity and density of cross-border transactions for countries in a particular world region.

Regardless of the underlying causes, regional clustering presents serious problems for theoretical generalization from particular case-studies. For instance, a study that relies on a few Latin American cases might overemphasize the role of diffusion, which clearly played a role in cases such as Argentina and Chile (Ramos, 1986; Brooks and Kurtz, 2012). Likewise, relying on the East Asian cases might lead to an overly optimistic assessment of state's role in managing distributional struggles.

Given that this book emphasizes distributional struggle as the most important determinant structuring the mechanisms leading to capital account liberalization, selecting cases to maximize variation in the degree of distributional struggle is the best strategy. However, measuring distributional struggle involves major conceptual and empirical problems (Korpi, 1980; Marshall et al., 1985; Przeworski and Wallerstein, 1982; Kelley and Evans, 1995; Boix, 2003; Marcel and Solimano, 1994; Shorrocks, 1983; Rodrik, 1996). The theoretical framework I adopt in this book compounds the existing problems even further, as I take into account not just intra- and inter-class struggles over the proverbial pie but also distribution relations between sectors and social groups such as debtors. Furthermore, as discussed in the previous sections, distributional cooperation and conflict are highly dependent on the elasticities of various macroeconomic aggregates such as investment.

One way to overcome such issues is to use a stock-measure of inequality as a proxy. Amsden (2001), in her influential study of economic development, relies on land Gini coefficients in the year 1960. Her reasoning rests on the thesis that economic development is ultimately a process of moving from exploiting primary products through unskilled labor to exploiting knowledge-based assets through skilled labor (2001, 2–4). Amsden (2001, 15–20) argues that countries that invested in national skills and national firms instead of importing technology through partnership with foreign capital were much more successful in achieving economic development. The countries that could successfully mobilize their population for "building at home" were also the countries with the least amount of inequality and distributional conflict (2001, 18):

> Countries that invested heavily in national firms and national skills—China, India, Korea and Taiwan—all had relatively equal income distributions. A national economy may be regarded as an organic whole. The greater income inequality (by social class, race, religion, or region), the more that organic whole is fractured, and the more difficult it is to mobilize support for national business enterprises and firm-specific national skills. After World War II, greater equality induced a relatively large flow of resources from primary product production to manufacturing and also resolved a policy paradox in industry's favor.

I employ a similar strategy in selecting the cases for examining capital account liberalization. Given that land distribution is remarkably resilient in the absence of a major political upheaval, I focus on three countries from different regions of the world with fairly different patterns of land distribution in 1960. South Korea in 1960, a few years after the Korean War and a major land reform, was one of the most equal countries in the world (Pak, 1956; Mitchell, 1949; Jeon and Kim, 2000; Kay, 2002).[31] In sharp contrast to the equal land distribution in East Asia, Latin American countries were characterized by vast inequalities in land distribution. Argentina's land Gini coefficient in 1960 was 0.86. The land Gini coefficient for Brazil in 1960 was 0.83. These coefficients confirm the remarkable level of land ownership concentration in these countries (Amsden, 2001, 18). Both of these countries would be good choices for an in-depth examination of alternative explanations of capital account liberalization. However, although the figures for land distribution in 1960 are missing for Chile, I focus in this book on Chile's experience with capital flows from the mid-1970s onwards. The reason is twofold. First, the extant historical scholarship leaves no doubt that Chile was in many ways similar to Latin American countries such as Argentina and Brazil in inequality and land distribution (Stallings, 1978; Mamalakis, 1976; Dorner, 1992; Kaufman, 1972; Bauer, 1975). Second, as will be discussed in a detailed manner in Chapter 2, Chile is a rather unique case among emerging economies in terms of capital account liberalization trajectory. Chile liberalized capital flows in a rapid manner in the late 1970s, which culminated in a major financial crash. In the late 1980s and early 1990s, when international investors were again interested in the Chilean assets, the Chilean authorities chose to curb capital mobility through innovative measures. This long trajectory of capital account reforms offers a valuable opportunity for within-the-case comparison, and I focus on Chile primarily for exploiting such an opportunity. Finally, Turkey, with a land Gini coefficient of 0.6, occupies a middle ground in terms of land distribution.

These three countries—Chile, South Korea, and Turkey—also exhibit quite different trajectories of capital account liberalization. Chile's first period is an example of hasty liberalization. Although the Chilean authorities shied away from the most volatile capital inflows with short-term maturity, they did not interfere with banks accumulating liabilities with shorter maturities than their assets. In the second episode, Chile favored long-term capital flows and effectively curtailed short-term movements. As opposed to such a liberalization trajectory, Korea's reforms in the 1990s encouraged short-term capital flows and maintained restrictions on long-term capital. The Turkish capital account reform in 1989 eliminated virtually all restrictions on capital mobility and made the Turkish lira convertible.

The value of comparative-historical research lies in the *thick* adjudication of evidence in light of alternative theories. In practical terms, rigorous comparative-historical research is some sort of detective work, where the researcher is in a (often desperate) search for smoking gun evidence to reject and confirm theories.

31 South Korea's land Gini coefficient in 1960 stood at 0.35 (Amsden, 2001, 17).

Such evidence rarely exists. Hence, it is imperative to use multiple sources of evidence including interviews, documentary sources, legislation, statistics, and sequence of events. Furthermore, the more exhaustive the search for alternative theories and evidence, the more rigorous the conclusions of the research.

The following methods and sources of data are used to carry out the empirical analysis. The field research in Chile, South Korea, and Turkey aimed to gather data through interviews and documentary sources. In total, 36 interviews were conducted with former high-level technocrats and politicians in these countries.[32] In terms of documentary evidence, the focus is on two types of sources. The first is the national news media, in order to track the public debate and significant events that influenced the financial opening process in each country.[33] The second is government (i.e., Ministries of Finance, Central Banks, and other government-funded institutions) publications on legal changes and government actions related to capital account transactions. These publications are used to track (1) the legal framework that applies to capital account transactions and (2) the monetary policies that have an effect on the capital account regime in each country. Finally, I rely extensively on the historical scholarship and policy analyses of capital account regimes in Chile, South Korea, and Turkey, which are quite rich for all three countries.

32 Please see Appendix E for a list of interviews conducted. These were semi-structured interviews of approximately 60-minute length. In cases where the respondent directly shaped the financial opening policy, longer and more detailed interviews (up to five hours) were obtained.

33 The following sources were used: *Qué Pasa* in Chile, *Business Korea* in South Korea, and the daily and weekly economic news bulletins of *ANKA Agency* in Turkey.

2 Boom, crash, restraint

The politics of taming capital flows in Chile

Chile confronted global capital inflows earlier than South Korea and Turkey. Following the military *coup d'état* that ended the democratically elected Allende government (1973), Chilean financial markets and capital account were deregulated in a swift and careless manner. This first episode of financial opening produced an economic boom that served the Pinochet regime in terms of political legitimacy. However, the economic boom was financial and to a large extent fictitious; by the end of 1982, Chile experienced the worst financial crash among all Latin American countries. Chile had access to international finance only through sovereign borrowing after the financial crisis. When voluntary capital inflows returned at the end of the 1980s, the newly elected center-left coalition government of President Aylwin did not blindly open up Chilean financial markets to the rest of the world. Instead, the Aylwin administration implemented—and in one case invented— sophisticated policies to curb short-term capital inflows to Chile.

Accordingly, this chapter compares two episodes of institutional change in Chile. The first episode is the financial opening between 1978 and 1982. The second episode is the period between 1989 and 1992, when capital controls—the most important being an unremunerated reserve requirement (the *encaje*)—were imposed on capital flows. The first episode brought the 1982 financial meltdown. The second episode and the decision to curb capital inflows were arguably why Chile could maintain admirable economic stability despite major crises in other emerging economies.

In each episode, I focus on the distribution relations and growth patterns that underpin the mechanisms of institutional change. The first episode of financial opening (1978–82) came after decades of anemic growth, high inflation, and antagonistic distribution relations. I examine how this history of distributional conflict and low growth enabled the rise of the Chicago Boys and prepared a fertile ground for one of the most radical neoliberal institutional changes in history. I show that once the capital account liberalization occurred, global capital flows—the majority of which were recycled petrodollars— led to an unprecedented boom in the Chilean economy. Such an economic boom provided the much-needed political legitimacy to the military regime; it thus reinforced the institutional change toward capital mobility. Furthermore, the most influential economic actors, big financial conglomerates, owed their power to their financial investments. Thus, despite significant appreciation in the real exchange rate, damage to small and medium businesses, and eroding competitiveness in export sectors, the Chicago Boys of the military regime did not see a need for restricting capital flows. The economic consequences were grave.

The institutional change between 1989 and 1992 stood in stark contrast to the first episode. In analyzing this episode, I first show how the 1982 crisis realigned political power in Chile and forced the Pinochet administration to abandon many of the ideologically driven economic and social policies. I then focus on the export-based growth dynamism of the 1980s in Chile. Once the 17-year Pinochet dictatorship was over, the strong growth pattern of the 1980s enabled the democratically elected Aylwin administration to implement various policies to address some of the worst excesses of the previous administration's neoliberal agenda. Tax and labor reforms provided the Aylwin administration the necessary fiscal ammunition for implementing successful policies to alleviate poverty. Furthermore, the new government achieved a modest but politically successful level of redistribution through its reforms. The strong export-based growth and the explicit redistribution agenda of the government changed the dynamics of capital account openness in the early 1990s. As growth resumed by the second half of the 1980s and as global economic conditions changed, Chile started receiving large amounts of capital, both in the form of FDI and short-term capital inflows. Such inflows put pressure on the exchange rate and threatened macroeconomic stability. The economic team in the Aylwin administration rejected short-term economic expansion and chose to defend a competitive exchange rate by implementing novel capital controls. The concern for long-term growth based on export dynamism was paramount in shaping this decision. The newly elected government after the military regime identified economic growth as originating in export sectors and designed its macroeconomic policies accordingly. The absence of distributional pressures was a crucial structural factor that enabled the new administration's stance toward international capital mobility.

This chapter begins by analyzing the neoliberal economic transformation after the 1973 *coup*—the background of dramatic institutional change on the issue of international capital mobility. It then examines the first episode of financial opening, which produced an economic boom as a result of unrestricted openness and terminated in a financial crash. The next section traces how the Chilean economy recovered from the debt crisis. It shows that the dynamism of the Chilean economy originated in the export sectors and then investigates the political consequences of export-based growth. The following section analyzes the implementation of capital controls when voluntary capital flows returned to Chile at the end of the 1980s.[1]

1 It should be pointed out that the literature on Chilean economic history and political economy is vast and of exceptional quality. Indeed, almost all the periods of Chilean economy between 1970 and 2000 have been the subject of able scholarship. In particular, I have benefited considerably from Fourcade-Gourinchas and Babb (2002), Silva (1991), and Silva (1996). Thus, in interpreting the broad contours of political and economic transformations in Chile, this research draws on various secondary sources in addition to the primary material.

Distributional conflict and neoliberal economic transformation

Unlike Argentina, where many years of strong GDP growth between the 1950s and 1970s alleviated distributional conflict, Chile had consistently low growth between 1955 and 1973 (Cortés Conde, 2009, 226–40; Fourcade-Gourinchas and Babb, 2002, 543; Hedges, 2011). The per capita GDP grew by only 1.4 percent between 1940 and 1960 and 2.6 percent between 1960 and 1970 (Mamalakis, 1976, 90). The high concentration of wealth was a significant contributor to this anemic growth performance, as it hindered much-needed advances in skill formation and technological progress (Mamalakis, 1976). As a result, distributional conflict was chronic in the post-war Chilean society. The Christian Democratic rule during the Frei presidency in the 1960s implemented reforms to redistribute wealth and tackle poverty. However, a persistently high inflation in a low-growth economy muted the positive effects of these reforms (Fourcade-Gourinchas and Babb, 2002; De Vylder, 1976; Stallings, 1978).

Increasing political mobilization during the 1960s accompanied distributional conflict (Landsberger and McDaniel, 1976). In this social context, the Chilean left under Salvador Allende's leadership found a strong cause for reform. Distributional reform and justice constituted a rallying cry for various politically mobilized social groups, as the heterogeneous elements of the Chilean left were united in the "belief that the historical distribution pattern within Chile's political democracy prevented economic democracy" (Mamalakis, 1976, 353). The political agenda of the Chilean left had some support from the urban bourgeoisie. However, the Chilean capitalist class was a vociferous opponent of an Allende presidency (Silva, 1996; Stallings, 1978). It is under such adverse conditions that Allende managed to win the presidency and unite various different political parties in a broad alliance—*Unidad Popular* (Popular Unity). Allende's policies were ambitious and wide-ranging. They included "the nationalization of the copper mines, extensive expropriations in land and industry, major increases in industrial wages, fixed consumer goods prices, and worker participation in running of state-controlled industries" (Fourcade-Gourinchas and Babb, 2002, 544). Most notably, the *Unidad Popular* government enabled a significant increase in the GDP wage share, which can be seen in Figures 2.1 and 2.2. Figure 2.1 presents the GDP wage share on the right axis as a number between 0 and 1. Although the wage share was relatively flat in the 1960s, it surged between 1970 and 1972. Correspondingly, the average profit rate decreased in this period. Furthermore, one of the reasons why the profit rate did not drop even more sharply was the anemic accumulation pattern since the 1960s, which can be observed in the negative growth rates of the per worker capital stock (Figure 2.2).[2] Given that capital productivity, labor productivity, labor force, and GDP growth rates did not diverge sharply from each other in this period (Figure 2.2), it is clear that the increases in wage rate and wage share were significant distributional gains for the working classes.

2 Please see Appendix A for the relationship between profit rate, capital productivity, and profit share.

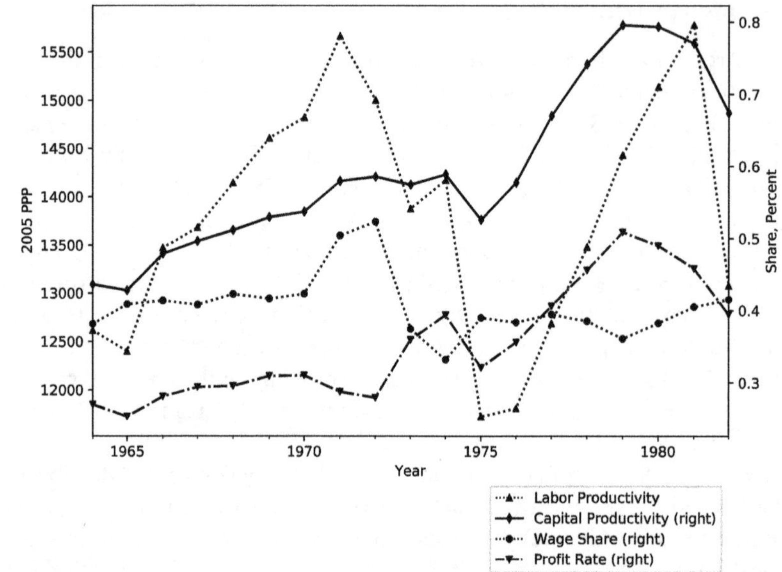

Figure 2.1 Distributional Dynamics, 1964–82.
Note: See Appendix A for the definition of variables and for the explanation of axes in this figure.
Source: Extended Penn World Tables v. 4 (Foley and Michl, 1999; Marquetti, 2003).

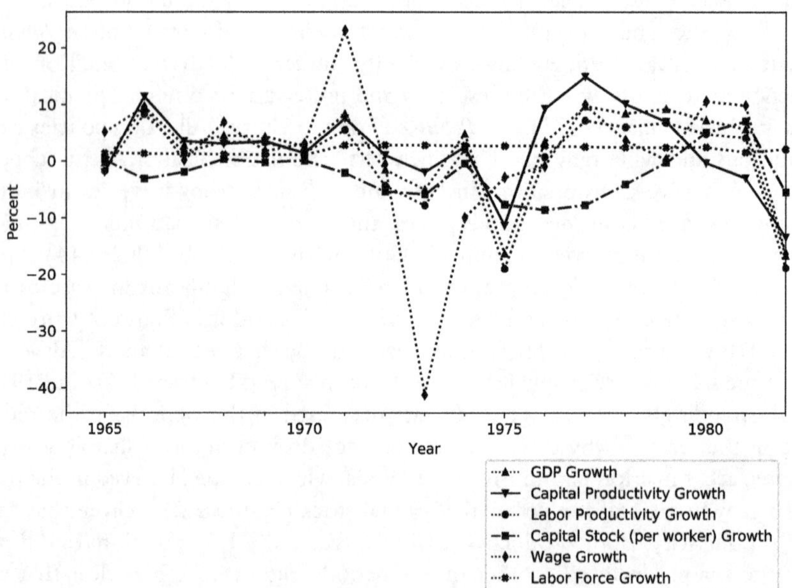

Figure 2.2 Growth Dynamics, 1964–82.
Note: See Appendix A for the definition of variables used in this figure.
Source: Extended Penn World Tables v. 4 (Foley and Michl, 1999; Marquetti, 2003).

Partially as a result of these distributional dynamics, the *Unidad Popular* government (1970–73) under the leadership of Salvador Allende led to a prolonged economic crisis (Collier and Sater, 2004, 346). Apart from the hostile capitalist class, the economic turmoil that developed in this period was a result of several factors: price controls, the mismanaged nationalization of mines, the expropriation of large private businesses, increasing labor militancy, declining agricultural as well as industrial production, and rampant inflationary pressures (Baltra, 1973; De Vylder, 1976; Collier and Sater, 2004; Landsberger and McDaniel, 1976). Furthermore, Chile faced a negative terms of trade shock because of falling copper prices. The combination of these factors caused a considerable deterioration in aggregate production. At the same time, aggregate demand rose due to wage increases. Excess demand was balanced by importing more, which led to a trade deficit. As copper prices fell, balance of payments problems and foreign exchange scarcity became acute. The Chilean economy came to a virtual stalemate by 1973 (Collier and Sater, 2004, 344–46).

Since the *Unidad Popular* policies faced strong opposition by the capitalist class, political chaos and polarization accompanied economic turmoil. The military, under the leadership of Augusto Pinochet, put a brutal end to the long tradition of democracy in Chile on September 11, 1973. Pinochet and his economic team implemented a radical and comprehensive transformation of the Chilean economy between 1973 and 1982, until these policies were interrupted by a severe financial crisis.

Neoliberal market reforms did not—at the beginning—have sufficient support within the military junta (Silva, 1991, 392). As various scholars show, in spite of the overarching thread of liberalizing Chilean markets, economic policies were piecemeal and there were important setbacks to implementing free market reforms.[3] For this reason, the period between 1973 and 1982 is best analyzed, following Silva (1996), in terms of two periods of policy formation: gradualism and radical neoliberalism.[4] While gradualism dominated between 1973 and 1975, radical neoliberalism ascended from 1975 onwards (Silva, 1996). What distinguished gradualism from radical neoliberalism was the extent to which deep structural reforms for the construction of unfettered markets were implemented. As shown below, the period after the second half of 1975 was markedly different in this aspect from the previous period. In fact, free market ideology exerted its influence most forcibly between 1975 and 1982.

Even before the end of the *Unidad Popular* rule through the military *coup d'état*, there were preparations for an economic plan and set of policies to counter

3 The neoliberal transformation under the Pinochet regime has been the subject of a vast literature. See the following notable works: Edwards and Cox (1987); Fortín (1989); Foxley (1983); Huneeus (2007); Kurtz (1999); Silva (1996); Ramos (1986).

4 However, despite the fruitfulness of Silva's distinction between gradualism and radical neoliberalism, economic policies under the military junta exhibited a monetarist tenor right from the beginning. Unlike the previous technocratic climate dominated by the structuralism of ECLAC (Economic Commission for Latin America and the Caribbean)—which advocated for a positive role of state in economic industrialization—, monetarism did not allot an active role to state. Indeed, the monetarist outlook was fiercely anti-government (Silva, 1991, 389–90).

the socialist reforms that shaped the period between 1970 and 1973. These preparations started with the Monday Club, which consisted of private business leaders who held regular meetings each week (Valdés, 1995, 247). It was at these meetings that a special group was established in order to analyze *Unidad Popular*'s economic policies. Initially, the group produced reports on the Chilean economy, gradually establishing deep ties with various business associations and the political opposition to *Unidad Popular* (Valdés, 1995, 248–49). In 1972, as economic conditions worsened, the group undertook the preparation of a new economic program (Valdés, 1995, 249–50).[5] The document was given the name *el ladrillo* (the brick). It outlined the measures that formed the backbone of economic policies in the post-coup era.

The team that produced *el ladrillo* consisted mostly of economists trained at the economics department of the University of Chicago (Collier and Sater, 2004, 365).[6] The immediate concern for the economic team at that time was the stabilization of the economy. The *Unidad Popular* government left an economy with a large public and trade deficit and severe balance of payments problems. The inflation rate reached 606 percent in 1973 (Edwards and Cox, 1987, 32). Furthermore, the market mechanism was no longer functioning properly. Accordingly, the immediate goal of the reforms between 1973 and 1975 was establishing macroeconomic equilibrium and reconstituting the market mechanism (Foxley 1983, 50–56; Ramos 1986, 12).

It was only by the mid-1975 that radicalism rather than gradualism began to dominate the reform strategy of the economic team employed by Pinochet. There are several reasons why gradualism dominated radicalism in economic policy-making (Silva, 1996). First, there was indeterminacy on the part of military rulers about which economic policies to adopt. After all, as Collier and Sater (2004, 364) argue, "The generals knew nothing much about economics." Thus, to a certain degree, the implemented economic policies were *ad hoc*, rather than being coherent (Stallings, 1989, 183). Second, the balance of power within the core capitalist group that influenced economic policy-making in the period immediately after the coup was in favor of "internationally competitive producers for domestic markets" (Silva, 1996, 76–78). To be sure, such conglomerates also wanted economic liberalization. However, given the high-levels of protection they enjoyed for decades, a rapid liberalization of tariffs would be detrimental for such businesses (Silva, 1996). Third, the core capitalist group, which had a key role in the preparation of *el ladrillo*, expanded to form a large bourgeois and upper-class coalition involving various business peak associations (Silva, 1996, 68–69). A gradualist reform agenda rather than a radical set of reforms was more instrumental for bringing such a diverse array of interests together (Silva, 1996, 69). Fourth, the military junta opted for gradualists rather than the more radical reformers associated with the *Universidad Católica* in its appointments for key

5 The request for a new program came from the Chilean Navy (Huneeus, 2000, 465).

6 Hence the famous name given to them: *los Chicago Boys*. See Silva (1991, 391) for a list of these economists.

macroeconomic management positions (Silva, 1991, 392). Radical reformers initially took secondary positions in key ministries and staffed ODEPLAN (Oficina Nacional de Planificación)—the State Planning Organization (Huneeus, 2000). Thus, they did not fully conquer economic bureaucracy until the second half of 1975. As a result, despite the free-market radicalism of some of these economists, structural reforms, such as drastic tariff reduction and financial opening, were not implemented (Silva, 1996, ch. 4).

Nevertheless, the economic policies between 1973 and mid-1975, despite their gradualism in structural reforms, were severe (Collier and Sater, 2004, 365). Immediately after the *coup*, in October 1973, prices—heavily regulated in the *Unidad Popular* era—were freed (Ffrench-Davis, 1983, 909–10). This was followed by a large devaluation (Ramos, 1986, 16). The economic team intended to address the problem of rampant inflation through a restrictive monetary and fiscal policy, cutting down the rate of money supply expansion and public expenditures (Foxley, 1983, 52–53). While monetary contraction was implemented swiftly, reduction in public expenditures did not occur until July 1974, when Jorge Cauas—an economist from the *Universidad Católica*—replaced Admiral Gotuzzo as the new finance minister (Foxley 1983, 55; Fontaine 1988, 79–83). In addition, wages were frozen and labor union activity was prohibited in order to control aggregate demand (Ramos, 1986, 16–17). The distributional effects of these policies were sharp, as they implied that the costs of macroeconomic stabilization fell largely on the working and middle classes, which can be observed in the large decrease of the wage share in GDP (Figure 2.1).

Contrary to the expectations of moderate policy-makers, the measures were ineffective in reducing inflation. The inflation rate was 369 percent in 1974 and 343 percent in 1975 (Edwards and Cox, 1987, 32). It was at this juncture that the radical Chicago Boys replaced moderates in key posts and gained control of economic policy-making (Silva, 1991, 393). Beginning in April 1975, a considerably more radical and extensive set of reforms were implemented. The first element of these reforms was a shock treatment. It consisted of a demand shock through drastic cuts in public employment and expenditure as well as further reduction in real wages (Foxley, 1983, 55–56). Starting in late 1974, fiscal contraction accompanied monetary contraction. As a result, real economic activity was severely depressed and the real GDP shrank by 16.3 percent in 1975 (Figure 2.2). Unemployment jumped from 4.8 percent in 1973 to 9.2 percent in 1974 and to 13.5 percent in 1975 (Edwards and Cox, 1987, 137).[7]

In addition, the economic team started implementing fundamental structural reforms. These reforms included tariff reduction, privatization, financial deregulation, and capital account liberalization. By 1979, all tariffs were lowered to a standard 10 percent (Foxley, 1983, 56–60). Financial deregulation started in 1974 by allowing special companies, *financieras*, to operate as financial intermediaries. It

7 Starting in 1975, the government implemented a minimum employment program (PEM— *Programa de Empleo Mínimo*) to counter the sharply rising unemployment. The numbers given in the text do not account for the percentage of the labor force employed in PEM. In 1975, this number was relatively low at 1.3 percent (Edwards and Cox, 1987, 137)

continued with the privatization of nationalized banks. External financial liberalization was done in an accelerated pace between 1977 and 1980, which allowed domestic firms and banks to obtain credit from abroad (Diaz-Alejandro, 1985).

Despite rapid reforms, the military regime did not privatize the lucrative copper mining company, CODELCO. This decision was to a large extent motivated by guaranteeing a comfortable level of revenues for the armed forces. Keeping CODELCO as a public company resulted in a stable source of revenues not only for the Chilean armed forces, but also for the Chilean state.

These structural reforms had significant consequences. Tariff reduction effectively killed the Chilean manufacturing industry and changed the structure of Chilean production. Despite domestic financial liberalization, real interest rates remained very high. Financial intermediaries, which belonged to big conglomerates, amassed large profits by borrowing cheap abroad and lending expensively in Chile. This, combined with hasty privatizations, led to the concentration of wealth and economic power in few hands (Collier and Sater, 2004; Edwards and Cox, 1987; Ffrench-Davis, 1983; Foxley, 1983; Ramos, 1986).

Financial opening: boom and crash under unrestricted openness

The economic policies started bearing fruit by 1977, producing an economic boom between 1977 and 1981 (Ffrench-Davis, 1983; Foxley, 1983; Ramos, 1986), with an average real GDP growth rate of 8.06 for this five-year period (Figure 2.2). However, the economic boom was highly fragile because one of the main engines of growth was the heavy influx of capital from the rest of the world (Ffrench-Davis, 1983, 916).

The economic boom between 1977 and 1981 came to an abrupt end with a financial meltdown. In fact, Chile had the most severe financial and debt crisis among all Latin American countries. As might be suspected, the main culprits were unrestricted financial opening and accommodating monetary policies. This section outlines how the crisis developed and then discusses the impacts of the crisis on the Chilean political economy. I conclude the section by examining how distribution relations and overt distributional conflict in Chile shaped the institutional change pertaining to the capital account.

Boom

The 1982 crisis originated in a classic loan-based boom. As such, it neatly fits into the general model of financial crises developed by Minsky (1982). This model specifies that a crisis originates in an exogenous shock to the financial system, such as a fundamental policy change or financial innovation. This "displacement" then leads to an expansion in bank credit and money supply, feeding an economic boom. At this stage various opportunities for expanded consumption, investment, and production emerge in the economy (De Antoni, 2006; Minsky, 2008 [1986]; Gemici, 2012, 2016). Exploitation of these opportunities creates a bubble, causing significant asset price increases. When the bubble bursts, euphoria leaves its place to panic; contraction in economic activity follows (Kindleberger, 2000, 14–18).

The events spurring an economic boom in Chile were financial deregulation and capital account liberalization. Domestic financial liberalization began in 1974–75. First, in 1974, the establishment of private financing societies (*financieras*) were allowed. These financial institutions were favored over commercial banks—which were nationalized under the Allende government—since there were effective controls on commercial bank interest rates (Ffrench-Davis, 1983). Second, in 1975, a large number of banks were privatized through auctioning (Harberger, 1985).[8] Third, in October 1975, controls on domestic interest rates charged by commercial banks were removed (Edwards and Cox, 1987, 54–55). Fourth, controls on credit allocation and credit maturity were abolished (Ffrench-Davis, 1983, 910–11). Finally, reserve requirements for banks were gradually lowered between 1976 and 1980, which allowed banks to create money through lending to firms and to the general public (Barandiarán and Hernández, 1999, 6).

Cross-border capital flows were deregulated between 1977 and 1982 (Foxley, 1983, 58). The first step in deregulation occurred in September 1977. Commercial banks were allowed to trade in capital inflows through the Article 14 of the Exchange Law (Corbo, 1985, 915). Initially, Article 14 of the Exchange Law imposed considerable restrictions on the movement of capital in and out of Chile. Two of these restrictions were particularly binding. First, the level of foreign liabilities of a bank was limited. Second, there was a constraint on how much a bank's foreign liabilities could grow each month (Edwards and Cox, 1987, 55–56). The first one was removed in June 1979, leaving no specific regulation on the level of foreign liabilities (Corbo, 1985, 915).[9] The second one, the flow constraint, was abolished in April 1980 (Barandiarán and Hernández, 1999, 9).

Chilean authorities did not allow short-run capital movements. This was done by prohibiting capital movements with maturity less than 24 months and by maintaining reserve requirements for capital movements with maturity between 24 and 66 months (Edwards and Cox, 1987, 55). However, the maturity restrictions on capital movements were not effective in curbing unbalanced fiscal expansion for two reasons. First, capital inflows from the rest of the world were intermediated by banks, who used these funds to lend in the domestic economy. While Chilean banks borrowed from abroad at long-term maturity, they lent with maturities of 30 to 90 days in the domestic economy. Second, banks overborrowed partly as a result of aggressive expansion strategies by large conglomerates and partly in order to roll over bad loans. This was possible because of lax financial supervision. As a result, the Chilean financial system as a whole accumulated a large amount

8 The auctioning of nationalized banks was done in the middle of the 1975 recession. As such, it is open to the criticism that the nationalized banks were sold to the large *grupos* for values not reflecting their real worth.

9 There was still a capital adequacy ratio of 5 percent applicable to the total of domestic and foreign liabilities (Barandiarán and Hernández, 1999, 9).

Table 2.1 Foreign Debt, 1978–82

Indicator	*1978*	*1979*	*1980*	*1981*	*1982*
Total Foreign Debt[a]	6,664	8,484	11,084	15,542	17,153
Public Debt[b]	70.7	59.7	45.7	35.7	38.8
Private Debt[b]	29.3	40.3	54.3	64.8	61.2
Foreign Debt/Exports[c]	2.3	1.8	1.9	2.8	3.7
Net Domestic Savings[d]	1.1	2.7	4.1	−1.2	−8.6
Foreign Savings[d]	4.8	5.9	8.5	14.5	9.2

a Stock value, 1982 prices, millions of U.S. dollars. *Source:* Edwards and Cox (1987, Table 3-8).
b Percent share in total debt, calculated from Edwards and Cox (1987, Table 3-8).
c Ratio of foreign debt to exports, calculated from flow value in 1970 prices. *Source:* Ramos (1986, Table 2.1).
d Percent share in GDP, calculated from flow value in 1977 prices. *Source:* Edwards and Cox (1987, Table 3-3).

of assets (loans to private parties) with short-term maturity. The magnitude of the credit boom became evident when foreign banks and financial institutions stopped lending to Chile.

The evolution of Chile's foreign debt between 1977 and 1982 illustrates the magnitude of the boom spurred by financial deregulation and capital account liberalization. Financial deregulation, coupled with capital account liberalization that was completed in 1980, allowed domestic firms and banks to borrow at an increasing pace from abroad. As can be seen in Table 2.1, Chile's foreign debt jumped from $6.6 billion to $17.1 billion between 1978 and 1982. What is striking in this increase is the composition of the foreign debt. Within the same period, the share of private sector debt increased from 29.3 to 61.2 percent of the total debt. The increase in the amount of public debt was only $1.9 billion, whereas the increase in private debt was $8.5 billion.

In fact, Chile was replacing domestic savings by foreign savings. The share of net domestic savings (savings adjusted for the consumption of capital) in GDP was 4.1 percent in 1980, −1.2 percent in 1981, and −8.6 percent in 1982. Within the same period, foreign savings' share in GDP was 8.5 (1980), 14.5 (1981), and 9.2 percent (1982). These figures clearly show the magnitude of foreign savings' contribution to consumption and investment before the crisis.

The surge in foreign indebtedness was predominantly due to borrowing by Chilean banks (Cowan and De Gregorio, 2007, 246). The excessive borrowing by the Chilean banks fed a spurious financial development. Between 1978 and 1982, financial assets in the Chilean economy grew at rates of 30 to 40 percent a year, several times more than the rate of GDP growth (Table 2.2). Indeed, for each year between 1978 and 1982, the growth rate of financial assets that were due to only foreign loans were higher than the real GDP growth.[10] Not surprisingly, the ratio of loans to GDP increased from 0.232 to 0.733, while the

10 This can be seen by comparing foreign-loan based growth rates in financial assets (Table 2.2) with real GDP growth rates (Figure 2.2).

Table 2.2 Financial Expansion, 1978–82

Indicator	*1978*	*1979*	*1980*	*1981*	*1982*
Ratio of Loans[a]	0.23	0.28	0.38	0.5	0.73
Ratio of Assets[b]	0.34	0.39	0.51	0.64	0.92
Change in Financial Assets[c]	41.3	29.6	40.3	11.3	22.6
Foreign-Loan Based[d]	10.8	7.5	11.3	11.4	20.5

a Ratio of total loans to GDP, inflation-adjusted values. *Source:* Barandiarán and Hernández (1999, Table 2-6).
b Ratio of total assets to GDP, inflation-adjusted values. *Source:* Barandiarán and Hernández (1999, Table 2-6).
c Percent annual change in total financial assets, inflation-adjusted values. *Source:* Barandiarán and Hernández (1999, Table 2-3).
d Percent annual change in total financial assets that was due to foreign loans, inflation-adjusted values. *Source:* Barandiarán and Hernández (1999, Table 2-3).

ratio of assets to GDP registered a three-fold increase between 1978 and 1982 (Table 2.2).

The massive amount of capital inflows caused a remarkable asset value boom in Chile. This was, as highlighted in the first chapter, due to the increasing availability of funds that put upward pressure on asset prices.[11] If the domestic absorption capacity of foreign inflows is limited, the magnitude of the upward pressure increases, since domestic residents use foreign funds to chase after a limited supply of assets. In a rare empirical examination of land, stock market, and housing prices between 1979 and 1982, Morandé (1992) shows that foreign capital inflows was the most influential determinant of asset prices in Chile during this period. Both housing and stock market prices registered spectacular increases in these years. For example, at its peak in 1982, the overall price index of housing was more than 2 times its value prior to capital account liberalization and 4.5 times its value in 1989 (Morandé, 1992, 118).

In addition, the macroeconomic policies of the authorities supported the booming economy. Two aspects of the implemented policies were particularly important. One was the exchange rate policy that went into effect in June 1979, which fixed the value of the dollar to 39 pesos (Corbo, 1985). The authorities intended to use the fixed exchange rate as an anti-inflationary tool. They envisioned that by fixing the exchange rate, prices in the domestic economy would be anchored to external prices, which would stabilize the domestic inflation rate. The other was the real wage indexation mechanism that the military government implemented in 1979. The wage indexation mechanism made it mandatory that wage readjustment in collective bargaining fully covered the cost of past inflation (Mizala and Romaguera, 2001, 207).[12]

Both measures pushed the aggregate demand upwards. First, the automatic price adjustment mechanism did not function as the authorities envisioned. As a result of massive capital inflows, the real exchange rate appreciated considerably, which led to higher demand for tradable goods. Second, the backward wage

11 See Appendices C and B for the consequences of such a boom in asset prices.
12 Collective bargaining was restricted to the firm level.

Table 2.3 Boom and Crash, 1977–83

Indicator	*1977*	*1978*	*1979*	*1980*	*1981*	*1982*	*1983*
Exports[a]	12.0	11.8	14.2	14.5	−9.0	4.5	0.1
Imports[a]	32.4	18.1	23.9	20.7	13.3	−34	−17.7
Current Account Deficit[b]	3.7	5.2	5.4	7.1	14.5	9.2	5.4
Gross Fixed Investment[c]	13.3	14.5	15.6	17.4	19.2	13.7	11.9
Real Interest[d]	8.8	18.9	6.8	5.9	26.5	19.5	4.5
Unemployment[e]	14.2	14.2	13.8	11.9	10.9	20.4	18.6

a Percent annual growth rate, calculated from series in 1977 prices. Source: *Indicadores Económicos y Sociales de Chile, 1960–2000*, Banco Central De Chile.
b Percent share in GDP, calculated from series in current prices. Source: Ffrench-Davis and Tapia (2001, Table 3-3).
c Percent share of gross fixed capital investment in GDP, calculated from series in 1977 prices. Source: *Indicadores Económicos y Sociales de Chile, 1960–2000*, Banco Central De Chile.
d Average ex-post real annualized deposit interest rates. Source: Edwards and Cox (1987, Table 3-6).
e Source: Edwards and Cox (1987, Table 6-1).

indexation mechanism ensured that real wages recovered slightly from already depressed levels, which boosted demand (Corbo, 1985).

All these factors turned the economic boom into a bubble. First of all, foreign funds that were in abundance in the Chilean economy did not particularly feed capital formation and productive investment. Gross fixed capital formation in Chile was moderate at best during this time. As can be seen in Table 2.3, except the years 1980 and 1981, fixed capital formation rates were low.[13] Furthermore, most of the increase in fixed investment was in the construction sector (Harberger 1985; Oppenheim 2007, 138). However, the bubble was accompanied by a significant increase in imports and the current account deficit (Table 2.3). Chileans were importing more. They were financing the cost of imports not with the revenue of exports, but with increasing foreign debt (see the figures on foreign debt over exports ratio in Table 2.1 and the figures on increasing current account deficit in Table 2.3). Hence, this was the period of high consumerism and economic euphoria in Chile (Silva, 1996, 137).

Crash

The bubble burst as the world economic climate changed from high liquidity and low interest rates to low liquidity and high interest rates, when Paul Volcker implemented tight money policies in the United States (Brenner, 2002). A major financial group went bankrupt in March 1981. Financial distress exacerbated in the second half of 1981, when international banks cut credit lines to Chile (Silva, 1991, 396–97). Concomitantly, the Chilean terms of trade deteriorated as the price of copper plunged. As a result, economic conditions in Chile worsened in 1982.

13 Nonetheless, even such low rates of fixed capital formation constituted an improvement, given the history of anemic capital accumulation and growth in Chile (Figure 2.2).

Despite an initial reluctance, the Chilean authorities had to abandon the fixed exchange rate policy in June 1982. As the early financial distress transmuted into a full-blown financial collapse, the government had to intervene and provide assistance to two large private banks. The monetary authorities intervened into 21 financial institutions between 1981 and 1986 (Barandiarán and Hernández, 1999, 42–43). This, in an ironic manner, constituted a re-nationalization of private banks (Rozas and Marín, 1989). In addition to active interventions, the government implemented various other programs (such as debt rescheduling, preferential exchange rates, and debt recapitalization) in order to overcome the financial meltdown and debt crisis.

As can be seen in Table 2.3, the economic and social consequences of the 1982 crash were disastrous. The value of imports collapsed by one third in 1982. The real interest rate jumped from 5.9 percent in 1980 to 26.5 percent in 1981 and to 19.5 percent in 1982. The share of gross investment in GNP decreased from 23.9 percent in 1981 to 9.6 percent in 1982. The real GDP declined by 16.6 percent in 1982 (Figure 2.2). When one takes into account the adverse effect of the concurrent terms of trade shock on national income, the fall in the real GNP was 19 percent (Edwards and Cox, 1987, Table 8-1). That was equal to the loss of one fifth of the Chilean gross national income. As capital inflows came to a halt, the drop in the real aggregate expenditure was even sharper: 24 percent (Edwards and Cox, 1987, Table 8-1). In 1982, the unemployment rate surged to 20.4 percent, one-fifth of the total labor force.[14] As of late 1983, those who were in absolute poverty constituted 50 percent of the total population (Barandiarán and Hernández, 1999, 1). In addition, Chile's total stock of external debt stayed at a level higher than its GDP between 1982 and 1987. The approximate annual amount paid as interest payment on this debt was equal to 8 percent of the Chilean GDP (Meller, 1996, 266).

Explaining financial openness

Why did Chile follow this particular trajectory of financial opening? At the most fundamental level, the long history of distributional conflict in a low-growth economy should be singled out because it led to a deeply polarized society. As Fourcade-Gourinchas and Babb (2002, 543) argue, "Such conflict ultimately exploded into more overt class warfare, exemplified by the Allende government's nationalization of private assets and the subsequent military coup backed by large business groups." It is significant that the various political factions united under Allende's political alliance had an explicit agenda for economic democracy, redistribution, and transformation in relations of production. It is also significant that the *Unidad Popular* registered large gains for the working and middle classes in a short amount of time (Figure 2.1). However, the *Unidad Popular* government's attempt to alter the existing balance of power in Chile was not successful. Such an

14 If the share of labor force employed in the minimum employment program is considered as unemployed too, the unemployment rate was approximately 30 percent.

attempt prodded the large business groups and the military to radically transform Chilean economy and society.

In line with the theoretical model outlined in the introduction, the balance of power dynamics arising from distributional conflict were crucial in creating the vacuum and thus the opportunity structure for a novel ideology—neoliberalism—to become dominant in policy-making circles. Neoliberal beliefs, ideas, and values triumphed only because distributional conflict underpinned a massive realignment of power.

Once in power—following a long period of economic stagnation that culminated in crisis—the Chicago Boys had an unprecedented license to implement their radical ideas. And they operated with an unwavering belief in the adequacy of the macroeconomic policies they implemented.[15] Such a conviction had a basis in the ideological purity of the Chicago Boys, illustrated in Sergio de Castro's unconditional belief in economic theory and market forces (Arancibia, 2006, 354):

> Cualquier economista que estudie Economía en cualquier parte del mundo, sabe que lo que nosotros hicimos fue aplicar la teoría económica a los problemas específicos que tenía Chile. Yo creo que solo hay una ciencia económica, cuyos principios tienen validez universal; lo que cambia es la aplicación de los mismos, sus énfasis, que es lo propio de la política económica.[16]

Textbook-style economic management guided by pure ideology was especially evident in the intended use of the fixed exchange rate as an anti-inflationary tool. The measure itself was inspired by the monetary approach to balance of payments that was gaining currency in orthodox academic circles at that time.[17] The Chilean economic team followed the monetary approach in a methodical manner and expected the automatic adjustment mechanism to function smoothly. This can be seen in the following lengthy passage by the finance minister Sergio de Castro (quoted in Edwards and Cox 1987, 46):

> The neutral monetary policy of the Central Bank implies that money is only created as a result of inflows of foreign exchange. If such inflows do not take place via a higher level of foreign loans, the private sector's desire to finance a high current account deficit will be simultaneously reflected in a loss of international reserves, and in an equivalent monetary contraction. This will raise the interest rate, generating a decline in expenditure and in the

15 Interviews with Manuel Marfán, Roberto Zahler, and Ricardo Ffrench-Davis, October–December 2006, Santiago, Chile.

16 "Any economist who studies economics in any part of the world knows that what we did was to apply economic theory to the specific problems Chile was having. I believe that there is only one economic science, whose principles hold universal validity; what changes is the application of these principles, their emphases, which is the essence of political economy." (Author's translation.)

17 The main implication of this approach was the view that all balance of payments disequilibria were monetary phenomena and that such phenomena were simply transitory (Johnson, 1977, 226–28). The economic team stipulated that under the fixed exchange rate system, an automatic adjustment mechanism through international capital flows would bring balance of payments equilibria. They saw domestic money supply as endogenously determined by domestic credit expansion and international capital flows (Fausten 1979, 661; Whitman 1975, 499).

demand for imports, to the level required to finance a current account deficit compatible with the level of foreign borrowing that the country can sustain.

This approach did not pay any attention to institutional factors and economic heterogeneity. Furthermore, the Chicago Boys systematically neglected the warning signs that would have been evident to a more pragmatic group of economists (Edwards and Cox, 1987; Ffrench-Davis, 1983).

In addition, the wave of capital account reforms that started in 1977 ushered an economic boom that enlarged the domestic pie considerably in Chile. The economic expansion was beneficial for the consumption of the majority of Chileans, including the middle classes whose disposable income rose considerably. However, the benefits accrued most clearly to large business groups. This was because the credit supply channel worked overwhelmingly for the benefit of big capitalists.[18] These were conglomerates with an international orientation and access to liquid assets. Furthermore, they controlled the majority of financial intermediaries in Chile (Silva, 1996). The large business groups also benefited from rising asset prices (see Appendix B). However, the external-finance originated bubble was to the detriment of small and medium-scale firms, as outlined in Appendix B. That is because: (1) these firms could not access foreign credit, (2) they faced very high real interest rates, and (3) asset price increases did not favor them (Ffrench-Davis, 1983; Rozas and Marín, 1989).

Exporters were the other victims of an economic expansion financed by international capital flows. Because of the fixed exchange rate regime, capital inflows, and high real interest rates, the Chilean peso appreciated considerably between 1979 and 1982. Figure 2.3 presents movements in the real exchange rate before and after the fixed exchange rate regime. It can be seen in Figure 2.3 that the appreciation of the Chilean peso started immediately after June 1979, when an important restriction on foreign borrowing was removed, and the fixed exchange rate regime was announced. The Chilean real exchange rate appreciated 35 percent between July 1979 and April 1982. As such, it damaged the competitiveness of Chilean products in world markets while making imports cheaper (Edwards and Cox, 1987, 129). In contrast, fixed exchange rate regime and high level of financial openness provided significant economic benefits to the conglomerates controlling financial intermediaries (Silva, 1996).

In other words, the full institutionalization of capital account liberalization occurred through the increasing returns generated by the distributional benefits associated with these neoliberal policies. To be sure, the benefits were not evenly distributed, and some groups such as exporters and domestic producers suffered under this institutional change. However, the economic boom was real. So was the euphoria associated with such spectacular expansion following decades of low growth in a high-inflation economy. Under such conditions, it is no wonder that the Chicago Boys and their neoliberal ideology enjoyed legitimacy and reinforced

18 The extreme concentration of wealth and economic power in few conglomerates exacerbated the uneven distribution of credit. See Appendix B for a theoretical model on the implications of credit supply channel under capital mobility for different social groups.

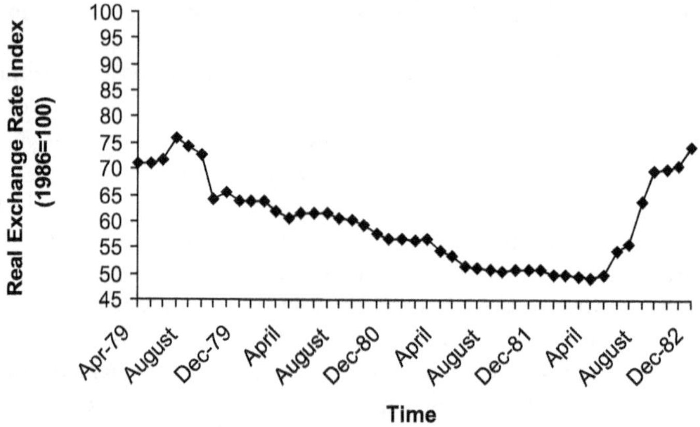

Figure 2.3 Real Exchange Rate, 1979–82.
Note: The real exchange rate series presented here take into account the structure of Chile's foreign trade, domestic inflation, and world inflation. A lower value on the real exchange rate index signifies appreciation of the domestic currency. Source: *Social and Economic Indicators, 1960–2000*, Central Bank of Chile.

the Pinochet dictatorship. As outlined in the introduction, unfettered capital mobility became a crucial instrument in the struggle for legitimizing an authoritarian regime through a fragile economic boom.

Thus, Chile became neoliberal *avant la lettre*, before Thatcher in the United Kingdom and Reagan in the United States. Until late 1981, the country was considered a success and a triumph story in implementing radical reforms. Furthermore, before the banking crisis erupted, there was no clear recognition of how fragile the financial expansion was. However, as the next section shows, the legitimacy of the regime and the fate of radical neoliberalism changed dramatically once euphoria left its place to hardship and despair.

The reordering of political and economic power

As observed by several scholars (Frieden 1991b, 427, 2006; Kaufman 1979; Silva 1991), the financial opening and economic growth between 1977 and 1982 was crucial for the progress of neoliberalism in Chile. The economic recovery following the 1975 recession became an economic boom between 1979 and 1981. It was this economic performance that produced a triumphalist discourse about the "Chilean miracle" (Vergara, 1985, 184–87). The economic boom was instrumental for the military rule and the neoliberal project. First, it helped consolidate Pinochet's hold on political power through a referendum in 1978 and then through the 1980 Constitution. Second, it provided the justification for implementing major neoliberal reforms, known as "seven modernizations." Third, economic growth was an indispensable component of a politically conservative vision for the future of Chile, defended by a certain faction of right-wing intellectuals.

As a result, the collapse of the economic growth in 1982 was a severe blow to the projects of political conservatism and economic neoliberalism in Chile. The 1982 crisis led to a transformation of political and economic power. Gradually, a less hawkish variety of neoliberalism replaced monetarism. Thus, this section traces the change in balance of power following the 1982 crisis.

Huneeus (2000, 468–71) argues that the Chilean state under Pinochet was a dualist state, employing distinct rationalities within the spheres of economy and polity. On paper and in terms of doctrinaire ideology, these two rationalities—one stressing minimal state and regulatory framework, the other embodying authoritarian and encompassing control over society—were seemingly contradictory. However, the two rationalities exhibited a strong affinity in denying legitimacy to democratic politics and in separating economy and politics (Block and Somers, 2014; Polanyi, 2001 [1944]). Furthermore, the two rationalities were linked to each other through the politics of growth. As Silva (1991, 395) argues, "[Pinochet] was well aware of the fact that for the definitive consolidation of his personal rule he needed the continuous achievement of successes on the 'economic front.' " Not only Pinochet, but a team of right-wing intellectuals, the *Gremialistas*,[19] envisioned economic growth as part of a comprehensive political model of limited democracy (Oppenheim, 2007, 115–19). In the words of Huneeus (2007, 357), "It was thought that the economic boom would take the country out of underdevelopment and further legitimize the regime, which was to progress gradually toward a limited democracy." Furthermore, as compellingly shown by Huneeus (2000), this group of right-wing intellectuals were closely linked to (or overlapped with) the Chicago Boys.

This political strategy found its expression in the 1980 Constitution, which was a coercive attempt to provide legitimacy to the military government and to the dictatorship of Pinochet (Silva, 1991, 396). The practical motivation for enacting the 1980 Constitution was twofold. On the one hand, the Constitution carried the objective of determining the successor regime, since the junta did not aim for a permanent authoritarian rule (Barros, 2002, 178–79).[20] On the other hand, because of internal and external pressures, the junta and Pinochet sought legitimacy for the military rule (Ramón, 2001, 250–52).[21]

19 The *Gremialistas* were a group of right-wing intellectuals headed by Jaime Guzmán, who founded *El Movimiento Gremial Universitario* in 1966 (Huneeus, 2000). Guzmán and the *Gremialistas* were the main political ideologues behind the military regime (Barros, 2002; Cristi, 2000; Huneeus, 2000). For example, it was Guzmán who wrote the famous *Chacarillas* speech of Pinochet, which laid out the program and goals of the military regime (Huneeus, 2007; Oppenheim, 2007). He was also one of the principal authors of the 1980 Constitution. Guzmán was assassinated on April 1, 1991 by *Frente Patriótico Manuel Rodríguez* (FPMR)—the Manuel Rodríguez Patriotic Front.

20 The junta and its ideologues envisioned a transition period after which a right-wing government could continue the conservative political project under democracy (Oppenheim 2007, 117–19; Ramón 2001, 254–55). The constitution named Pinochet—the only individual recognized in the constitution—as president until 1989, which could be extended until 1997 through a plebiscite (Barros, 2002; Ramón, 2001).

21 The intellectual motivation was the notion of "autocratic, protected, and technified democracy" that was thought of as the *sine qua non* of transitioning into a better government (Ramón, 2001, 250–58). "Autocratic, protected, and technified democracy" aimed to limit separation of powers

The constitutional reform and the concurrent economic boom instituted the political basis for implementing encompassing neoliberal reforms that targeted a structural change in state-society relations (Huneeus 2007, 166; Silva 1991). This was achieved through modernizations in seven major areas, including labor, health, education, pension, judiciary, administrative, and agricultural reforms (Délano and Traslaviña, 1989, 79). All of these reforms invoked replacement of functions carried by the state with market forces. Furthermore, they embodied the atomization of economic relations. There was a close affinity between Pinochet's desire for a politically atomized society and the Chicago Boys' project for an economically atomized society (Oppenheim, 2007, 133), which implied strong complementarity between the Pinochet regime and neoliberalism.

The triumphalism of radical monetarists came to an end in mid-1982 as the deteriorating economic conditions obligated concessions in hard-line economic reforms and management. The team led by Sergio de Castro (the finance minister) proposed to address the economic crisis by further privatizations and wage cuts (Huneeus, 2007, 362–63). However, as the economic boom turned into a major crisis, such measures became politically unacceptable. Instead of following his proposals, Pinochet replaced de Castro in April 1982 (Rozas and Marín, 1989, 45).

The firing of de Castro marked the defeat of monetarist neoliberalism in Chile. The fixed exchange rate and thus the "automatic adjustment" policy was abandoned in June 1982. Until April 1984, there was a quick succession of finance ministers coming from the ranks of Chicago Boys. As these technocrats shared the same ideological rigidity with their predecessors, the policies they implemented failed to address the ongoing economic crisis (Valdés, 1995, 262–63). In addition, these technocrats were forced, in the midst of a financial meltdown, to implement policies that were diametrically opposite to their project (e.g., providing public guarantees to private debts).

Meanwhile, massive social protests shook Santiago and the whole of Chile in 1983 and 1984.[22] Protests began in May 1983 under the initial leadership of the Copper Workers Federation (CTC) (Garréton, 2001, 266; Schneider, 1995).[23] The unemployed from middle and lower-class backgrounds, university students, shantytown dwellers, and workers from various sectors participated in

and political participation; it aspired to enact a form of government which was "purified of the vices and bad habits" (quoted in Huneeus 2007, 142).

22 The Pinochet dictatorship was marked by state violence and oppression. However, between 1973 and 1983, the opposition and protest against the military rule and dictatorship did not involve mass mobilization. Instead, political defiance and opposition were local and fragile (Schneider, 1995, 3). This changed in 1983. The sudden increase in unemployment and poverty following the 1982 financial crisis spurred dissatisfaction with the dictatorship's economic policies (Martínez and Díaz 1996, 18–19; Stallings 1989).

23 The economic and political weight of the CTC was critical in turning the movement into a national uprising (Martínez and Díaz, 1996, 22). The CTC carried a significant political legacy: it was copper workers who took a dominant role in the October 1972 strike against the Allende government, which was a turning point in the chain of events leading to the 1973 *coup* (Huneeus, 2000, 477).

these protests (Oxhorn, 1995; Schneider, 1995).[24] Although the government responded to protests by repressive measures, such regular protests with participation from various social groups limited the level of repression that could be used (Garréton, 2001).[25]

As a result, Pinochet was forced to make a limited set of concessions in order to control the increasing opposition. A major concession was the appointment of an interior minister coming from the old right, Sergio Onofre Jarpa Reyes. Sergio Jarpa followed a policy of political opening. Likewise, the military government started responding to demands from groups such as small-size business owners and sectoral associations. In other words, as Vergara (1985, 240) puts it fittingly, the military government transitioned from essentialist politics to *transactional* politics as a result of the economic crisis.

At the same time, conglomerates such as *Vial* and *Cruzat-Larraín*, whose economic strengths were based on the burgeoning finance sector and financial openness, took a heavy blow during the crisis. This implied that a different segment of capitalists, which included exporters and producers for domestic sectors, began articulating economic demands and propositions (Silva, 1996, 176).

The realignment of power prepared the ground for another institutional change. In this institutional change, a pragmatic and heterodox type of neoliberalism played a key role. This variety of neoliberalism also shared the vision that economic growth and development originated from free markets. However, it was more flexible and allowed controls, regulations, and incentives that complemented the operation of markets. In the words of Valdés (1995, 269), "The dogmatic approach to economic science was rejected, given its failure to deal with an economic reality that it found evasive and unmanageable." Furthermore, a strong export boom in the second half of the 1980s reinforced such institutional change.

Recovery, export miracle, and its political consequences

Given the severity of the 1982 crisis and the atmosphere of gloom that characterized Latin America in the 1980s, the Chilean recovery that began in 1984 and 1985 was remarkable and unexpected even to most perceptive observers. Indeed, the Chilean disaster became the Chilean economic miracle in a few years; the real GDP surpassing the peak performance of 1981 in 1988 (Barandiarán and Hernández, 1999).

The rapid Chilean economic recovery was possible due to the combination of several factors. A crucial component was the pragmatic macroeconomic policies that allowed Chilean exports to expand and diversify at a rapid rate. Chilean

24 The protests were, at least at their initial stages, widely supported by middle classes (Garréton, 2001).

25 The protests continued until 1986 (Schneider, 1995, 4). Hence, the financial crash and the subsequent economic crisis paved the way for a mass uprising that effectively challenged the military rule (Martínez and Díaz, 1996, 18–20). Furthermore, as Schneider (1995, 13) notes, "[The] economic crisis created the political context for the reemergence of political parties, unions, and nongovernmental organizations."

economic authorities implemented monetary and fiscal policies that maintained stability in key macroeconomic aggregates. Chile was also successful in establishing a policy to convert accumulated foreign debt to equity through an innovative policy instrument, which subsidized foreign direct investment in export sectors. Furthermore, financial regulation and supervision infrastructure were modernized. There was improvement in Chilean terms of trade. The exchange rate was sustained at competitive levels. All of these factors enabled the build-up of productive capacity in sectors such as agriculture and fishing to be transformed into an export boom.

This section explains the development and origins of the Chilean economic boom in the second half of the 1980s. The economic performance in this period is important because Chilean economic growth and dynamism originated in export sectors. Thus, a competitive level of exchange rate became a top priority for the most dynamic sectors of the economy. Furthermore, policy-makers began to recognize competitive exchange rate policy as an indispensable component of Chilean economic growth.

The rise of the export sector

The banking system was in a major disarray after the 1982 crisis. The Chilean economy faced a massive current account deficit. As access to international finance halted, financial collapse led to a balance of payments crisis. The Chilean authorities had to enter into debt negotiations involving international banks and the IMF (Somerville, 1992, 108). These negotiations resulted in a provisional agreement with international banks and in a structural adjustment program that provided much-needed external finance (Meller, 1991, 1550). However, because of the magnitude of the Chilean debt, the external finance guaranteed in the early period of the debt crisis was insufficient. Furthermore, the stock of private foreign debt, which was partially nationalized through the Central Bank after the 1982 crisis, imposed heavy interest payments on the Chilean state. Such onerous payments led authorities to seek macroeconomic policies that would increase the level of public saving and domestic private saving. This was also the strategy that the international financial institutions favored.

Generating a trade surplus became an explicit economic goal during this period. This necessitated reducing imports and expanding exports through carefully designed macroeconomic and structural reform policies (Ffrench-Davis, 2002, 164–65). As the control of monetarists over economic policy loosened, the implementation of heterodox policy measures began in 1983 (Silva, 1996, 181–93). For example, small and medium-sized businesses obtained preferential exchange rates for their debts (Silva, 1996, 179). In 1983, the uniform tariff rate was increased to 20 percent. Later, in 1984, the tariff rate was increased again, this time to 35 percent. Additional surtaxes for a number of products were also put into practice (Stallings, 2001, 30).

The exchange rate policy was initially an area of experimentation and inconsistency after the initial financial meltdown. Thus, as Meller (1991, 1548) points out, the Chilean authorities implemented several distinct exchange rate regimes between June and September 1982. The exchange rate policy was later fixed in a crawling peg (Ffrench-Davis, 2002, 226). The crawling peg was utilized for establishing a competitive level of exchange rate. This was achieved through orderly depreciation as well as large one-time devaluations (Agosin 1999, 90; Ffrench-Davis 2002, 226). Consequently, the real exchange rate exhibited a secular trend of depreciation after 1983, as can be seen in Figure 2.4.

The competitive exchange rate policy promoted the transfer of resources to export sectors and specifically to sectors producing tradable goods. Policies aiming at a rapid growth in exports were not limited to this. Another major component was a significant fall in real wage, as reflected in Figures 2.5 and 2.6. Although the data are missing for 1983 and 1984, these figures show a marked downward trend in real wage and wage share. The decline in real wage ensured that the labor cost of producing tradable goods decreased (Meller, 1991, 1555–57). Other data sources offer information on the magnitude of distributional losses for the working classes for the years 1983 and 1984. If one takes the level of real wage in the 1980–81 period as the base, real wage was 8.9 percent lower in 1983 (Meller, 1991, Table 9). The fall continued in the following years. At the end of 1985, the level of real wages was 20 percent lower compared to the 1980–81 period (Meller, 1991, Table 9). The real wage remained at low levels, despite great cost to wage-earners, until 1988, as can be seen in Figure 2.5 (Labán and Larraín, 1995, Table 4.1). However, such distributional repression was instrumental in enabling an increased profit rate for the Chilean private sector, as can be seen in the rising profit rate in Figure 2.5.

Similarly, there was a change in monetary policy (Budnevich and Cifuentes, 1993, 36). Beginning in 1984, the Central Bank of Chile implemented policies

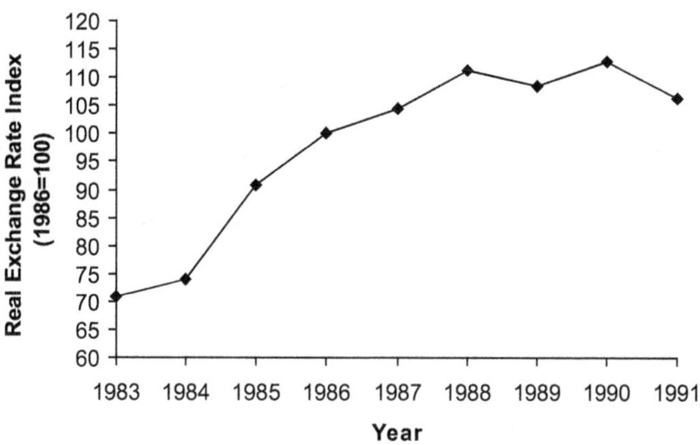

Figure 2.4 Real Exchange Rate, 1983–91.
Note: The real exchange rate series presented here take into account the structure of Chile's foreign trade, domestic inflation, and world inflation. A higher value on the real exchange rate index signifies depreciation of the domestic currency. Source: *Social and Economic Indicators, 1960–2000*, Central Bank of Chile.

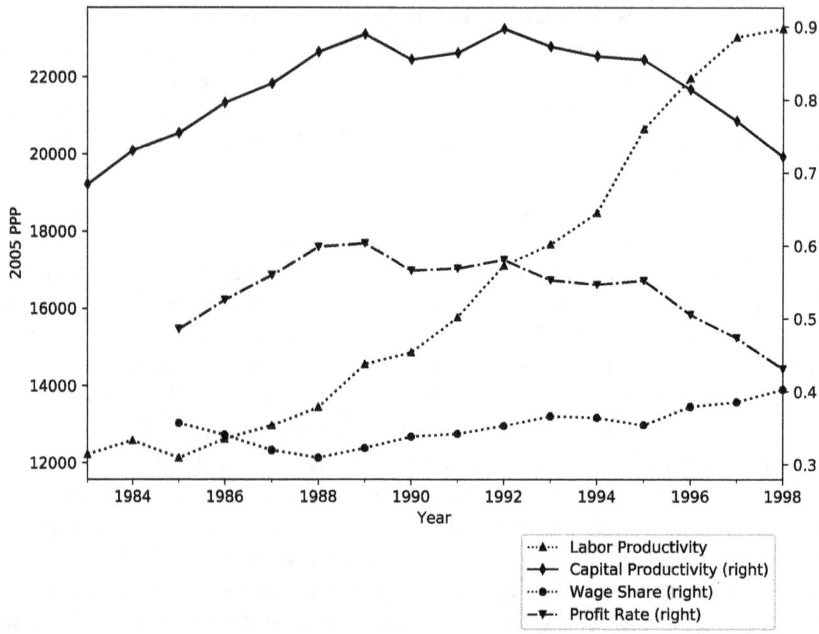

Figure 2.5 Distributional Dynamics, 1983–98.
Note: Wage share and profit rate are missing for 1983 and 1984 in the Extended Penn World Tables v. 4. See Appendix A for the definition of variables and for the explanation of axes in this figure.
Source: Extended Penn World Tables v. 4 (Foley and Michl, 1999; Marquetti, 2003).

targeting a decrease in real interest rates. The goal of this policy was to stimulate private investment (Fontaine, 1991, 121).

In addition, while keeping the vision of economic development and growth driven by private business and markets (and specifically by export industries), the Chilean state took an active role in the economy (Martínez and Díaz, 1996; Moguillansky, 1999). This active role was best exemplified in the export promotion policies adopted after 1985. These policies included various drawback systems,[26] recuperation of duties and taxes paid for inputs used in exported goods, and exemption of tariffs on capital goods (Agosin 1999, 93; Ffrench-Davis 2002, 167; Moguillansky 1999, 48).

The most unusual aid to export sectors involved the use of debt-equity swaps. In simple terms, debt-equity swaps allowed Chilean debtors to convert their debts—bought and sold in international markets—to equity claims (Ffrench-Davis, 2002, 148). Because of the particularities in the implementation, debt-equity swaps involved a preferential exchange rate for creditors and thus amounted to a net subsidy (Ffrench-Davis, 2002, 158–59). The Central Bank leaned heavily toward the authorization of conversions in activities and projects

26 These systems are designed so that the exporter receives cash subsidies for exports up to a certain volume.

related to export sectors.[27] This resulted in an indirect subsidy to export sectors.[28] In sum, as Agosin (1999, 94) observes, "The authorities made a virtue out of necessity and applied an industrial policy under another name."

Another example of the changing role of the state was the regulation and supervision of the financial system, which was enacted in 1986. This law greatly strengthened the supervisory role of the state, established rules and regulations on risk, and determined adequate capitalization requirements (Stallings, 2001, 32). Furthermore, the authorities imposed limitations on credits allocated to related firms (Held and Jiménez, 2001, 157–58). Except for small investor deposits, all guarantees on deposits were abolished (Held and Jiménez, 2001, 159).

In brief, the 1982 crisis—and the transformation of economic and political power that followed the crisis—led to significant changes in Chilean economic policy. To a large extent, the working and middle classes bore the cost of adjustment (Figure 2.5). However, the repression of wages enabled a major reordering of distributional dynamics between the different segments of the capitalist class. Notable changes in economic policy occurred in tandem. Instead of an orthodox set of economic measures and automatic adjustment mechanisms, economic authorities initiated "the realignment of relative prices to increase exports" (Martínez and Díaz, 1996, 54). This realignment involved mini-devaluations, control of interest rates, low real wages, and adjustments in tariffs (Martínez and Díaz, 1996, 54–55). Furthermore, the state took an active economic role through its various macroeconomic and export-promotion policies. Moguillansky (1999, 16) calls this role a new "dirigism," which discriminated between sectors and types of economic activities. The next section traces the outcomes of these policies.

Recovery and growth based on export dynamism

The realignment of political economy around the export sector provided the much-needed economic growth and dynamics in Chile. Figure 2.6 illustrates the recovery of the Chilean economy following the financial meltdown in the early 1980s. As can be seen, economic growth was quite strong in the second half of the 1980s. From 1986 onwards, the real GDP grew at a rate consistently above 5 percent, registering a remarkable 7.3 percent in 1988 and 10.8 percent in 1989. Unlike the previous periods, the economic growth in the second half of the 1980s was accompanied with increasing domestic saving and gross fixed capital formation (Figure 2.7).

The growth performance was reflected in unemployment figures as well. As can be seen in Figure 2.8, which presents the evolution of unemployment between 1980 and 1991, unemployment started to increase by the end of 1981. It peaked in the second half of 1982 and stayed at high levels until the end of 1985.

27 For further details and evidence, see the reappraisal of this program—enacted through the Chapter XIX of the Exchange Law in 1985—by the Chilean officials who took a role in debt management and renegotiations with international creditors: Somerville (1992) and Mayorga and Alvear (1992).

28 The magnitude of this subsidy is significant but difficult to measure. For further details, see Ffrench-Davis (2002) and Moguillansky (1999).

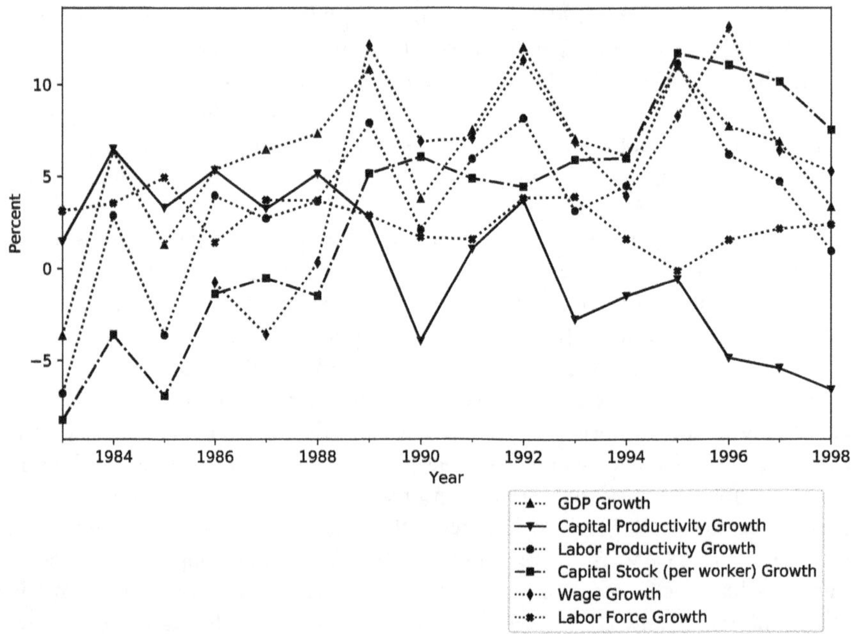

Figure 2.6 Growth Dynamics, 1983–98.
Note: Wage growth rate is missing for 1983 and 1984 in the Extended Penn World Tables v. 4. See Appendix A for the definition of variables used in this figure.
Source: Extended Penn World Tables v. 4 (Foley and Michl, 1999; Marquetti, 2003).

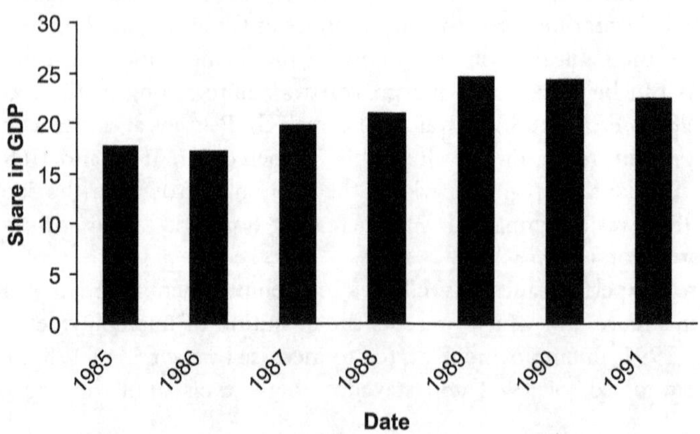

Figure 2.7 Gross Fixed Investment, 1985–91.
Note: The share of gross fixed capital formation in GDP, 1986 prices.
Source: *Social and Economic Indicators, 1960–2000*, Central Bank of Chile.

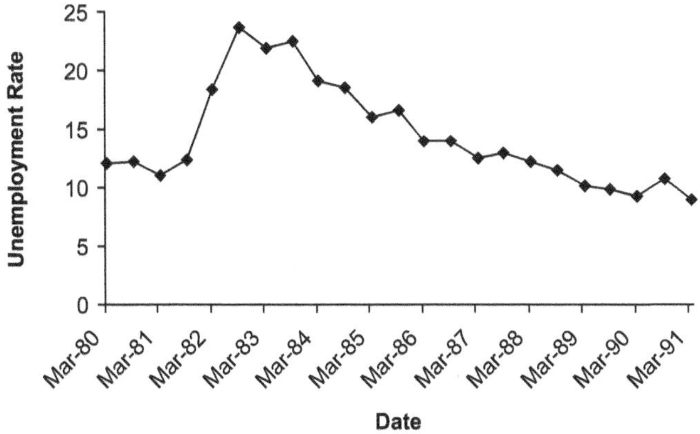

Figure 2.8 Unemployment Rate, 1980–91.
Source: *Social and Economic Indicators, 1960–2000*, Central Bank of Chile.

Through a secular trend of decline, the Chilean economy reached 9 percent unemployment rate in the first half of 1991. Considering that minimum employment programs such as PEM were terminated by the end of the 1980s, these numbers show a significant trend of recovery and growth.

Within the same period, gross fixed investment rate also recovered from the low levels of the 1970s and early 1980s (Figure 2.7). While gross fixed investment constituted only 17.1 percent of GDP in 1985, it jumped to 22.4 percent in 1991. At its peak, in 1989, it reached 24.5 percent of GDP. These numbers show that there was a significant momentum in business confidence and investment activity by the end of the 1980s.

The source of the economic dynamism and recovery was exports, which registered the highest rate of growth. Indeed, the evolution of exports since the fall of the Allende government shows a remarkable increase in how much exporting activity contributed to the Chilean GDP. In 1974, exports constituted only 14.5 percent of the Chilean GDP (Figure 2.9). The share of exports in GDP increased steadily during the 1970s, and it stood at 25 percent by the end of 1980. Despite a decrease in 1981, the high growth trend continued throughout the 1980s, with significant acceleration in the second half of the 80s. By the end of 1991, the share of exports in the Chilean GDP was 34.7 percent. In other words, exports became the chief source of dynamism and growth of the Chilean economy.

For much of its history in the twentieth century, Chilean exports were dominated by copper. This began to change after the international opening implemented during the 1970s. While copper continued to hold its dominant position, there was also a remarkable diversification in the Chilean exports. As can be seen in Figure 2.10, in 1974 copper exports constituted 75 percent of the Chilean exports. This percentage decreased in the 1970s. In 1978, copper and non-copper exports had equal weight in the total value of the Chilean exports. The ratio of

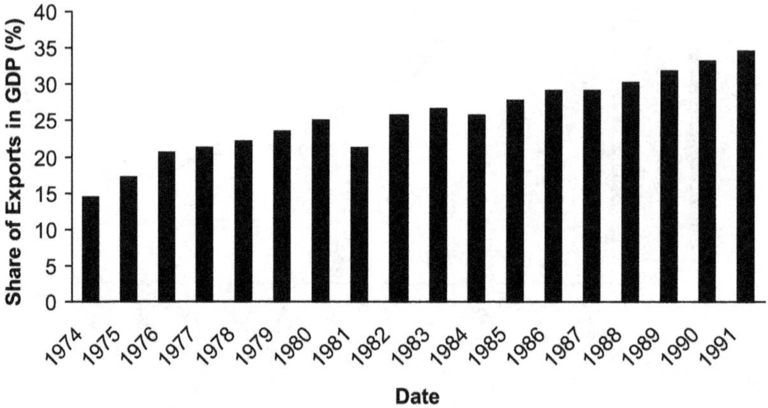

Figure 2.9 Share of Exports in GDP, 1974–91.
Note: The share of exports in GDP, calculated from expenditure on GDP Series, 1986 prices.
Source: *Social and Economic Indicators, 1960–2000*, Central Bank of Chile.

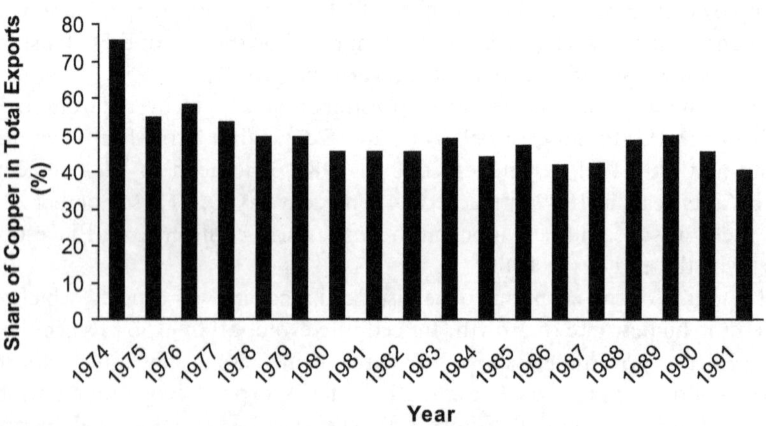

Figure 2.10 Share of Copper in Total Exports, 1974–91.
Source: *Social and Economic Indicators, 1960–2000*, Central Bank of Chile. The percentages are calculated from balance of payments data, current prices in US dollars.

copper in total exports continued its downward trend throughout the 1980s. At the end of 1991, copper constituted only 40 percent of the Chilean exports.

The extent of export diversification is illustrated in Table 2.4, which presents the annual average growth rates of export volumes by types of goods (Agosin, 1999, 84). In all the periods under examination, the growth rate of copper exports was lower than total non-copper growth rates. Furthermore, many export industries registered quite strong—if not spectacular—growth rates between

Table 2.4 Export Growth Rates by Types of Goods, 1974–95†

Product	*1974–81*	*1982–89*	*1990–95*
Copper	7.8	4.6	7.8
Other Minerals	6.7	6.5	3.4
Agricultural Products	32.6	11.8	7.0
Fishmeal and Fishery Products	45.8	11.1	3.0
Wood and Wood Products	41.0	7.3	4.3
Pulp and Paper	18.5	0.8	22.7
Other Manufactures	38.6	9.2	12.7
Total Non-Copper	12.0	6.5	9.0

† All numbers are in percentage terms. Source: Agosin (1999, Table 2).

1974 and 1991.[29] While all types of goods, except copper and various other minerals grew at exceptionally strong rates, the strength of the growth was particularly noticeable in agricultural, fishery, and wood products. It should be observed that the export volumes of these goods continued high growth rates (i.e., in double digits), even after the first decade of opening to international trade.

Ramifications: a solid export coalition and export-based growth

Chilean economy was volatile under the military rule: it experienced a major depression in 1975, a boom between 1978 and 1981, a major crisis in 1982–83, and finally a period of high growth after 1985. The main achievements of the military rule were: (1) a decisive transformation of the Chilean economy and society,[30] (2) the integration of the Chilean economy with the rest of the world, and (3) an export-led growth strategy that capitalized on rich natural resources in Chile (particularly after the 1982 meltdown).[31]

Chile became increasingly unequal during this period. Apart from the artificial boom of 1977–82, the real wage declined in a secular manner. As a result, Chilean wage-earners overwhelmingly bore the cost of neoliberal policies (Figures 2.1 and 2.5). The average salary during the sustained economic boom period (1985–89) was 13 percent lower than the average salary in 1970 (Stallings, 2001, Table 5.1). In 1987, the richest 20 percent's share of income was 56.3 percent, while the poorest 20 percent's share was 4.5 percent (Torche, 2000, Table 10). The poverty level was even more alarming. 45 percent of the population was under poverty level in 1987 (Stallings, 2001, Table 5.1).

29 The growth rates in the first period (1974–81) are—to a certain extent—artificially high because of economic depression and underuse of capacity during the *Unidad Popular* government.

30 See the book *Chile: The Great Transformation* by Martínez and Díaz (1996) on this point.

31 The impressive export growth and diversification observed in this period had deeper roots. As observed by various authors (Martínez and Díaz, 1996; Meller, 1996; Riesco, 1999), the export boom in Chile reflected a complex amalgam of policies and economic transformations, including: (1) decades of investment in human capital in sectors such as agriculture and fishery, (2) a comparative advantage emanating from richness in natural resources, (3) filling particular niches such as wine and fish products in industrialized country markets, and (4) the land reforms during the Frei and Allende administrations. Due to these complex origins, Chile had a solid export-led growth at the end of the 1980s.

It is clear that, during the 1980s, the Chilean state reorganized itself and the rules and regulations pertaining to the operation of markets around export-led growth. This model provided ample success and growth in the second half of the 1980s. The successful realization of the export-led growth had several political implications.

First, despite rising income inequality and the decline in real wages after the crisis, the Chilean economy started growing at a fast rate. This time, the economic growth was not fictitious. Nor was it fragile. For a country that experienced anemic growth for the entire post-war period and entered the 1980s with a financial meltdown, the gains were substantial.

Second, this economic growth led to the formation of a bloc of capitalists whose interests lay in competitive exchange rates. In the period after the 1973 *coup*, the Chilean economy was dominated by conglomerates that expanded through investment in financial intermediation. In the period after the 1982 crash, the center of gravity in the economy moved toward exporters, comprising small and medium-sized companies as well as large conglomerates (Meller, 1996; Martínez and Díaz, 1996).

Third, such a transformation in the Chilean economy resulted in the identification—on the part of Chilean policy-makers—of exports as the key to the Chilean economic growth. This brought forth a preference for the promotion of exports as well as the maintenance of a competitive level of exchange rates.

Capital mobility restrained

As argued above, Chile's access to foreign capital markets came to a sudden stop in mid-1981. Throughout the 1980s, Chilean authorities battled high interest payment on the stock of foreign debt without access to global financial markets. External finance was obtained through international financial institutions (i.e., IMF and World Bank), and the debtor was the Chilean state. As the Chilean economy recovered in the late 1980s and as its export industries soared, Chile again became an attractive country for foreign investors.

The massive surge in capital inflows to Chile occurred during the "transition" to democracy after 17 years of military government. However, unlike the period between 1978 and 1982, Chilean authorities exercised caution and prudence in their management of capital flows. This was achieved through an innovative policy measure, the *encaje*, which was an unremunerated reserve requirement on capital flows with short-term maturity. This policy tool was further strengthened by other economic measures, such as a stamp tax on capital flows and allowing capital outflows. Given high income inequality, it was remarkable that Chilean authorities did not pursue policies that would rapidly expand the economy. Instead, Chilean authorities aimed moderate redistribution.

What made Chilean authorities exercise caution in the face of increasing capital inflows? It is obvious that the objective of defending a competitive exchange rate level underpinned the decision to follow a prudent approach to managing capital account openness. This explains, as a first approximation, why the authorities aimed at shielding Chilean markets from massive capital inflows. However, the decision to defend a competitive level of exchange rate was just the tip of the iceberg. A thorough understanding of capital controls in Chile can be obtained only by looking into the dynamics of distribution and growth during the transition period.

The end of the Pinochet regime and the priorities of the Concertación government

The 1980 Constitution ordained a plebiscite that would allow Pinochet to remain as president for an additional eight years. In October 1988, Chilean people voted for whether or not to continue with Pinochet as president. In line with the rules laid out in the 1980 Constitution, the defeat in the 1988 plebiscite forced Pinochet to hold free elections in 1989.[32] Facing a highly probable defeat, the authoritarian regime constrained future democratic governments by implementing various institutional ties such as the binomial electoral system, appointed senators, and a conservative supreme court (Loveman, 1995, 309). In the 1989 elections, the right-wing candidate—the former finance minister, Hernán Büchi—was defeated by Patricio Aylwin—the candidate of the *Concertación*.[33] Aylwin's government took power in March 1990. Pinochet remained as the head of armed forces. This meant that, despite Pinochet's continuing role in the armed forces and despite institutional ties, Chile began its transition to democracy. The comprehensive social, economic, and political transformations under the authoritarian rule shaped the nature of this transition.

The initial period under the *Concertación* government was marked by various uncertainties associated with transition from authoritarian rule to democracy (Boylan, 1996). First, there was uncertainty about the future and scope of democracy. Although the government came to power as a result of free elections, Pinochet was still the head of the armed forces; he wielded both military and political power. Second, there was uncertainty arising from mistrust toward *Concertación*'s economic policies. Business organizations, powerful media with a salient right-wing bias, and conservative political parties suspected that the *Concertación* would pursue redistributive policies, abandon free market reforms, and activate a greater presence of the state in the economy.[34] For example, the influential weekly *Qué Pasa* editorialized that had the transition occurred in 1984 and 1985, the free market model in Chile would have been abandoned.

Facing uncertainty, mistrust, and a hostile Pinochet who continued to hold power, the *Concertación* followed a strategy of compromise and prudence in almost all policy fronts (Huneeus 2007, 485; Ramón 2001, 287; Valdés 1995,

32 54.6 percent of the electorate followed the opposition who campaigned against Pinochet and voted *No* (Correa et al., 2001, 336).

33 Aylwin won a landslide victory, obtaining 55.2 percent of the vote, whereas Büchi gained only 29.4 percent (Drake and Jaksić 1995, 14–15; MacDonald and Fauriol 1997, 48).

34 Interview with Manuel Marfán (macroeconomic coordinator and main advisor to the minister of finance in the transition government), November 6, 2006.

254–56). The determining factor was the strong desire to guarantee a smooth transition to democracy (Boylan, 1996; Drake and Jakšić, 1995; Loveman, 1995; Oppenheim, 2007; Silva, 1996). As such, political polarization and redistributive mobilization were perceived as perilous by *Concertación* leaders (Loveman, 1995, 305). Yet, moderation, prudence, and consensus-building involving a diverse set of actors—including right-wing parties—entailed some difficult choices. Most significantly, a full-scale investigation of human rights violations during the authoritarian rule could be carried only after the year 2000.

In its economic policies, the *Concertación* opted for continuity rather than a break (Huneeus, 2007, 461–63). Unlike the previous administration, who managed the economy in a heavy-handed manner, the Aylwin administration paid attention to building consensus.[35] The following quote from Alejandro Jadresic, the sectoral policies coordinator of the Ministry of Economy at the time, illustrates the tone and tenor of the *Concertación*'s approach to macroeconomic management:[36]

> En esencia, la política económica no ha cambiado. Sigue siendo manejada en forma técnica, pero con un poco más de apertura y humildad. . . . Los economistas del gobierno pasado eran un poco dictadores. Nosotros, en cambio, hacemos un esfuerzo por reconecer y escuchar a quienes no son economistas.[37]

The success of a calibrated set of neoliberal policies in the second half of the 1980s was a key factor in shaping this policy. As Silva (1991, 399) put it,

> Despite the general criticism of the negative social aspects of the neoliberal model, many people within the leftwing political parties admit (openly or tacitly) that at present the Chilean economy functions well and that it is now in better shape than at any other point during the last 25 years.

The economic growth driven by the export sector was both a constraint and opportunity for the new government. It was a constraint to the extent that it set the expectations for the continuation of an export-driven, internationally open economic model of growth. It was an opportunity simply because growth enabled, as will be shown below, a redistributive agenda.

It should be noted that continuing the neoliberal economic model was a sensitive topic at the time, especially within the *Concertación*.[38] The economic team headed by Alejandro Foxley (the Minister of Finance), which consisted of economists educated in U.S. universities, identified quasi-orthodox measures

35 This can be seen through an examination of various speeches given by Alejandro Foxley during this time, collected in his aptly titled book *La economía política de la transición: el camino del dialogo* (The Political Economy of Transition: The Path of Dialogue) published in 1993.

36 *Qué Pasa*, April 15, 1991, pp. 26–27.

37 "In essence, political economy has not changed. It is still managed in a technical way, but with a little bit more openness and humility. . . . The former administration's economists were somewhat dictatorial. We, on the other hand, make an effort to recognize and listen to those who are not economists." (Author's translation.)

38 See Foxley (1993) and Valdés (1995).

such as controlling inflation and fiscal prudence as keys to economic growth.[39] Hence, the Aylwin administration opted for economic stability and continuing the economic growth trend of the late 1980s (Silva, 1991, 405). The *Concertación* government was well aware that the political success of the transition and return to democracy were closely related to economic growth.

Consequently, one of the first priorities of the transition government was the promotion of export-led growth. Foxley made the commitment to export-led growth strategy amply clear in a meeting with business leaders on November 8, 1990 (1993, 111):

> Queremos nada menos que exportar un 35% de nuestro Producto en bienes en el año 1995. Y ese 35% del Producto debiera estar constituido en un 70% por bienes de exportación diferentes del cobre. Si afrontamos esta tarea adecuadamente, el desarrollo exportador va a empujar y arrastrar a todo el país detrás de sí. Va a transformar la estructura productivo chilena.[40]

Another priority for the Aylwin government was fiscal prudence. Aylwin administration aimed to avoid the economic populism they observed in other Latin American countries during transition from authoritarian rule to democracy.[41] Chilean authorities were aware that their economic policies would have long-term effects on the fate of democracy in Chile. For this reason, a pattern of economic populism that could lead to macroeconomic instability was perceived as a threat to the long-term stability of democratic rule.[42]

Fiscal prudence gained further urgency because of high government expenses at the end of the Pinochet regime. With the hope of increasing Pinochet's popularity and the chances of Hernán Büchi in the presidential election, his economic team pursued populist policies between 1987 and 1989 (MacDonald and Fauriol, 1997, 49). Hence, the fiscal and monetary policies of the military government in 1988 and 1989 were expansionary and imprudent (Foxley, 1993). The expansionary measures adopted included lavish corporate tax cuts, an increase in the money supply, and exchange rate appreciation (Huneeus 2007, 440; Ffrench-Davis 2002, 145–46). Due to macroeconomic imbalances, the Chilean economy showed clear signs of overheating by the second half of 1989 (Ffrench-Davis, 2002, 146): inflation was higher, imports exploded, and interest rates once again reached very high levels. (Ffrench-Davis, 2002, 146).

Tight monetary policies targeting macroeconomic adjustment started in January 1990 through interest rate increases.[43] The Aylwin administration backed monetary adjustment by following a prudent fiscal expenditure policy.

39 The other influential figure was Carlos Ominami, who was the Minister of Economy. See Silva (1991) and the April 15, 1991 issue of *Qué Pasa* on "los nuevo boys" who ran the Chilean economy during the transition to democracy.

40 "We want no less than to export 35% of our goods product in the year 1995. And that 35% of product should be constituted 70% in goods other than copper. If we face this task in an adequate manner, the export growth will carry the whole country along. It will transform the Chilean productive structure." (Author's translation.)

41 Interview with Manuel Marfán, November 6, 2006. For a further discussion, see Foxley (1993).

42 Interview with Manuel Marfán, November 6, 2006.

43 *Qué Pasa*, various issues, January-March 1990.

Table 2.5 Nonfinancial Public Sector, 1985–91†

Sector	*1985*	*1986*	*1987*	*1988*	*1989*	*1990*	*1991*
Government Saving[a]	−0.94	0.9	2.3	5.8	7.3	4.9	4.6
Government Surplus[b]	−3.65	−1.8	−0.7	3.9	5.4	3.1	2.3
Public Companies Surplus	1.06	−0.3	0.5	−3.8	−4.1	0.5	0.1
NPS[c] Surplus[d]	−2.59	−2.1	−0.2	0.2	1.3	3.6	2.4

† All numbers are percentages of GDP. Source: Larraín and Vergara (2000, Table 3).
a Government Saving = Current Income − Current Expenditure.
b Government Surplus = Government Saving + Capital Income − Capital Expenditure.
c Nonfinancial public sector.
d NPS Surplus = Government Surplus + Public Companies Surplus.

The economic team was careful to send signals to the private sector through an announced inflation target.[44] Furthermore, the government made a clear commitment to generating fiscal surplus, as can be evidenced by looking into nonfinancial public sector surplus (Table 2.5). The nonfinancial public sector surplus, which is the sum of government surplus and public companies surplus, rose from 1.3 percent of GDP in 1989 to 3.6 percent (1990) and 2.4 percent (1991) under the first *Concertación* government.

Thus, the *Concertación* government adopted the neoliberal economic model. Yet, the government's commitment to macroeconomic stability, fiscal prudence, and export-led growth presented a significant challenge. The *Concertación* triumphed over the Pinochet regime not only because of the collective memory of a past laden with repression but also because of disenchantment with poverty and economic inequality. The coalition capitalized on economic inequality and poverty heavily in its electoral campaign, with the promise of fighting poverty and inequality. Indeed, "growth with equity" (*crecimiento con equidad*) was one of the most salient slogans of the *Concertación* (Frank, 2002; Weyland, 1997). However, its commitment to continuing the neoliberal economic model—thus its commitment to controlling inflation, maintaining low corporate taxes, and fiscal prudence—was not particularly conducive to redistributive policies that could alleviate extreme poverty and decrease income inequality. Hence, the continuity of the neoliberal model carried the danger of embittering the electoral base of the *Concertación*.

The *Concertación* government addressed this problem by implementing tax and labor reforms. The tax reform, while moderate, had the objective of creating revenue in order to increase social spending. The labor reform, less successful than the tax reform, aimed to give rights and greater bargaining power to workers (Ffrench-Davis, 1999, 150–53). The next section focuses on the tax reform to illustrate how fiscal balance and high government saving empowered the Aylwin administration to implement moderate redistributive policies.

44 Interview with Manuel Marfán, November 6, 2006.

Redistributive policies

Changes in corporate tax, personal income tax, and value-added tax rates constituted the main body of the 1990 tax reform (Labán and Larraín, 1995, 134–36). In terms of taxation, Chilean corporations were enjoying very low rates compared to other developing countries. For example, in 1987, the corporate income tax was 35 percent in Brazil and Mexico, 33 percent in Argentina, 32 percent in Colombia, and 30 percent in Uruguay. In Chile, this figure was a mere 10 percent.[45] Given such a low tax rate, the government opted for increasing corporate tax rate by 50 percent, from 10 to 15 percent. Furthermore, the 1990 reform expanded the tax base for corporate taxation (Labán and Larraín, 1995, 134).

In terms of personal income taxes, the administration chose to leave the tax rates intact, but changed the structure of income tax brackets. The effect was an increase in the level of personal income taxes (Labán and Larraín, 1995, 135). The value-added tax (VAT) was increased from 16 to 18 percent (Marcel, 1997).

In reality, the 1990 reform was more audacious in rhetoric; at the end, the revenue gains were moderate. Furthermore, as Boylan (1996) observes, the government was careful to not attract the ire of the business class.[46] However, given the depressed levels of social spending during the Pinochet regime, the increased revenue through the 1990 tax reform enabled the transition government to increase social spending. This, in turn, made possible to design policies to fight extreme poverty in Chile, especially through increased spending on health and education (Larraín and Vergara, 2000; Weyland, 1997). As a result, social spending increased at a rate of 10 percent annually between 1990 and 1993, surpassing the GDP growth rate (Marcel, 1997, 39). Naturally, after 17 years of economic hardship from which Chilean middle and lower classes suffered disproportionally, these were novel and popular reforms.

Such reforms were possible because the Chilean economy was increasing its rate of national saving consistently in the 1980s. The role of nonfinancial government saving was pivotal in this increase (Vial, 1998, 184–87). As can be seen in Table 2.5, government saving was positive between 1986 and 1991. This trend was replicated in government surplus figures and was reflected in the total nonfinancial public sector surplus, which was 3.6 percent in 1990 and 2.4 percent in 1991 (as percentage of GDP). Furthermore, thanks to CODELCO being kept as a public sector company under the Pinochet regime, the Chilean state had access to significant resources. The magnitude of CODELCO's contribution to the fiscal power of Chilean state cannot be overemphasized.[47]

45 All statistics given are for corporate direct investment income tax. Source: Boylan (1996, 20).

46 Boylan (1996, 12) shrewdly observes this characteristic of the 1990 tax reform and the nature of the political bargain it involved: "Despite the rhetoric of social justice surrounding this reform, careful examination of its specific components suggests that the government was much more attuned to the interests and needs of the business class. Aware of this class's fears regarding an uncertain economic feature, the government sought to design a tax reform that would not alienate the support of this crucial actor in transition. Thus, while the primary burden of this modest reform fell on capitalists, it was a small price to pay for the socioeconomic peace and stable economic environment achieved in return."

47 See Riesco (1999, 101) for an extended discussion on this point.

Thus, despite macroeconomic prudence, the Chilean state was able to implement redistributive policies rather effectively. The Aylwin administration could address redistributive demands by creating additional fiscal resources through a moderate tax reform. Higher levels of social spending through a tax reform was feasible because (1) Chilean tax rates were already low, and (2) fiscal resources enabled the expansion of spending without threatening the capitalist class. The results can be observed in Figures 2.5 and 2.6. The wage share in GDP started to increase beginning in 1989, a trend that continued in a secular fashion during the 1990s under the *Concertación* governments. Similarly, the real wage grew at a faster rate than GDP, while the profit rate declined under the *Concertación* rule.

Surge in capital inflows

As President Aylwin assumed power in March 1990, the Chilean economy confronted, once again, the return of voluntary capital inflows. Table 2.6 presents the magnitude and composition of capital flows to Chile between 1985 and 1991. In 1985, almost all inflows to Chile were in the form of sovereign borrowing. Thus, capital inflows to the public sector were 8.4 percent of GDP in 1985. Voluntary capital inflows to Chile began in 1986 with debt-equity swaps (Ffrench-Davis et al., 1995). Between 1987 and 1989, debt-equity swaps generated net capital inflows that fluctuated between 3 and 4 percent of GDP, approximately equaling total net inflows for each year. Beginning in 1990 Chile faced a massive surge in capital inflows. In 1990, total net inflows were equal to 9.6 percent of GDP, more than two times their magnitude in 1989.

While FDI continued to be strong in 1990 (5.7 percent of GDP), the sudden increase was largely due to portfolio inflows and short-term private credits. One of these items, portfolio investment, consisted of funds brought into Chile through two new channels: foreign investment funds and American Depository Receipts (ADRs) (Ffrench-Davis et al., 1995, 101).[48] Portfolio inflows amounted to 1.2 percent of GDP in 1990. Short-term private credits constituted 2.9 percent of GDP in the same year. In total, the increase due to portfolio and short-term credits was 4.1 percent of GDP.

Debt-equity swaps, no longer an attractive option for foreign investors because of increasing discount prices of these instruments in international markets, decreased substantially to 1.1 percent (Agosin, 1998; Ffrench-Davis, 2002; Ffrench-Davis et al., 1995; Labán and Larraín, 1994). It should be observed that medium and long-term private credits, long an outflow item in the Chilean balance of payments, were only 0.2 percent in 1989 and 0.4 percent in 1990.

The sudden increase in *hot money* to Chile was based on the burgeoning opportunities for arbitrage and the perception of a strong Chilean growth prospect among international investors (Agosin, 1998; Ffrench-Davis et al., 1995; Labán and Larraín, 2000; Laurens, 2000; Cowan and De Gregorio, 2007). The key was the high domestic interest rate that prevailed in the Chilean market at

48 ADRs were traded in the same manner as any other stock in the U.S. financial markets. As such, they enabled foreign firms to raise capital in the U.S. financial markets (Ffrench-Davis, 2002, 218).

Table 2.6 Net Capital Inflows, 1985–91†

Sector	*1985*	*1986*	*1987*	*1988*	*1989*	*1990*	*1991*
Total Net Inflows	8.0	5.4	4.1	3.7	4.1	9.6	3.4
FDI	0.8	2.2	5.5	5.9	6.5	5.7	2.6
Regular Inflows[a]	0.6	1.1	2.1	2.3	2.6	4.6	3.1
Debt Swaps	0.2	1.1	3.4	3.7	3.9	1.1	−0.1
Outflows	–	–	–	−0.1	–	–	−0.4
Net Portfolio Inflows	–	–	–	–	0.3	1.2	0.7
M. & L. Term Credits[b]	−2.2	−4.4	−5.3	−4.6	0.2	0.4	–
Short-Term Credits[c]	1.0	2.7	−1.1	−1.0	1.1	2.9	2.1
Public Inflows	8.4	4.9	5.1	3.3	−4.0	−0.7	−2.0

† All numbers are percentages of GDP at current prices. Source: Agosin (1998, Table 5.1).
a Private credits. Includes credits associated with FDI.
b Private medium- and long-term credits. Includes errors and omissions.
c Private credits. Includes errors and omissions.

that time and the low domestic interest rates in international markets, especially the United States.

An examination of inflation-adjusted real interest rate differentials between Chile and the United States shows the arbitrage opportunities created by high levels of domestic interest rates. The adjusted real interest rate difference was −5.7 percent in 1986, −0.5 percent in 1987, and 0.5 percent in 1988. It leapt to 2.4 percent in 1989 and to 4.7 percent in 1990 (Budnevich and Cifuentes, 1993, Table 1). In addition, the strong Chilean growth performance raised expectations about appreciation in the Chilean currency and gains in the stock market (Agosin, 1998). Thus, Chile was a highly profitable emerging economy for international investors looking for large gains in the short run.

Table 2.7 illustrates the use of capital inflows by different sectors between 1985 and 1991. Two points are worth emphasizing. First, in sharp contrast to the 1978–81 economic boom, the banking sector was not the primary contractor of capital inflows (Budnevich and Cifuentes, 1993). As can be seen in Table 2.7, the banking sector registered outflows rather than inflows during this period.

Table 2.7 Private and Public Sectors' Use of Capital Inflows, 1985–91†

Sector	*1985*	*1986*	*1987*	*1988*	*1989*	*1990*	*1991*
Public Sector	3.9	2.8	1.6	3.5	1.6	0.9	−2.0
Central Bank	3.7	−0.5	0.5	−2.1	3.4	−0.8	−0.2
Banking Sector	0.1	−1.7	−2.6	−1.9	−1.7	−1.0	−0.9
Private Sector	0.0	1.9	0.6	0.5	2.3	9.0	4.6
Short Term	2.1	3.7	−0.4	−1.6	0.0	4.0	2.6
M. & L. Term[a]	−2.1	−1.7	1.1	2.1	2.3	5.0	2.0

† All numbers are percentages of GDP at current prices. Due to different sources utilized in constructing Tables 2.6 and 2.7, slight discrepancies between the two are normal. Source: Budnevich and Cifuentes (1993, Table 3).
a Medium- and long-term capital flows.

Second, the private sector was the main contractor of capital from the rest of the world. Indeed, private sector's use of funds—FDI, portfolio flows, short-term trade credits, etc.—from the rest of the world reached 9 percent of GDP in 1990.

Naturally, the high inflow of funds from the rest of the world to the private sector in Chile put tremendous appreciation pressure on the domestic currency. The magnitude of this pressure is traced out in Figure 2.11, which presents the level of real exchange rate, its trend over time, and the percentage change month by month. The real exchange rate appreciated sharply beginning in February 1991, immediately after a significant amount of foreign funds entered into the economy. The next section examines how Chilean authorities reacted to the appreciation pressures.

Curbing capital inflows

Beginning in 1990, the appreciation of the Chilean peso became a major policy concern. The Aylwin administration employed a number of tools to counter the over-abundance of capital inflows. One measure utilized, especially during 1990, was sterilization (Labán and Larraín, 1994, 135–36). As Labán and Larraín (1994, 135–36) observe, this strategy was to a certain extent effective. While the exchange rate was in a trend of appreciation in the first half of 1990, this trend was partially reversed in the second half (Figure 2.11), when the Central Bank used sterilization at an increasing rate (Ffrench-Davis et al., 1995, 120–21). However, as discussed in Appendix C, sterilization entailed costs. Specifically, the Central Bank—and thus the Chilean economy— incurred operating losses stemming from supplying domestic bonds and accumulating foreign exchange reserves.

Yet, the effectiveness of sterilization was short-lived. In February 1991, the real exchange rate was at the 115.3 point level. The index came to 111.7 in March 1991, a 3.1 percent appreciation (Figure 2.11). Then, the next measure adopted was introducing greater uncertainty into the foreign exchange market. This was achieved by pegging the Chilean peso to a basket of currencies composed of the dollar, the deutsche mark, and the yen (Labán and Larraín, 1994, 134–35). Given high fluctuations observed among exchange rate parities, such a strategy aimed at obstructing prediction of Chilean peso's future movements (Agosin, 1999; Ffrench-Davis, 2002).

Despite the introduction of uncertainty into foreign exchange markets, the trend of appreciation continued in April, May, and June of 1991—a period during which exchange rate appreciation on a monthly basis was consistently higher than 3 percent. In June 1991, the exchange rate index was at 102.5 points.

A speech by Foxley given in September 1991, just after the heavy influx of capital to Chile, illustrates that the economic authorities at the time identified the pressure on the exchange rate as a central policy issue (1993, 174–75):

> En vez de hablar acerca de la crisis de la deuda, estamos empezando a hablar acerca del «problema de la enfermedad holandesa»: ¿cómo absorber un flujo masivo de capitales sin dañar seriamente las exportaciones? Un movimiento

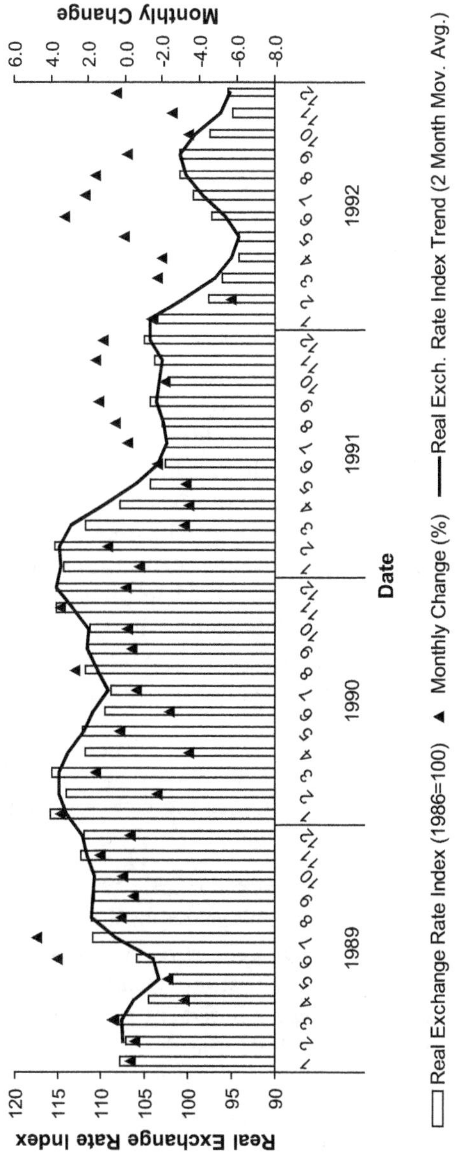

Figure 2.11 Real Exchange Rate Index, 1989–92.

> masivo de capitales externos pone presión sobre la tasa de cambio, induciendo una apreciación de la moneda doméstica, y eventualmente pone en riesgo el desempeño exportador. Eso obliga a concentrarse en los aspectos que verdaderamente importan para el éxito económico de largo plazo.[49]

Thus, Chilean authorities had a clear recognition of the challenges presented by massive capital inflows. As can be seen in the above quote, Chilean policy-makers identified exchange rate appreciation as an undesirable effect of capital inflows.

It should be observed that exchange rate appreciation is not *per se* an undesirable consequence. In fact, exchange rate appreciation might be conducive to certain policy goals. In the context of Chilean economy during late 1980s and early 1990s, the most prominent of these monetary goals was the control of inflation. A higher exchange rate could—in theory—decelerate economic activity in an open economy like Chile. Roberto Zahler, then a member of the Central Bank Board and later its governor, summarized the allure of domestic currency appreciation in the period between 1990 and 1991, when inflation was high:[50] "It would have been very easy for us. . . . If you allow the currency to appreciate, inflation will go down. It's the best of all worlds."

However, policy-makers recognized that exchange rate is a crucial price for the Chilean economy, given its high level of openness and the growing size of the export sector. This price had to be competitive in order for Chile to take advantage of further trade integration with the rest of the world. In addition, this price had to be stable and predictable for ensuring the long-term development and success of the export sector. For Guillermo Le Fort, who took an active role in the management and design of the *encaje* after 1992, this was one of the main motivations of the capital control scheme implemented in Chile:

> Chile being an open economy, a country that had to develop on the basis of the development of its exports, you need to have a strong and well-diversified export base. For that to happen, you need to have some stability in the real exchange rate.[51]

Hence, as Labán and Larraín (1995, 125) put it aptly, "It was recognized that external markets provide the best opportunities for small economies, and thus the government must try to maintain a competitive real exchange rate." To forestall the continuing pressure toward the appreciation of Chilean peso, Chilean authorities introduced the *encaje*—an unremunerated reserve requirement for foreign loans —in June 17, 1991 (Laurens, 2000, 71).[52] As Cowan and De Gregorio

49 "Instead of talking about the debt crisis, we are beginning to talk about the 'dutch disease problem': how to absorb a massive inflow of capital without seriously hurting exports? A massive movement of foreign capital puts pressure on the exchange rate, leading to an appreciation of the domestic currency, and eventually puts export performance under risk. That forces us to focus on the aspects that really matter for economic success in the long run." (Author's translation.)

50 Interview with Roberto Zahler, November 30, 2006.

51 Interviews with Roberto Zahler, Ricardo Ffrench-Davis, Jorge Desormeaux, Pablo García, Guillermo Le Fort, and Manuel Marfán, November 2006.

52 An additional measure was making foreign credit subject to stamp tax (Ffrench-Davis, 2002, 223).

(2007, 249–50) note, "The *encaje* required that a fraction of the capital inflow be deposited in a non-interest-bearing account in the Chilean central bank." The initial rate of this reserve requirement was 20 percent. The *encaje* was an innovative and market-based tax on capital flows, similar to the famous Tobin tax (Labán and Larraín, 1994; Tobin, 1978). As such, it functioned as a market-based capital control.[53]

The *encaje* was designed to discourage capital inflows. This was achieved by imposing a minimum holding period for all foreign loans. The initial implementation imposed a differentiated structure of holding times. The minimum holding time was 90 days. The holding time was the whole period until the maturity for loans with maturity between 90 days and a year. For long-term loans with maturity exceeding one year, the holding period was only one year (Laurens, 2000, 71). According to Ffrench-Davis (2002, 231), the implicit cost of the *encaje* fluctuated—depending on the LIBOR rate—between 1.2 and 1.4 percent in the initial period.

Although the *encaje* was effective in curbing capital inflows, its power to preclude capital inflows was eroded as the real interest rate difference between Chile and the United States continued to rise.[54] As a result, authorities took additional steps to discourage capital inflows. First, in January 1992, the scope of the *encaje* was extended to sight and term deposits in foreign currency. Second, in June 1992, the reserve requirement was increased from 20 to 30 percent. In addition, the minimum holding period was fixed at one year, regardless of the maturity of foreign loan (Cowan and De Gregorio, 2007, 286–87).

The design achieved by the additional measures in 1992 was particularly onerous for short-term loans with maturity less than 90 days. This was primarily due to the one-year minimum holding period, which was enforced regardless of the maturity of foreign loan. For example, the cost for loans with three-month maturity was 6.4 percent in 1992 (Ffrench-Davis, 2002, 231). The tax imposed by the *encaje* decreased as the maturity of the loan increased (Laurens, 2000). For long-term loans with maturities exceeding a year, the cost was a fixed 1.5 percent in 1992 (Ffrench-Davis, 2002, 231).

Explaining the restraints on capital mobility

The performance of export sector as the source of dynamism and economic growth in Chile had an important role in shaping how Chilean policy-makers perceived capital inflows. Jorge Desormeaux, an influential economist who later became Vice Governor of the Central Bank, expressed this point in unequivocal terms:[55]

> The export sector was … the darling of the economy and policymakers went to great lengths basically to protect the profitability of the export sector.

53 One difference with the Tobin tax was that the *encaje* was asymmetric in the sense that it targeted exclusively capital inflows (Laurens, 2000, 70).

54 This difference was around 7 percent in 1992, almost double the 1991 rate (Laurens, 2000, 72).

55 Interview with Jorge Desormeaux, November 1, 2006.

> That's why the encaje appeared, because the last thing we wanted in the economy to happen was to have the exchange rate to appreciate. So basically we tried everything that was in the book and what wasn't in the book we invented it, you know, in order to protect the export sector.

Hence, the *encaje*—in addition to other measures—was utilized as a tool to defend the competitive alignment of domestic currency with world currencies. As Ffrench-Davis et al. (1995, 100) claim, "The main aim has been to prevent an exchange rate appreciation like the one experienced in the previous period of abundant capital inflows (1978–81), and to make space for domestic monetary policy."

Such a policy implied the rejection of economic expansion through capital inflows. The economic team at that time was aware that capital inflows presented opportunities for expansionary policies.[56] However, the Aylwin administration aimed to avoid excess spending through rising external debt (be it private or public), as illustrated in the following statement by Alejandro Foxley (1993, 100):[57]

> Durante algún tiempo hemos tenido problemas con el dólar por un exceso de entradas de capital. Aquí se da la paradoja de que nosotros como gobierno estamos tratando de disminuir el número de créditos externos hacia Chile—le estamos diciendo al Banco Mundial y al Banco Interamericano que queremos disminuir el flujo de créditos—y le estamos diciendo al sector privado que no debe salir a endeudarse en forma indiscrimanada—como hizo a comienzos de los años 80—porque ahora tenemos un nivel de ahorro interno muy alto.[58]

The statements by Desormeaux and Foxley are telling, because they point out the structural conditions enabling a cautious approach to financial integration with the rest of the world. Three factors worked to the advantage of the Aylwin administration when Chile faced a surge in capital flows from the rest of the world. First, the Chilean economy was on a strong growth path, much of it enabled by a burgeoning non-copper export sector. Second, the new administration did not have to deal with budgetary pressures, as the government and public companies registered a surplus in the early years of the *Concertación* government (Table 2.5). The strong growth certainly had a major role in alleviating any potential budgetary problems. In addition, the Aylwin administration's tax reforms contributed to the increase in revenues. Third, the new government implemented a modest but effective set of redistributive reforms. Such reforms were crucial in addressing poverty in Chile. Furthermore, the redistributive reforms had political and symbolic importance. After all, Chile was a country that experienced a

56 Interview with Manuel Marfán (November 6, 2006) and Guillermo Le Fort (December 5, 2006).

57 The quote comes from a speech made in November 1992.

58 "For some time we have had problems with the dollar due to an excess entry of capital. Here we have the paradox that we as a government are trying to decrease the amount of external credits toward Chile—we are telling the World Bank and the Inter-American Development Bank that we want to decrease the flow of credits—and we are telling the private sector they should not go out and create debt in an indiscriminate manner—as they did at the beginning of the 1980s—because now we have a much higher level of domestic saving."

17-year dictatorship, much of it shaped by a radical neoliberal ideology and increasing concentration of wealth. The redistributive reforms signaled that Chile was entering a new era in terms of income distribution.

It would have been fairly difficult for the Aylwin administration to restrain international capital mobility without such a strong growth performance and without redistributive reforms. Large business groups and much of the capitalist class approached the new administration with a suspicion. A lingering question was whether the new administration was going to change track in economic policies. Furthermore, the *Concertación* government did not yet have a firm grip on political power. Had the economy been stagnant and had the distribution relations been conflictual, all of these factors would have exerted considerable pressure on the Aylwin administration to keep the financial markets open and to expand the economy through capital inflows.

Conclusion

This chapter compared two episodes of institutional change in Chile. In each episode, I have shown how distribution relations and growth dynamics were the structural factors that enabled particular mechanisms of institutional change.

The first episode of institutional change followed decades-long conflict over how to divide the economic pie in Chile—a country with a remarkable record of low economic growth in the postwar period. Such conflictual distribution relations created the political conditions that led to the rise of the Chicago Boys. These ideologically motivated technocrats had the support of Pinochet in implementing a radical institutional change in Chile. When combined with abundant capital inflows, their policies engendered a significant economic boom between 1978 and 1982. This economic boom supported a sense of euphoria in the Chilean society. Consumption surged, growth was strong, and construction activity boomed. The main beneficiaries of the rapid growth and expansion were the large finance-based *grupos*. Although export sectors were building up dynamism as a result of greater integration with the rest of the world, the neoliberal economists at the time were blind to the adverse affects of appreciating domestic currency. The Chilean economy boomed, regardless of export sectors' performance. The Pinochet regime focused on solidifying an authoritarian regime and its technocrats spent their energies in establishing a market society. The existing balance of power and financial openness reinforced each other.

The economic boom came to an end with the financial meltdown in 1982 and left Chile with a massive debt crisis. The crisis undermined the legitimacy of the Pinochet regime and caused a realignment in the balance of power in the Chilean society. Such adverse conditions underpinned the change in the orientation of Chilean policy-makers. It was necessary to have large trade surpluses, so that Chile could service its debt payments and could overcome the crisis. The Chilean state not only promoted macroeconomic policies conducive to strengthening export performance but also subsidized the export sectors. Export sectors, already with significant potential as a result of decades-long accumulation, took advantage of

Chile's comparative advantage in natural resources. The result was a remarkable recovery based on export dynamism.

At the end, it was the export dynamism combined with redistribution that determined the course of institutional change when confronted with a massive amount of capital inflows. The Chilean policies in the early 1990s were remarkable because they embodied an institutional change in a direction quite different from many emerging economies. The early 1990s were the peak point of the Washington Consensus (Williamson, ed, 1994). There was a considerable alignment of ideological, political, and economic forces at the international level behind the project of financial liberalization. Furthermore, as can be seen in Figure 1.2 of the introductory chapter, the overall trend in the world was unequivocally in favor of capital account liberalization. It was all too easy for Chile—a country that was desperate for international capital for much of the 1980s—to jump on the bandwagon. After all, the institutional framework regulating capital mobility in Chile at the time—a remnant from the Pinochet era—did not present barriers to international capital mobility. However, the Aylwin administration—despite the market-friendly tendencies of its technocrats— implemented polices that curbed capital inflows.

3 Embracing hot money, rejecting cold money in South Korea

South Korea had a remarkable record of economic development in the twentieth century, during which the country transformed itself from an agricultural economy to an industrial powerhouse.[1] The roots of rapid industrialization originated in the interwar period, when Korea was under the Japanese colonial rule (Cumings, 1984b). The Japanese colonial rule introduced industrial production into Korea and was instrumental in the creation of modern infrastructure (Kuznets, 1994). This rule ended in 1945 and the subsequent division of the peninsula into two nation-states culminated in the Korean War. The war was devastating for the newly established Republic of Korea (ROK). The severity of the devastation and the loss of life in the Korean War left South Korea in a desolate state and the country faced severe economic problems in the 1950s and the early 1960s. Yet, the economic growth after 1965 was in double digits for many years. By the end of the 1980s, Korea was an industrial economy and Korean firms were competing in global markets. Rapid economic growth halted in 1997, when an unprecedented financial crisis shook the Korean economy. South Korea's opening to international capital flows was arguably the main factor behind the crisis.

The Korean capital account reforms during the 1990s were perilous. The newly elected Kim Young-sam government liberalized various short-term capital inflows and outflows while maintaining restrictions on long-term capital flows. Such policies enabled domestic firms to borrow heavily, either directly from international markets or through banks and non-bank financial institutions. Korean financial institutions borrowed short-term from international markets, but they lent with longer-term maturities. The economy grew quickly as a result of heavy investment by big conglomerates. However, increasing amounts of short-term liabilities and long-term assets by domestic financial intermediaries fueled the strong investment in the early 1990s. The growing dependence on external financing created a significant maturity risk for the Korean financial institutions. Equally important was the currency mismatch risk, since the Korean financial institutions borrowed in foreign currencies but supplied credit in domestic currency.

1 Despite the 1997 financial crisis, Korean real GDP per capita grew at 6.2 percent between 1961 and 2003. This figure is based on the World Development Indicators Database of the World Bank.

The perilous trajectory of the capital account reforms in Korea resulted from the gradual collapse of the developmental alliance between the Korean state and big business groups (*chaebols*). The alliance between the capitalists and the Korean state was successful, for a number of reasons, in bringing forth industrialization between 1965 and 1979 (Hundt, 2009). The most proximate factor was the high level of investment in productive capacity, which persisted because Korean firms were successful in finding demand for their products in export markets. Furthermore, the Korean economy could maintain a remarkable level of investment in productive capacity because the Korean state undertook the role of nurturing big business and their entrepreneurial activities through its control over credit supply and allocation. High levels of debt and thus elevated corporate leverage financed the remarkable performance of the *chaebols*. This growth pattern was risky, but the Korean state socialized the risks by guaranteeing funds to successful companies, even when they were under stress and even when this supply of financial funds required the redistribution of the fruits of economic growth from workers and ordinary savers to the *chaebols*. In return, the Korean state's control over finance enabled it to discipline the *chaebols* and to pick the best performing firms. Thus, there was a particular constellation of state power, finance, and distribution relations that sustained high levels of productive investment and rapid economic development.

For various reasons, which are analyzed below, the alliance between the Korean state and the *chaebols* started to crumble in the 1980s. Then, the balance of power between the Korean state and the *chaebols* began to favor the *chaebols*. The development of private financial intermediaries in the 1970s weakened the Korean state's control over finance. Piecemeal liberalization reforms in the following decade further loosened the state control over the financial system. By the early 1990s, Korean firms were eager to move into the next stage in the product cycle and explore production in high value-added activities such as electronic goods. However, by this time, the Korean state was not capable to provide the necessary credit for such investment. In this context, the surging capital flows provided an attractive financing opportunity for the *chaebols*. Korean authorities were aware of the dangers of rapid liberalization of capital flows, but the economic bureaucracy was neither coherent nor strong enough to resist the pressures for rapid liberalization. Furthermore, a newly elected government under Kim Young-sam came to power with the mantra of change and liberalization. This new government saw globalization as a viable solution to the problems of the Korean economy and society. The resulting set of capital account reforms amounted to embracing hot money and partially rejecting cold money. Such a combination contributed greatly to the financial meltdown during the 1997 Asian crisis.

Distribution, finance, and Korean development

Korea developed rapidly thanks to elevated debt levels, high shares of investment in GDP, and a considerable degree of economic concentration (Kohli, 2004). In an underdeveloped and impoverished country like Korea in the 1960s and 1970s, such a development course was possible only by allocating scarce capital to high value-added economic activities—economic activities that would spur further industrialization in the long run (Cumings, 2005; Woo, 1991; Cho, 1989; Cole and Park, 1983). However, the very policies that promoted economic development also embodied a persistent redistribution of the fruits of development from small and medium-scale enterprises, savers, laborers, and middle-classes to the *chaebols*.

The political economy of Korean development

Sustained levels of high investment by Korean industrialists, who competed among themselves to export manufactured goods, was the economic mechanism that enabled the Korean rapid development. But why did industrialists in a small economy like Korea prefer to undertake risky investments oriented toward uncertain export markets? That is a question worth posing because it is erroneous to assume that capitalists would be naturally inclined to invest and compete for export markets. In fact, the opposite course of economic development, one where domestic capitalists have been oriented toward their own markets and capital accumulation has been slow, characterizes Latin American economic history (Hirschman, 1968, 17–22).

There are a number of different answers to this question, which mainly fall into two broad groups. The neoclassical explanation attributes the success of the Korean development to free-market oriented policies (Krueger, 1979, 1997). In this view, institutional measures such as trade liberalization and letting the market mechanism to determine prices were the main causal factors behind the rapid Korean economic growth.

The statist explanation, in contrast, shows that there was widespread state intervention and guidance of industrial policies (Jones and SaKong, 1980; Amsden, 1989; Wade, 1990; Chang, 1993; Weiss and Hobson, 1995). Hence, heavy state involvement in markets and an explicit industrial transformation agenda shaped the Korean economic development (Haggard and Moon, 1993, 52). Furthermore, state guidance of the markets was often effective. Unlike developing countries in other parts of the world (such as Latin America), the Korean state played a leading role in fostering economic development.

Evidence points to the statist approach as being superior to the neoclassical model in explaining the Korean trajectory of development (Stubbs, 2009; Hundt, 2009; Park, 2011). However, it is important not to overstress the state's role. If presented as a monocausal explanation of the Korean development, the statist explanation is not particularly illuminating. Calibrating the statist approach is necessary to obtain an accurate model of Korea's rapid economic development. First, state intervention worked in Korea because it took the form of cheap financing conditional on success in export markets. Second, state intervention was not effective at the expense of capitalists. To the contrary, the state and the capitalist class were in a coalition from which both parties gained (Kim, 1994). The state had a very strong hand over particular capitalists, but was in a pact with the capitalist class (Chibber, 2003). Third, the Korean state heavily repressed working and middle classes, both politically and economically. In fact, labor repression and the low cost of labor were essential to maintaining global competitiveness (Deyo, 1989b, 155). Fourth, there were a number of conjectural factors that cannot be fitted into one single model. One is the role of Japan and Japanese capital in launching the Korean development in the early 1960s. Another is the Vietnam War, which boosted the Korean balance of payments during the initial take-off.

Fifth, and the one emphasized in this chapter, is that the Korean state acted as midwife to the Korean capitalist class. The "midwife" role considered here is, to a certain extent, different than what is found in Evans (1992, 1995), who coined the term. Evans (1995, 13) portrays state midwifery as the capacity to "assist in the emergence of new entrepreneurial groups or to induce existing groups to venture into more challenging kinds of production." What Evans (1995, 14, 249) considers under state midwifery are various industrial planning and sector-specific promotion policies.[2] However, creating finance capital goes beyond promoting industrial transformation through sector-specific policies; it involves taking a primary role in the formation of *entrepreneurs* and *capitalists*.[3]

Sixth, there was a bias toward "large business groups with proven track records," which led to the neglect of small and medium-scale enterprises (SaKong, 1993, 36–37). In other words, the Korean state actively encouraged national champions to spearhead economic growth, even at the expense of accumulating large amounts of debt. The *chaebols* adopted the policy of economic expansion as a strategy for economic survival and growth. These large firms were acting with the strategic goal of increasing their size to make their failure costly for the Korean state. By making themselves "too big to fail," the *chaebols* ensured a steady supply of resources from the Korean developmental state (Woo-Cumings, 1997). The result was a curious phenomenon. While industrialists in Latin America were risk-adverse capitalists who were reluctant to undertake expansionary investment oriented toward export markets, industrialists in Korea were *all too eager* to take such a role.

The sum total of these factors was a unique developmental model, and it is important to recognize what Cumings (2005) calls the "Schumpeterian" element in the Korean development. For Schumpeter, economic development stems from innovation and the agents of innovation are entrepreneurs (1983, 74–79). The innovative activities carried out by entrepreneurs expand the productive capacity of an economy by establishing new lines of industry, new markets, and new products. Furthermore, the "creative destruction" described by Schumpeter is

2 Evans (1995, 80) gives the following list as examples to midwifery policies: "Erecting a 'greenhouse' of tariffs, import prohibitions, and investment restrictions in order to protect infant sectors from external competition is the most obvious example. Providing subsidies and incentives is likely to be part of the midwife role."

3 The following remarks about *producing* rather than *reproducing* social relations resonate with this argument (Woo-Cumings 1997, 65, [original emphasis]): "The historical mission of the Korean state has been not so much one of reproducing social relations, as state theorists argue, but *producing* them: aborting labor organizations through repression and nurturing big business by supplying financial resources."

possible only if the finance industry acts as a midwife to capitalists' entrepreneurial endeavors (Bertocco, 2008, 1167).

The Korean case, admittedly very different from the free-market environment that Schumpeter had in mind, shows that the principle described by Schumpeter was essential in late development as well. Financial policies were a central component of the Korean state's involvement in the economy. Indeed, as Cho (1989, 95) remarks, it is possible to identify a particular "Korean" approach to finance and development (Amsden, 1990b, 27). This approach, which took shape after 1964–65, involved the mobilization of domestic and foreign funds—and thus a plentiful supply of credit—to export industries until the implementation of the HCI (Heavy and Chemical Industry) drive in the 1970s. After that period, the Korean state channeled the credit supply particularly to large-scale investment projects. In other words, the Korean state controlled the financial system to ensure that Korean financial intermediaries, private or public, provided ample credit to the *chaebols*. Chang (1993, 138–39) aptly labels this approach "investment management" and stresses the anti-consumption and pro-investment nature of the adopted policies:

> To Korean policy-makers, economic development required giving priority to investment ... macroeconomic policy was geared towards the need to create an expansionary environment—if necessary through inflationary measures — which was seen as vital for a sustained high level of investment.

In both periods, a defining feature of the Korean economic development was the suppression of long-term interest rates that made large-scale investment possible (Amsden, 1990a, 72). This implied that the cost of credit was low for favored firms and industries.

The *chaebols* were not in the business of inventing new products and technologies, especially at the early stages of the Korean take-off. However, they focused their energies, with the help of cheap finance, into exploiting export markets and creating a niche for themselves in world markets.[4] Thus, the Korean state played the leading role in *the supply of finance-capital* for investment projects that exploited the static and dynamic comparative advantage of Korea in international markets. And this role was possible because the Korean state subsidized the investment activity of the *chaebols* at the expense of workers, whose wages were repressed; at the expense of savers, as the structure of interest rates favored the *chaebols*; at the expense of middle classes, as consumption was curtailed; and at the expense of small and medium-scale enterprises, who lacked access to credit.

This trajectory of economic development, enabled by a remarkable repression of wages, can be seen in Figure 3.1. What distinguished the Korean development from, for instance, a case like Chile (Figure 2.1), was the feverish rate of capital accumulation, which translated into a rapid rise in labor productivity and an

4 See Cumings (1984b) for the importance of the international division of labor in Korea's take-off.

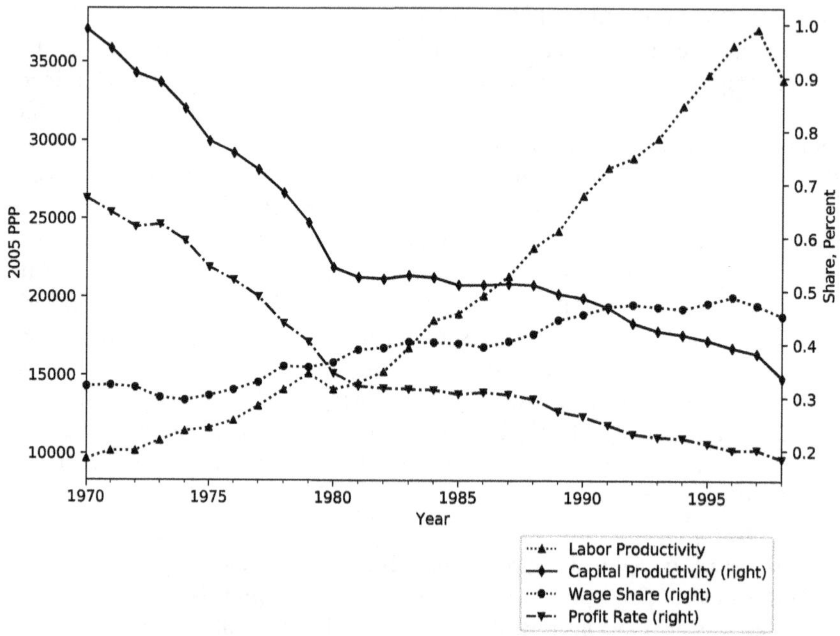

Figure 3.1 Distributional Dynamics, 1970–98.
Note: See Appendix A for the definition of variables and for the explanation of axes in this figure.
Source: Extended Penn World Tables v. 4 (Foley and Michl, 1999; Marquetti, 2003).

accompanying fall in capital productivity.[5] Had such a trajectory of capital accumulation occurred organically, it would have generated an accompanying decline in profit rates and a concomitant rise in real wages (Foley and Michl, 1999). However, by selecting few firms as "national champions" and by repressing labor, the Korean state under Park Chung Hee kept profit rates high and the wage share in Korean GDP relatively stagnant during the 1970s, despite remarkable growth rates of GDP and labor productivity (Figure 3.2).

The historical origins of the developmental alliance

The developmental alliance between the state and the capitalists had its origins in the Japanese colonial rule. However, the land reform after the Korean War played a much more important role in shaping the Korean developmental alliance. The land reform made Korea a remarkably equal country by eliminating the landlord class. As a result, compared to most other developing countries in the world at the time, social relations in Korea were conducive to a successful developmental alliance between the state and capitalist class. Nonetheless, the developmental

5 See Appendix A on the trajectory of labor and capital productivity in the course of economic development.

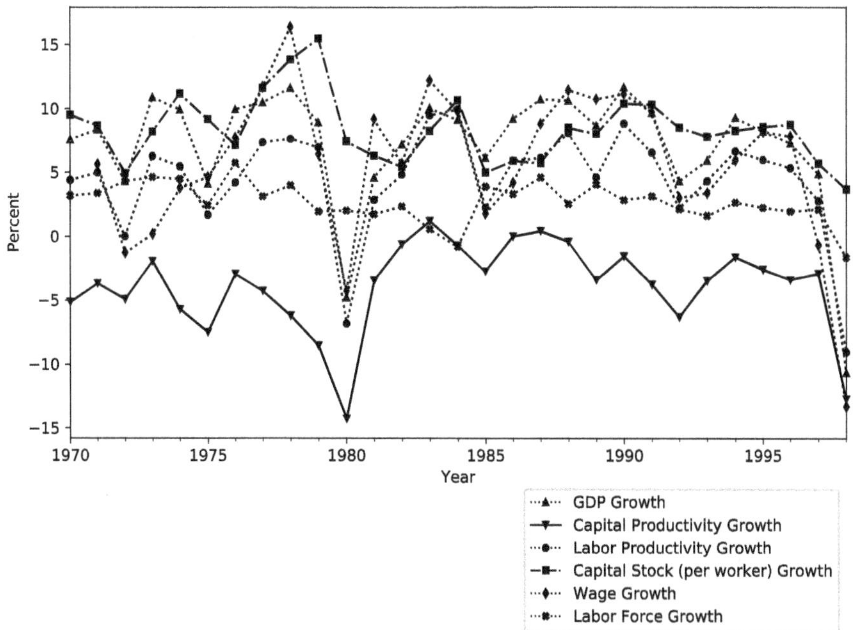

Figure 3.2 Growth Dynamics, 1970–98.
Note: See Appendix A for the definition of variables used in this figure.
Source: Extended Penn World Tables v. 4 (Foley and Michl, 1999; Marquetti, 2003).

alliance that enabled the rapid development was not a given outcome; many other unintended causal factors contributed to its gradual emergence.

Distribution relations after the Korean war

Following decades of intervention in the Korean peninsula, Japan annexed Korea in 1910, five years after emerging victorious in the 1904–05 Russo-Japanese War. The Japanese rule was predatory and harsh. Until 1930, it primarily consisted of the exploitation of Korean labor for the procurement of raw materials and agricultural products. In addition, Japan used Korea as a captive market for Japanese manufactured goods (Ban et al. 1980, 163–65; Cho and Kim 1991, 4; Woo 1991, 21–23). In spite of the evils of colonialism, agricultural techniques, productivity, and production in this period showed remarkable growth (Myers and Yamada, 1984; Kohli, 1994, 1997).[6]

By the late 1920s, Japan's imperial ambitions widened; and, its colonial policy and exploitation changed character (Woo, 1991, 24–25). Besides agricultural production, the Japanese colonial administration initiated an industrialization

6 According to the most recent estimates of the Korean GDP in the colonial period, agricultural production increased 63 percent between 1911 and 1930 (calculations based on GDP expenditure series in 1935 prices estimated by Cha and Kim 2006, Table B).

drive (Woo, 1991). This drive expanded the Korean manufacturing base, which grew by an average annual rate of 12 percent. With such annual growth, the Korean manufacturing capacity increased by 232 percent between 1929 and 1940.[7] There was also significant investment in physical infrastructure, including transportation and communication infrastructure (Chung, 2006). Furthermore, the Japanese colonial government founded a modern financial system, including a bank devoted to industrial financing (Cole and Park 1983, 44; Woo 1991, 29).[8] The financial system in 1940 comprised the Bank of Choson (which acted as the central bank), the Korean Agriculture-Industry Bank, the Korea Savings Bank, commercial banks, and a large number of financial associations.[9] This organizational infrastructure played an important role in channeling funds to Japanese investors in Korea.[10]

Big Japanese firms—the *zaibatsu* groups—had access to adequate financing, cheap labor, and low taxes. As a result, they were the pivotal agents of a significant increase in economic production and growth (Woo, 1991, 31–35). This model, which can be summarized as the government-sponsored mobilization of domestic and external saving channeled to private investment through government-controlled financial intermediaries (Chung, 2006, 305), is the prototype of state-finance-entrepreneurship constellation analyzed theoretically at the beginning of this chapter. As will be examined below, it would play an indispensable role during the export boom and the industrial push under the Park Chung Hee regime.

The Japanese domination over Korea came to an end in 1945. The Soviet Union and the United States occupied Korea and divided it into two areas at the 38th parallel. Most of the heavy industry (e.g., chemicals and manufacturing) and mining remained on the northern side, while the South kept light industries such as textiles (Jones and SaKong, 1980, 27).[11] With the involvement of two superpowers, who were becoming increasingly antagonistic toward each other in the aftermath of World War II, two regimes with different characteristics and ideologies emerged in the Korean peninsula: the Democratic Republic of Korea in the North (DPRK) and the Republic of Korea in the South (ROK). The two regimes clashed when the DPRK assaulted the South in 1950. The war lasted

7 The Korean GDP grew at an annual average rate of 5.7 percent in the same period. In 1940, it was 77.7 percent higher than the 1929 level. The share of manufacturing expenditure in the GDP increased from 9.1 percent in 1929 to 17 percent in 1940. (All calculations are based on GDP expenditure series in 1935 prices estimated by Cha and Kim 2006, Table B.) However, the majority of new plants and businesses belonged to Japanese firms and nationals (Jones and SaKong, 1980, 25).

8 Woo (1991, 30) observes that the financial system built by the Japanese colonial administration was "remarkably developed" for an agricultural economy like Korea at that time.

9 The number of bank branches were over 200 (Cole and Park, 1983, Table 9).

10 As Chung (2006, 304) claims:

> The magnitude and the nature of private investment were largely influenced by financial incentives provided by the government through fiscal and financial policies favorable to investors. … Another important, perhaps crucial, instrument for promoting private investment was the extension of loans for financing investment to designated industries and agriculture.

11 The majority of rice paddies remained in the South, while arable land was divided approximately equally. See Mason et al. (1980, 86–87).

three years, claimed millions of lives, and brought economic devastation to North and South Korea (Buzo, 2002; Cumings, 2005).[12]

Despite the subsequent destruction of physical capital during the war, the colonial period contributed greatly to the human capital development in Korea, especially in the form of a select group of industrial elites and entrepreneurs who became pivotal in shaping the Korean industrialization after 1964 (Lim, 1999). The colonial rule also shaped the future Korean bureaucracy, state organization, and military leadership (Cumings, 1984a). Equally important were the memory and knowledge of a "development model" that produced results.[13] Thus, despite severe economic exploitation and political repression under the Japanese rule, certain long-term elements of the Korean growth originated in the colonial period (Kohli, 1994, 1997, 2004; Cumings, 1984b; McNamara, 1990; Woo, 1991).[14]

However, as Amsden (2001) suggests, the land reform that occurred after World War II was an even more important factor than the colonial period's legacy for the subsequent trajectory of Korean development. In 1945, the U.S. Military Government began the process of land reform by consolidating and administering fertile farm lands owned by the Japanese. In response to mounting pressures from the peasant class, the South Korea Interim Legislative Assembly discussed enacting land reform in 1946 and 1947 (Mitchell, 1949) and the constitution of the newly-established Republic of Korea involved an article on land reform (Jeon and Kim, 2000, 254). As a result, even before the enactment of land reform and its implementation, the anticipation of a comprehensive land reform spurred the direct market exchange of approximately half of farmland (Ban et al. 1980, 285; Jeon and Kim 2000, 255). There were two other factors that forced landlords to sell their lands before the implementation of the land reform. First, both the U.S. Military administration and the Korean government were favoring tenants over landlords, partially in order to subdue peasant rebellions and to defeat the rise of communism in South Korea (Shin, 1998). Second, the compensation scheme proposed by the Korean government was unfavorable to landlords. These factors compelled many big landlords to sell their farmlands in the market (Ban et al. 1980, 287–91; Jeon and Kim 2000; Mitchell 1949; Pak 1956). The U.S. authorities distributed the consolidated land in 1948 (Whang, 2001). The South Korean government continued to redistribute the vast majority of the remaining farm land in the following decade.

12 As might be expected, there are different views on the causes of the Korean War. See Bruce Cumings' two volume study (1981; 1990) as well as the masterful analysis in his *Korea's Place in the Sun* (2005, ch. 5), Oh (1999), Kang (2005), and Buzo (2002) for different accounts with pointers to the relevant literature.

13 Jones and SaKong (1980, 18) succinctly summarize the legacy of the colonial period for the subsequent growth of South Korea: "The putative bureaucrats, entrepreneurs, and managers had largely 'learned by watching' rather than by 'doing,' but had, nonetheless, learned a great deal." Similarly, authors such as Kohli (1994, 2004) and Woo (1991) emphasize the "cognitive model" of economic development that was readily available to the bureaucratic cadre educated under the colonial rule.

14 The colonial legacy in Korean development is a matter of ongoing scholarly dispute and there are many dissenters to the view that the colonial period had an enduring contribution to Korean economic growth. See Haggard et al. (1997) and Yang (2004).

The land reform made South Korea a remarkably equal country compared to the rest of the world (Amsden 2001, 17; Song 1997). Such a drastic social change had several social-structural consequences. The first was the virtual elimination of the landlord class and its economic basis. Equal distribution of agricultural land meant that rents arising from landownership were quite difficult to obtain in the aftermath of the Korean War. Hence, a common problem blocking economic take-off in many underdeveloped societies—the effective hindrance of industrialization by an agrarian-based economy and landlord class—did not pose a barrier to development in Korea (Kay 2002; Kil 2001, 46; Shin 1998, 1313–14). Second, the great leveling of economic fortunes also avoided a class conflict between landlords and landless peasants, which would have been politically destabilizing had it occurred.[15] Both of these factors prepared the ground for a developmental alliance between the state and the *chaebols*.

The beginnings of chaebols

Even though the colonial period and the land reform created an opportunity for rapid economic growth in Korea, the take-off did not materialize in the immediate aftermath of the Korean War. There were several impediments to an economic take-off. First, the destruction of physical capital during the war was a major obstacle. Second, South Korea featured an autocratic and corrupt government, which was ineffective in its administration of the economy. Syngman Rhee, a U.S.-educated veteran politician with a doctorate from Princeton University, headed this government. Rhee ruled South Korea from its establishment in 1948 as the First Republic of Korea until his ouster in 1960. Lacking a political base of his own, Rhee repressed the opposition and his regime was particularly brutal toward social activists and the left. Although his legitimacy diminished rapidly, Rhee stayed in power between 1953 and 1960 thanks largely to massive infusions of U.S. aid. However, this period of political corruption, economic dependency, and neglect of economic policies was also a reconstruction period (Woo, 1991). The literature on Korean development often draws a sharp contrast between the Syngman Rhee government and the subsequent Park Chung Hee regime. Yet, the vastly different historical conditions during the Rhee and Park regimes render such comparisons problematic. It is much more fruitful to approach the evaluation of the Rhee regime in light of the continuities and discontinuities with the Park Chung Hee regime.[16] This section highlights the elements of the Rhee period that continued to have an effect on the Korean development, while the next section evaluates some of the drastic changes that fueled the economic take-off.

15 As Pak (1956, 1021) puts it:

> The most significant result achieved by land reform during the war was the allaying of social and political unrest. In fact land reform saved human lives, particularly for landlords because there could have been serious rioting against landlords by landless peasants.

16 See Kang (2002), Lie (1998), and Woo (1991) for a criticism of the literature along these lines.

The Rhee period contributed to building capacity in at least two areas, which had lasting consequences. First, high levels of reconstruction and reorganization were achieved despite the political corruption of the Rhee government. Second, this was a period of capital accumulation for a large number of entrepreneurs, who would become the leading industrialists of Korea in the Park Chung Hee era.

In the 1950s, Korea followed import-substitution policies aiming to foster production in light industries such as textiles and food processing. A significant amount of U.S. economic and military aid facilitated the implementation of these policies (Cumings, 1984b). A persistent inflation and an overvalued exchange rate bedeviled the industrialization efforts in this period (Mason et al., 1980, 460–62). Although the industrial production growth rate was high compared to other developing countries, the prospects for future growth through light industry were dim. At the end of the 1950s, there was over-investment in a key industry such as textiles (Amsden, 1989, 39–42).

Despite these shortcomings, there was significant investment in rebuilding infrastructure and a considerable effort to establish state institutions. First of all, the Rhee government founded several state organizations, including the Ministry of Reconstruction and the Economic Development Council (Cheng et al., 1999, 100). Second, the Rhee administration was effective in two key areas: police force development and tax collection (Kohli, 2004, 66–68). Third, expenditure on economic and social services as well as fixed capital investment increased steadily. As can be seen in Figure 3.3, non-defense expenditure as a share of GNP increased from 5 percent in 1953 to 12.2 percent in 1960. Economic and social services received the lion's share of this expenditure. For example, the share of education in social services was a remarkable 61 percent in 1958 (Mason et al., 1980, 313). Similarly, the majority of fixed capital investment during this period went into housing, nonresidential building, and machinery. Investment in housing and nonresidential building constituted 17.9 and 25 percent, respectively, of total fixed

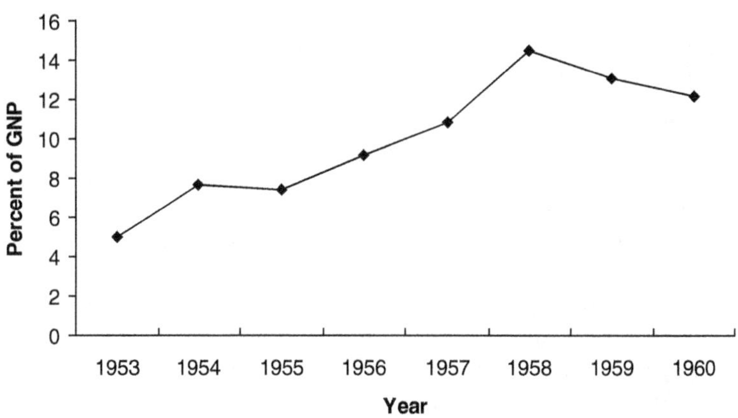

Figure 3.3 Non-defense Expenditure as Percent of GNP, 1953–60.
Source: Mason et al. (1980, Table 75).

investment between 1953 and 1961. Investment in housing and nonresidential building did not reach such high levels for the next three decades (Chung, 2007, Table 3.2).

The *chaebols* emerged as significant economic actors in this period. As Mason et al. (1980, 249–50) argue, "The foundations for a number of entrepreneurial fortunes of later members of the *chaebŏl* were laid during this period. A by-product of this system was … the development of considerable entrepreneurial talents." Collusion between the state and the *chaebols* was rampant; and, this collusion was instrumental in making the fortunes of few select entrepreneurs. A case illustrating the nature of collusion was the sale of Japanese-owned businesses. It was the U.S. Military Government that initiated the sales of these businesses. However, the Rhee government sold the majority of Japanese-owned enterprises (Kang, 2005, 274–76). The terms of these sales were highly favorable to buyers (Amsden, 1989, 39). As a result, a few Korean-owned enterprises emerged as dominant actors by the end of the Rhee regime. The distribution of U.S. aid further increased the size of the *chaebols.* The Korean economy relied heavily on U.S. aid, and the processing of aid in foodstuff and raw materials was a major business activity. The Rhee government politicized the distribution of foreign aid by favoring few large enterprises that contributed to the regime's political machinery (Cumings 2005, 308; Woo 1991).

The growth of the financial system was stagnant until the end of the Korean War.[17] As the war ended, two new financial institutions emerged: the Korea Development Bank (KDB) and the Korea Agricultural Bank (Cole and Park, 1983, 52–53). Despite the establishment of the KDB and the agricultural bank, the Korean financial system was largely ineffective in the mobilization of domestic saving. This was, as Chung (2007, 217) argues, partly due to low income and economic insecurity that characterized the period following the Korean War. In addition, low interest rates and high inflation implied that placing savings in Korean banks was not economical (Cole and Park, 1983, 262–65).

The leap forward and the state-big business pact

In April 1960, the Rhee regime collapsed following election fraud that triggered widespread student protests (Oh, 1999, 40–42). The April Revolution, as it came to be known, led to the establishment of the Second Republic of Korea as a parliamentary regime. Chang Myon—a social activist, former diplomat, and opposition politician during the Rhee regime—won the elections in July 1960 and formed the government as the first prime minister of the Second Republic (Kang, 2005, 201–03). Korea's experience with genuine—but politically unstable—democracy was short-lived; the Chang Myon government ended with a military coup in May 1961. Park Chung Hee was one of the military officers who staged the coup, but he was not late in establishing his leadership (Buzo, 2002, 112). His authoritarian

17 As Cole and Park (1983, 48) put, "At the end of World War II, Korea had the shell of a modern financial system—and a modern economy—but lacked sufficient people experienced in running it."

regime lasted until 1979—the year he was assassinated by the chief of the Korean Central Intelligence Agency (KCIA).

The military junta saw economic development as an imperative for national security, but failed to implement coherent economic policies until 1964. However, after 1964, the focus of economic policy-making shifted to exports and export industries (Haggard, 1994b). From this point onwards, Park Chung Hee and his economic administration zeroed in on the idea of promoting exports. They employed several measures to achieve this end. The first one was the large devaluation of the exchange rate from 130 won to the dollar to 255 in May 1964 (Haggard et al., 1991, 864). In addition, the Park government enacted various export-promotion measures, including tax concessions for exporters, preferential loans for exports, and overseas marketing support (Kim, 1991, 109–10). In other words, the Korean state subsidized the export sector through various instruments such as multiple exchange rates and preferential credit allocation. At the same time, the Park administration protected the domestic market through import barriers, which eliminated foreign competition that could have hindered the growth of the *chaebols* (Amsden, 1989, 70). The preferential treatment of export-oriented firms was subject to minimum export requirements and conditional on their continuing to export to world markets (Amsden, 1989; Kim, 1991).

What led to this turn toward export-led industrialization (ELI) strategy? Chibber (2003), in a compelling analysis, argues that the growing alliance between Korean and Japanese capitalists exercised the determining influence on the Park regime's turn from *ad hoc* industrial expansion policies toward orchestrated export-promotion efforts. He posits that a growing alliance between Korean and Japanese capital in the first half of the 1960s provided the window of opportunity for the Korean firms to be successful in foreign markets (Chibber, 2003, 72–79).[18] This window of opportunity, in turn, enabled the developmental pact between the Korean state and the Korean capitalist class, since the Korean firms' success in export markets made ELI a profitable business strategy (Chibber, 1999, 312).

The Park regime enacted two major changes in the financial system, which were crucial in fueling the ELI drive. The first one was a system of foreign loan guarantees (Mason et al., 1980, 350). Conditional on the approval of the Economic Planning Board (EPB), the government-controlled banks guaranteed the foreign borrowing of Korean firms. The second change was a comprehensive financial reform that began in 1964. The goal of the reform was to mobilize domestic savings (Cumings, 1984b).

The financial reform had a clear bias in favor of the *chaebols*. The distributional mechanism was a wedge between deposit rates and loan rates. By setting loan rates lower than the deposit rates, the Park administration subsidized capital accumulation and growth in the Korean corporate sector (Kim and Im, 2001, 20–21). The Ministry of Finance opposed the financial subsidy to the corporate sector, which

18 This argument is not entirely novel (see, in particular, Cumings 1984b and Woo 1991). However, Chibber (2003) corrects the statist bias in the literature by showing that the East Asian context, with the heavy presence of Japan, was particularly beneficial for the Korean take-off.

violated the principle that the forces of supply and demand determine equilibrium interest rates in financial markets. The EPB, in contrast, championed this particular distributional preference. Enjoying the support of Park Chung Hee, the policy remained firmly effective and cost the Ministry of Finance dearly. As Kim and Im (2001, 20) suggest,

> Park sided with EPB by firing its minister [Minister of Finance] (three times between 1964 and 1967) to send a clear signal to the state bureaucracy and business community that he was prepared to sacrifice financial stability for industrial growth.

The financial measures and the ensuing allocation of funds from savers to the corporate sector had a positive effect on the Korean financial development. Previously, the credit channel in the economy was limited and foreign exchange came through U.S. aid. After the reforms, foreign borrowing and domestic saving replaced foreign aid as the main source of finance capital (Cho, 1989). This can be seen in Table 3.1 and Figure 3.4. Domestic saving increased from 6.5 percent of GDP in 1965 to 10.7 in 1966. In 1969, it stood at 17.8 percent. Credit—and thus finance capital—grew at a rapid pace during the same period (Figure 3.4).

The examination of credit sources in the Korean economy between 1965 and 1975 shows that the volume of foreign credit was close to that of domestic credit, especially in the second half of the 1960s. The normalization of diplomatic and economic ties with Japan after 1965 was a crucial factor in the steady flow of capital to Korea (Rhee, 1973, 679). The expansion and deepening of the financial system through the mobilization of domestic saving and the inflow of foreign

Table 3.1 Select Macroeconomic Indicators, 1961–72†

Year	*GDP Growth*[a]	*Manufacturing*[b]	*Saving*[c]	*Investment*[d]	*Fixed Capital*[d]
1961	5.9	4.0	2.0	12.0	11.8
1962	2.1	11.7	3.0	11.8	13.8
1963	9.1	16.1	8.0	17.0	13.6
1964	9.7	9.9	8.1	13.2	11.4
1965	5.7	20.5	6.5	14.1	14.9
1966	12.2	17.3	10.7	20.4	20.6
1967	5.9	21.6	9.9	20.9	21.8
1968	11.3	27.2	13.9	24.9	25.4
1969	13.8	21.6	17.8	27.9	26.1
1970	8.8	19.9	15.9	24.3	25.1
1971	8.5	18.6	14.7	24.8	22.5
1972	4.8	14.0	16.2	20.9	20.7

† All numbers are in percentage terms.
a Real GDP annual growth rate. As the Extended Penn World Tables v. 4 do not offer data on the early 1960s for South Korea, the figures on GDP growth presented here rely on Chung (2007, Table 2.2).
b Manufacturing annual growth rate. Source: Chung (2007, Table 2.2).
c Domestic saving as percent of GDP. Source: Chung (2007, Table 10.1).
d Percent of GDP. Source: Chung (2007, Table 3.1).

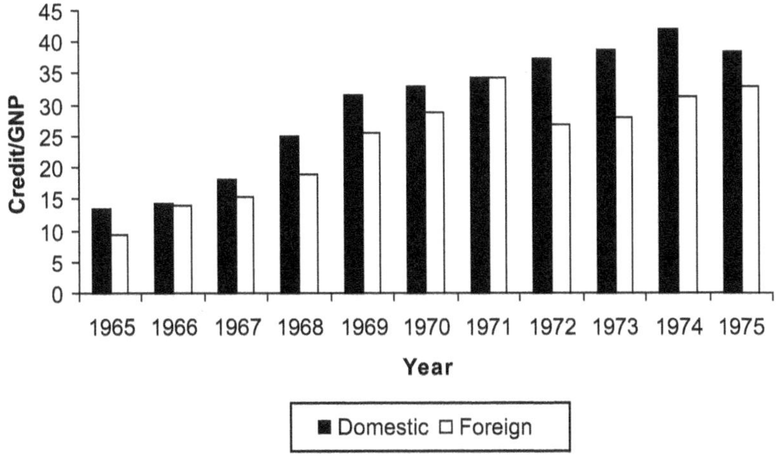

Figure 3.4 Domestic and Foreign Credit as Percent of GNP, 1965–75.
Source: Mason et al. (1980, Table 88).

capital (subject to authorization) enabled the Korean State to implement credit programs targeting export sectors (Cho, 1989, 92). Through its control over financial intermediation and foreign borrowing, the state dominated the credit allocation in the Korean economy.

As a result, high investment and exports became the engines of growth in the 1960s (Cheng and Chu, 2002, 33). The share of exports rose from 5 percent to 29 percent of the GDP between 1961 and 1973 (WDI 2014).[19] The center of production (and thus of exports) in this period was labor-intensive industries such as textiles and apparel (Bridges, 2001). Manufacturing industries grew at the average annual rate of 21 percent between 1965 and 1971. Domestic investment boomed, increasing from 14.1 percent of the GDP in 1965 to 20.4 percent in 1966 (Table 3.1). At the end of the 1960s, total domestic investment constituted approximately 25 percent of the Korean GDP. Even more remarkable was the share of fixed capital investment in total domestic investment. As can be seen in Table 3.1, fixed capital investment was consistently over 90 percent of total domestic investment.[20] Not surprisingly, the GDP growth was very strong (see Table 3.1).[21].

19 World Development Indicators, World Bank.

20 Furthermore, fixed capital investment surpassed total domestic investment in various years, which means that it often compensated for negative inventories.

21 Korea's involvement in the Vietnam War was another factor contributing to the post-1965 take-off. In fact, from 1966 onwards, Korea accrued significant foreign earnings as a result of its participation in the Vietnam War. As (Kim, 1970, 519) reports, "The 1968 earnings of $180 million represented 16% of the total receipts of foreign funds and 2.8% of South Korea's GNP." For an economy such as Korea in the second half of the 1960s, these foreign funds were a significant help in maintaining balance of payments and reducing debt-service to exports ratio (Kim, 1970)

The increasing preponderance of chaebols

The 1960s were a period of rapid economic growth for Korea. However, the early 1970s presented several challenges. First, maintaining strong economic growth became more difficult in the 1970s (Haggard, 1994b). Labor-intensive industries, which could compete effectively in world markets thanks to low wages, underpinned the Korean economic development throughout the 1960s. Labor-intensive, export-oriented development ran into various difficulties in the early 1970s, including increasing balance of payments problems, labor shortage, and wage increases (Im, 1987; Jeon, 1994; Rhee, 1973). As can be seen in Table 3.1, the GDP growth dropped from 13.8 in 1969 to 8.8 in 1970, to 8.5 in 1971, and then to 4.8 in 1972. Second, by the late 1960s and the early 1970s, the post-war high growth in the world came to an end. The global economy featured higher inflation, unemployment, and interest rates (Brenner, 2002; Eichengreen, 1996). Thus, the slowdown of the world economy accompanied the domestic economic problems in South Korea. Third, President Nixon's 1969 speech in Guam signaled a potential reduction of military support to the allies (Kimball, 2006), which naturally created anxiety in South Korea.

Finally, the Park regime faced increasing political competition and opposition. Although Park Chung Hee increased his votes by a small margin in the 1971 presidential election, his party suffered a major loss of seats in the National Assembly (Kim, 1972). This stood in contrast to Park Chung Hee gaining a third presidential term through a constitutional reform in 1969, which the Korean voters supported. The 1969 constitutional reform and the 1971 presidential election were political successes for Park Chung Hee, while the loss of seats was a relative failure.[22]

The Park regime's response to these political and economic challenges was twofold (Jeon, 1994): the imposition of the *Yushin* Constitution on the political front and the drive toward heavy and chemical industry (HCI) on the economic front. The *Yushin* Constitution, which became effective in 1972, was an anti-democratic set of rules that abolished various human rights and violated the principles of legislative and judicial independence. It thus bolstered the already formidable power that Park Chung Hee wielded in Korean politics and society (Kang, 2005, 207–10).

Following the strengthening of the authoritarian system, Park Chung Hee launched a program aiming at the development of heavy and chemical industry (HCI) in 1973. The Korean economic bureaucracy selected six key industries including shipbuilding, iron and steel, machinery, and chemicals for the industrial push. Select *chaebols*, at the behest of the Park regime, undertook large-scale industrialization projects designed directly by the Korean economic

22 This can be explained by the paradoxical nature of the Park regime. As Kim (1972, 223–24) succinctly argues, Park disdained politics and empowered technocratic rule. Park's disdain for politics resulted in his inability to transform the approval of his economic management to greater political success. Furthermore, strong regionalism followed by Park paved the way for the political success of Kim Dae-jung, his main competitor in the 1971 election, who was widely supported in a region ignored by the Park regime.

bureaucracy.[23] Although there were strong industry-specific incentives to carry these projects, there was also an unmistakable element of coercion (Krueger 1997, 315; Lee 1991). As suggested at the beginning of this chapter, this is another evidence of the Korean state's capacity, under the Park regime, to produce rather than simply reproduce social relations at the critical junctures of the Korean development trajectory. The Korean capitalist class, despite the pressure that fell on individual *chaebols*, was a willing partner in this path of industrial transformation. The important point is that it is doubtful whether the Korean capitalists would have undertaken such a massive industrial transformation project without the state's guidance, guarantees, and resources—resources that the Korean state harnessed by redistributing the benefits of rapid growth from ordinary savers and wage-earners to the *chaebols*.

A complex array of factors were at the roots of the HCI drive. The Park regime saw industrial diversification and production of intermediate and capital goods as a solution to the potential loss of international competitiveness and slowdown in economic growth (Haggard, 1994b, 33). However, more important than the pure economic reasons were the strategic and political ones. Park Chung Hee prioritized self-sufficiency and industrial development and the Korean bureaucracy viewed economic independence as a panacea to the various problems the country was facing (Chang, 1993, 138). The goal of industrial self-sufficiency crystallized as early as the Second Five Year Plan (1967–72), which underlined independent national economic structure as an essential objective (Rhee, 1973, 680). Furthermore, Park Chung Hee and the Korean economic bureaucracy saw the successful example of Japanese industrialization as a feasible path to follow in economic development (Lee, 1991, 439).

The implementation of the HCI program was a success. As Lee (1991, 449–50) argues:

> Most of the big business groups in Korea were scrambling for a ride on the HCI bandwagon expecting to reap huge benefits from the new incentive system rather than from profitability of the ventures. Such eagerness on the part of Korea's major business groups enabled the HCI investment plan to be implemented successfully, and between 1977 and 1979 investments in HCI accounted for more than 75 percent of all investments in manufacturing.

As a result, the share of the HCI in production rose steadily in the 1970s, which led the economic center of gravity to switch from labor-intensive to capital-intensive industries (Wade, 1990, 319–20). This transformation can be tracked in Table 3.2. The share of the HCI in credit allocation was 35.6 percent in 1973. In 1975, the respective shares of heavy and light industries were reversed. While heavy industries received 65.8 percent, the light industries' share in credit allocation dropped to 34.2 percent of the total credit allocation. The credit allocated to the HCI remained in the vicinity of 60 percent throughout the decade. Similarly, the share of the HCI in manufacturing rose from 40.9 percent in 1973 to 54.9 percent in 1979.

23 A list of these projects can be found in Lee (1991, 433).

Table 3.2 HCI Drive†

Indicator	*1973*	*1974*	*1975*	*1976*	*1977*	*1978*	*1979*
Credit Allocation[a]							
Heavy Industry	35.6	32.2	65.8	60.0	60.7	55.7	58.4
Light Industry	64.4	67.8	34.2	40.0	39.3	44.3	41.6
Manufacturing Share[b]							
Heavy Industry	40.9	49.9	47.9	49.3	51.5	53.0	54.9
Light Industry	59.1	50.1	52.1	50.7	48.5	47.0	45.1
GDP Growth[c]	10.9	9.9	4.1	9.9	10.5	11.6	8.9

† All numbers are in percentage terms.
a Credit allocation to different sectors, as percent of total credit allocation by deposit-money banks and the Korea Development Bank. Source: Lee (1991, Table 17.6).
b Share of total manufacturing. Source: Chung (2007, Table 2.5).
c Real GDP annual growth rate. Source: Extended Penn World Tables v. 4 (Foley and Michl, 1999; Marquetti, 2003).

The initiative toward the HCI bore fruit especially in the second part of the 1970s, as manifested in increasing exports and growth rate (Haggard, 1994b, 41–43). The real GDP growth rate was 9.9 percent in 1976, 10.5 percent in 1977, and 11.6 percent in 1978 (Table 3.2 and Figure 3.2). Furthermore, as can be seen in Figure 3.5, the share of exports in GDP rose in tandem with the large current account deficits caused by the heavy importation of machinery and equipment needed for large-scale investments. In 1970, the HCI produced only 18.2 percent of total exports. This figure rose to 33.9 percent in 1975 and to 47.6 percent in 1980 (Lee, 1991, 452).

Such a rapid accumulation process spurred a remarkable change in the Korean economy. The capital-intensive growth model, with its reliance on elevated levels of corporate debt, naturally rewarded economies of scale. The successful *chaebols* in this period grew at an accelerating rate, since the Korean financial system channeled greater amounts of investment to enterprises with a proven track record. In this process, the *chaebols* became indispensable economic actors. Their political weight remained fundamentally curtailed by the *Yushin* Constitution and the accompanying political oppression that the Park regime exercised. However, the seeds of a fundamental change in the balance of power between the state and big business emerged during the HCI period (Cheng et al., 1999; Kim, 1994; Kim and Im, 2001).

At the same time, the HCI drive had many defects. High inflation, which the Park regime tolerated to accommodate high growth in select industries,[24] the high debt share in the GDP by the late 1970s, and the rising manufacturing wages (Figure 3.1 and Figure 3.2) exposed the vulnerabilities of the Korean development model (Amsden, 1989; Cheng and Chu, 2002). Formidable economic and political factors underpinned the rise in wages. On the one hand, as the Korean economy became more capital-intensive, the high demand for skilled labor

24 The evidence for this point can be found in an interview with the deputy prime minister Nam Duck Woo, quoted in Haggard (1994b, 42).

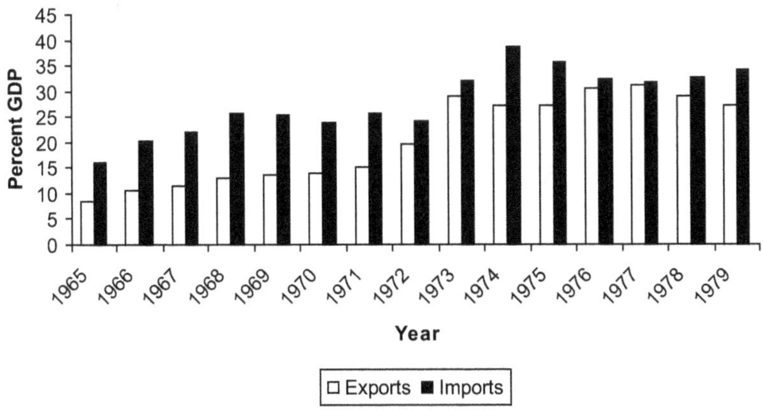

Figure 3.5 Exports and Imports as Percent of GDP, 1965–79.
Note: Author's calculation from time series in Korean *won*, current values.
Source: IMF, International Financial Statistics, May 2008.

in the manufacturing sector naturally pushed wages upward. On the other hand, as political and social mobilization against the *Yushin* regime solidified, wage repression through political and social control became much more difficult to implement. The resulting distributional pressures can be observed in Figure 3.1, which illustrates the upward trajectory of the wage share in the Korean GDP from 1975 onwards. Another side-effect of the export-oriented economy was the shortage of consumer goods—a shortage that the rising wages and living standards made more salient (Lee, 1980, 65). The Park regime's response to the mounting problems came in late 1978 and included tighter monetary policy measures, which led to a recession (Lee, 1980, 65–66). Coupled with the second oil shock and a depressed world economy in 1979, the problems in the Korean economy intensified.

The developmental alliance under strain

The Park regime relied heavily on the Korean Central Intelligence Agency (KCIA) in maintaining its authoritarian rule. As Cumings (2005) remarks, at the end it was that same powerful agency that terminated the Park regime in an unexpected manner. Park Chung Hee was assassinated by Kim Jae-kyu, the chief of the KCIA, during a private dinner on October 26, 1979 (Lee, 1980). For a brief period, South Korea was under martial law and a transition government, while the future of the political system remained uncertain. General Chun Doo-hwan's rise to power in 1980 dashed hopes for democratization and meant a new bout of authoritarian rule (Haggard 1994a, 50; Lee 1981; Lie 1998, 120–25).

A myriad of problems thwarted the Chun administration's plans of establishing a legitimate regime. First, Chun Doo-hwan lacked political legitimacy since he came to power through a military coup d'état. Second, his government crushed the widespread democratization expectations in a ruthless manner, which further delegitimized the Chun government.[25] Third, the economy had entered into a major slowdown by 1979 (Figure 3.2). Furthermore, high inflation and a significant foreign debt stock, one of the largest among developing countries at the time, accompanied the economic slowdown (Hundt, 2009).

Most importantly, the Chun government faced a political environment where it was politically more costly to repress labor (Koo, 1990, 2001). To be sure, under the Chun government, the draconian restrictions on trade unions, strike activity, and shop floor organizing remained in place (Deyo, 1989a).[26] However, the Chun government had less room to repress wage growth. The outcome of the Chun government's diminished capacity to continue the distributional bias of the Park regime can be seen in the contrast between the first half of the 1970s and the period after 1975, both in terms of wage share in the GDP and the growth rate of average real wage. Although the growth rate of average real wage was much lower than the GDP growth rate until the late 1970s, the real wage growth caught up with the GDP growth rate and even surpassed it for many years during the 1980s (Figure 3.2). The result was a steady increase in the wage share and a corresponding decline in the profit rate (Figure 3.1).

The Chun government responded to these challenges in a multitude of ways. Three of its policies are noteworthy because of their effects on the subsequent transformation of the Korean political economy. First, Chun Doo-hwan initiated a substantial "clean-up" of the state bureaucracy. The new authoritarian administration purged hundreds of senior and thousands of lower level officials from economic bureaucracy as well as state-controlled firms and banks (Lee, 1980, 135).[27] As a result, a new group of technocrats, much more liberal than their predecessors, took the helm of economic policy-making (Lie 1998, 124). Kim Jae-ik, an economist with a doctorate from Stanford and considerable experience in Korean economic bureaucracy, was the most influential figure among the "liberalizers." Chun appointed Kim Jae-ik as his top economic advisor in September 1980. Apart from Kim Jae-ik, the liberalizers included technocrats at the top levels of economic bureaucracy: Kang Kyong-shik (Minister of Finance) and Kim Ki-hwan (President of Korea Development Institute).

Despite occupying the high echelons of economic decision-making, the liberalizers faced resistance from the "traditionalists," which included the majority of middle and lower levels of economic bureaucracy, in addition to top-level cabinet members such as Kim Dong-hwi (Minister of Commerce and Industry). The liberalizers' influence in the early phases of the Chun administration was not entirely surprising, given that Chun rose to power in a macroeconomic context characterized by high inflation (both at home and abroad), debt overhang,

25 The most egregious example of such repression was the massacre after the Kwangju uprising (Lie, 1998, 120–22).

26 United States. Central Intelligence Agency. CIA - RDP86T01017R000606090003 - 7. *South Korea's Labor Record: Balancing Political and Economic Priorities*. June 11, 1986. Web.

27 As Kim (1994, 52) argues, "The loss of numerous senior economic bureaucrats considerably weakened the economic bureaucracy."

and over-investment in multiple industries. In such an environment, Kim Jae-ik's program of austerity and market reforms was necessary to avoid an economic crisis in the near future. Furthermore, the liberalizers offered the promise of modernizing the Korean economy by adhering to internationally sanctioned market principles. Nonetheless, Kim Jae-ik's reforms were limited to trade and domestic financial liberalization. The liberal reforms were gradual and of modest scope. Furthermore, the influence of the liberalizers was already in decline by 1983. The comparison with Chile after 1975, where the Chicago Boys—a much more cohesive group of radical reformers—had complete control over the economy, is instructive. Like Chile, the liberalizers had direct influence over the President. However, unlike Chile, they faced effective opposition within the Korean economic bureaucracy.[28] The killing of Kim Jae-ik by a bomb in Myanmar during an official state visit in October 1983 further curtailed the influence of the liberalizers in the 1980s.[29]

Second, the Chun administration targeted the *chaebols* and devised policies to weaken their economic power. Chun Doo-hwan favored such policies, as he aimed to gain legitimacy through liberalization reforms oriented toward middle classes (Moon, 1994, 152). On the one hand, the Chun government aimed to encourage further market competition by enacting a trade and monopoly regulation law in 1981 (Kim 1994, 53; SaKong 1993, 83). On the other hand, the Chun administration liberalized imports from 1981 onwards (Kim 1994; Krause 1997, 121). The Korean economic bureaucracy accelerated tariff reduction plans in 1984 and sought to liberalize tariffs on "monopolistic and oligopolistic products" at a much faster pace (SaKong, 1993, 89). Even more importantly, the cornerstone of Korean industrial policy—"picking winners"—was abandoned for a more modest role of state intervention and promotion (SaKong, 1993, 75).

Third, and most important of all, the Chun government began adopting a series of measures in order to liberalize financial markets. Paradoxically, some of these liberalization measures originated in the 1970s, during which the HCI drive magnified the state's role in the financial system.[30] However, there were also pressures toward the liberalization of the financial system during the HCI drive. First, privately owned non-bank financial institutions (NBFIs) were increasing their share of resource allocation in the economy by addressing the capital demand of firms other than the *chaebols* (Sikorski, 1996).[31]

28 United States. Central Intelligence Agency. CIA - RDP84S00553R000100050006 - 8. *South Korea: Economic Decision-Making in Transition.* January 1983. Web.

29 The Rangoon bombing, which was a North Korean assassination attempt against Chun Doo-hwan, took the lives of many senior Korean cabinet members and advisors, including Kim Dong-hwi, the Minister of Commerce and Industry (Hundt, 2009, 78).

30 The greater presence of the state in the financial system had to do with the financing requirements of the HCI drive. The Park regime directed credit to target sectors and subsidized large-scale investment in heavy and chemical industry by allocating credits through the newly established Industrial Rationalization Council (Cho 1989; Haggard 1994b, 33). As a result, state-directed credit allocation dwarfed private transactions in the financial system (Cho 1989; Haggard 1994a, 51).

31 NBFIs were financial intermediaries such as mutual savings institutions that could not accept deposits from the public. Their emergence had important consequences for corporate finance in Korea. As Cho (1989, 94) notes:

Second, by the end of the 1970s, there was disappointment with misallocated investments in HCI (Park, 1991, 53). Third, given the scarcity of capital, the informal curb market began allocating an increasing share of funds (Park 1991; Sikorski 1996, 230).[32] These factors, combined with the fragility of the Korean financial system, led the economic bureaucracy to view the privatization of commercial banks and deregulation of interest rates as potential solutions to mounting financial difficulties (Sikorski, 1996, 232).

Nonetheless, it is doubtful that the Park regime, had it continued, would have taken widespread financial liberalization measures as eagerly as the Chun government. Considering the quintessential role that the control over finance played in the Korean development, the Chun government's liberalization measures were remarkable. First, the government privatized commercial banks by selling its shares between 1981 and 1983 (Nam 1994, 190; SaKong 1993, 72). Second, the Chun government passed measures to encourage private ownership in the financial sector, including reducing barriers to entry and allowing new private commercial banks to be established (Nam 1994, 190; SaKong 1993, 73). Third, the administration began to dismantle the policy of applying differential and favorable interest rates to promote investment projects (Nam, 1994, 191). Fourth, the government implemented a program of interest rate structure simplification and a modest deregulation of lending rates (SaKong 1993, 73), followed by a major deregulation of interest rates in 1988 (Nam 1994, 191).[33]

These gradual reforms toward financial liberalization initiated, in fact, the abandonment of the Korean state's role in the provision of entrepreneurial capital. In other words, the state gradually quit acting as a financial midwife to big businesses during the 1980s. As such, the Korean state began to abandon its role in nurturing the *chaebols*. Obviously, such a process also led to the loss of state's control over the *chaebol* economic activities (Woo-Cumings, 1997).

The *chaebols* favored financial liberalization, but they showed strong opposition to interest rate deregulation (Choi, 1993, 42). The reasons for this somewhat ambiguous stance were not hard to decipher. Big conglomerates, having become mature economic corporations that commanded vast resources, were not particularly fond of the Chun government's interference with their economic decisions. Financial liberalization, as it would weaken the government's power over the *chaebols*, was an attractive policy. However, weak capital structure and high

Banks and foreign loans were the major source of corporate finance in the 1960s and 1970s. For example, they accounted for 75 per cent of total external funds raised by corporate firms during 1965–69. However, their share decreased to 30 per cent while NBFIs [nonbank financial institutions] and securities markets accounted for 67 per cent of total external funds raised during 1980–84.

32 The curb market in Korea was the name given to the operation of brokers who intermediated funds between a group of borrowers and lenders by using the formal banking system. The transmission of funds was based on trust, as these brokers did not have an official license for such financial intermediation.

33 However, this liberalization attempt was not successful and the government revoked most of the measures at a later date.

corporate leverage were the two economic pillars on which the strength of the *chaebols* rested. Hence, a potential rise in interest rates following interest rate deregulation was a significant worry for the *chaebols* (Choi, 1993).

The Chun administration had the goal of reducing the power of *chaebols*. Yet, the factors considered above changed the balance of power between the state and the *chaebols* dramatically in favor of the latter. This can be seen in Figure 3.6, where the share of top 30 *chaebols* in value-added GNP—already high by international standards—kept rising between 1985 and 1995. In retrospect, this was not surprising. Given their dominant position in the Korean economy, their large size, and control over resources, the *chaebols* had a clear advantage in keeping and strengthening their positions. The Chun government pursued liberalization reforms, but as is the case with almost all developing countries enacting market-friendly reforms, they neglected that freer markets require more rules and regulations to ensure competition, to use Vogel's (1996) felicitous phrase. The result was the partial breakdown of the developmental alliance between the state and the *chaebols*:

> Under circumstances in which the state did not take on regulatory functions in the interest of maintaining fair competition and consumer protection, the principle of free competition ... merely exacerbated the already excessive concentration of industry and economic power in the hands of the conglomerates. ... [T]he model of "private-sector industrial guidance" under the Chun regime boiled down to a "*jaebul*-guidance" model (Kim 1994, 54–55 [original emphasis]).

The change in government-business relations notwithstanding, Korea had a quick recovery from the 1979–82 recession. Several factors contributed to the recovery, including wage repression, disinflationary policies, a rise in productivity, and good export performance (Amsden, 1989; You and Lee, 2001). By 1986, inflation was

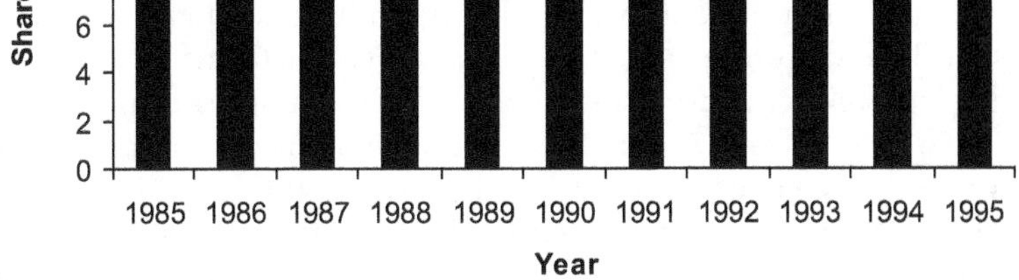

Figure 3.6 Top 30 Chaebols' Share in Value-Added GNP, 1985–95.
Source: Jwa (2002, Table 3.1).

Table 3.3 GDP Growth and Balance of Payments, 1987–97

Year	*GDP Growth*[a]	*Current Account*[b]	*Capital Account*[c]
1987	10.7	10.1	−8.9
1988	10.6	14.5	−4.2
1989	8.6	5.3	−2.6
1990	11.6	−2.0	2.9
1991	9.6	−8.4	6.7
1992	4.3	−4.1	7.0
1993	5.9	0.8	3.2
1994	9.3	−4.0	10.7
1995	8.2	−8.7	17.3
1996	7.3	−23.2	24.0
1997	4.9	−8.4	−9.1

a Real GDP annual growth rate. Source: Extended Penn World Tables v. 4 (Foley and Michl, 1999; Marquetti, 2003).
b Current Account Balance, billions of dollars. Source: IMF, *International Financial Statistics.*
c Capital Account Balance, billions of dollars. Source: IMF, *International Financial Statistics.*

under control. The industrial capacity built by the HCI program also contributed to this strong recovery. Furthermore, the Plaza Accord in September 1985 led to the appreciation of the Japanese *yen*, which improved the competitiveness of Korean products in international markets. Real GDP grew at 10.7 percent in 1987 and 10.6 percent in 1988. Rapid growth continued in 1990 and 1991 (Table 3.3 and Figure 3.2). The strong export performance that underpinned the accelerated growth trajectory can be tracked through the current account surplus between 1987 and 1990.

The political and social pressures on the Chun government increased significantly in 1986 and 1987 (Hundt, 2009, 80). Various groups challenged the Chun government, but student mobilization was a central element of the resistance against the authoritarian state. An eclectic set of demands underpinned the dissident mobilization. Crucially, the groups that took to the streets demanded greater democracy and broader social rights. They also made explicit appeals to the notion of Korean nation as a group of people oppressed by stronger powers such as China, Japan, and the United States. Implicit in these demands was the criticism that the Chun government, like its predecessor Park regime, has been a willing instrument in the Cold War rivalry, even if this henchman role required oppressing its own people.[34] Leftist groups as well as Christian activists were sympathetic to this set of demands. However, what distinguished the social mobilization in 1986 and 1987 from the social mobilization against the Park regime was the participation of organized labor. The surge in strike activity in this period turned the social mobilization against the Chun government into a major political and social crisis for Chun Doo-hwan. Given that neither the Korean military

34 United States. Central Intelligence Agency. CIA - RDP89M00699R002201800006 - 1. *The Radicalization of Dissent in South Korea*. September 1987. Web.

nor the United States was tolerant of an even more repressive South Korea, Chun Doo-hwan had little choice other than accepting some of the demands for greater democracy and broader social rights raised by workers, students, and various other social groups.[35]

Hence, the pressures for greater democratization and distributional demands by workers set the stage for the gradual transition to a more democratic state-society relations in Korea. The Chun presidency ended in 1987 and his close collaborator and another former military general, Roh Tae-woo, became president through a fair and democratic election. The key to Roh's success was the democratic rights declaration and the constitutional amendments implemented by him and Chun Doo-hwan in 1987. Additionally, the opposition was divided between Kim Young-sam and Kim Dae-jung (Oh, 1999, 98–112). In this political context, Roh shrewdly distanced himself from the Chun regime and chose to remove barriers to democratization (Bedeski, 1994).

The politics of embracing hot money

Thus, the Korean economy entered into the 1990s, a period during which global capital inflows would surge dramatically, with a fundamental change in its political system and political economy. Furthermore, at the end of the 1980s, Korea was again facing several problems that reduced the prospects of rapid growth in the 1990s (You and Lee, 2001). The transition to democracy enabled labor to raise its voice after a long period of wage repression, as can be seen in Figure 3.1 (Deyo, 1989a). The resulting increase in real wages, high growth, and increase in domestic consumption levels had the impact of overheating the economy (Figure 3.2). These factors contributed to inflationary pressures. By 1990, increased levels of wages and consumption, combined with the appreciation of the *won* against the dollar, generated a deficit in the current account (Table 3.3). This deficit increased to 8.4 billion dollars in 1991 and was 4.1 billion dollars in 1992. Capital inflows financed the Korean current account deficit. The gradual capital account liberalization after 1992 accelerated the Korean economy's reliance on external finance. The increasing dependence on external finance made South Korea, then a newly industrialized country and a manufacturing powerhouse, vulnerable to the whims of international capital flows.

In Korea of the early 1990s, banks and non-bank financial intermediaries dominated credit and money creation, despite the domestic financial liberalization reforms of the 1980s. Equity and security markets were on the rise, but these markets were still weak compared to banks and non-bank financial intermediaries in the supply of finance capital. Finance capital was scarce, and there was high demand for credit. Interest rates continued to be under the control of the state, and the differences between domestic and foreign interest rates were sizable. In what follows, I first revisit the pre-liberalization structure of the Korean financial system and how that structure supported a particular economic distribution.

35 United States. Central Intelligence Agency. CIA - RDP88G01116R000901160003 - 2. *South Korea: The Time Bomb is Ticking*. November 25, 1986. Web.

I then examine how the change in distribution relations shaped the course of capital account liberalization in the 1990s.

Distribution relations and the pre-liberalization structure of the Korean financial system

As argued previously, the Korean state kept firm control over the financial system in order to pursue rapid economic growth through cheap credit for selective sectors. The key to this system was twofold. First, Korean authorities exercised direct control over the decisions of financial institutions. Second, Korean authorities controlled domestic interest rates in a manner that favored the corporate sector in South Korea over ordinary savers. Korean banks were either under the administrative control or the effective guidance of the state. The bank operations consisted of collecting deposits, guaranteeing foreign loans, and providing loans to firms operating in selective sectors and meeting various performance criteria (Cho 2002, 17–18; Choe and Moosa 1999, 1073–74; Kishi 1998, 104–05). Public and semi-public financial institutions such as the Bank of Korea (BOK) and the Korea Development Bank (KDB) backed bank loans, by discounting such loans at low interest rates (Cho, 2002, 1989; Cole and Park, 1983; Park, 1991). Furthermore, the state provided loans with negative or negligible real interest rates to the *chaebols*. Export loan rates were consistently below inflation rates. The loans supplied by the National Investment Fund (NIF) provided finance capital for the HCI drive in the 1970s. The interest rates on these loans throughout the 1970s were either below inflation rates or slightly above them (Cho, 2002, 24–26).

Interest rate control was essential for the functioning of this financial system. Korean financial markets were underdeveloped, and finance capital was a scarce commodity. Complete liberalization of interest rates would lead to very high interest rates under such conditions (Demetriades and Luintel, 2001). The interest rates in the curb market, where lending and borrowing were not regulated by monetary authorities, was direct evidence to this claim. For example, in 1970, the bank loan rate was 24 percent whereas the curb market rate was 49.8 percent (Dalla and Khatkhate, 1995, 8). Since the consumer inflation rate was 15.4 percent in the same period, the real interest rate was a staggering 34.4 percent in the curb market. The significant spread between the regulated bank rates and curb market rates did not disappear in the 1980s and 1990s.

The curb market became a particular concern to the Korean policy-makers during the 1970–72 slowdown in economic activity. In 1971, the total liabilities to net worth ratio in the manufacturing industry stood, on average, at 394.2 percent (Cho, 2002, 24). Due to the slowdown in economic activity and high corporate leverage, many firms came under pressure and bankruptcies began to rise. The curb market loans, which fulfilled the function of short-term finance, became a heavy burden for the corporate sector. Under pressure from the corporate sector, the government declared a package of emergency measures (the Emergency Decree for Economic Stability and Growth), which imposed a moratorium on the curb market, and forced curb market lenders and borrowers to register (Cho 1989, 93; Kim 1988). The curb market policies and the accompanying measures under the Emergency Decree constituted a blatant bailout for the Korean corporate sector, where the losses of the *chaebols* were socialized (Kim and Im, 2001, 20–21).

It is in this context that the Korean government authorized non-bank financial institutions (NBFIs) to operate in the financial markets. The purpose was to forestall the growth of the curb market (Kishi, 1998, 105). Privately owned NBFIs gradually replaced government-controlled commercial banks in the Korean financial system. In 1992, the NBFIs received 63.8 percent of total deposits and commanded 51.7 percent of total loans (Lee et al., 2002, Table 1).

The Korean economic bureaucracy under the Park regime impeded the development of other types of financial intermediation, such as equities and securities markets, either through prohibition or through their control over interest rates. The securities market began to play a role in corporate finance only in the 1970s, following the economic slowdown between 1970 and 1972 (Dalla, 2002; Choe and Moosa, 1999). However, this role became consequential by the 1980s as a result of the Chun government's domestic liberalization reforms. The *chaebols* began to rely on medium to long-term bonds at an increasing rate to raise finance capital. The share of corporate bonds in GDP rose from a mere 0.8 percent in 1972 to 10.3 percent in 1990 (Nam, 1994, Table 8.5).

The development of capital markets notwithstanding, the Korean interest rates were still high compared to the rest of the world in the early 1990s. Between 1988 and 1997, the minimum interest rate gap between the yield of domestic corporate bonds and LIBOR (the London Inter-Bank Offered Rate) was no less than 5.9 percent. The spread between domestic and foreign interest rates was even larger in the early 1990s. For example, in 1993 the gap between corporate bonds and LIBOR was 9.3 percent (Cho, 2002, 45). As it will be shown below, the large difference between the domestic and foreign interest rates was one of the proximate reasons why the Korean economic bureaucracy opposed a comprehensive capital account liberalization.

The making of Achilles' heel

In contrast to the piecemeal financial liberalization reforms of the 1980s, the scope of the financial reforms in the 1990s was wide (You and Lee, 2001, 287). The real reforms toward capital account liberalization started after 1990, under the Roh government. The Kim Young-sam government, which came to power in 1993, accelerated capital account reforms and widened the scope of external financial liberalization. Three aspects of the capital account reforms should be noted. First, the Korean economic bureaucracy liberalized capital outflows ahead of capital inflows. Second, both the Roh and Kim governments implemented significant steps toward the liberalization of inward and outward FDI. Third, the reforms under the Kim Young-sam government amounted to liberalizing short-term capital inflows while keeping restrictions on medium to long-term borrowing (Agosin, 2001; Dooley and Shin, 2000; Kim et al., 2001; Noland,

2005; Moon and Rhee, 2000; Chang et al., 1998).[36] This type of capital account liberalization was perhaps the most perilous way—particularly in the context of the early 1990s, when global financial markets were flush with liquidity—in which a developing country could embrace global capital flows (Appendix C). Thus, the Korean capital account liberalization trajectory was surprising, given the high degree of competence that made the Korean economic bureaucracy famous around the world. But then the key factor that had enabled the rapid Korean development—the developmental alliance and the distributional bargain that underpinned it—was already defunct by the late 1980s.[37]

Yet both the *chaebols* and the Korean governments continued following policies of high growth and productive capacity expansion underwritten by large amounts of foreign debt. Until the late 1980s, the costs of rapid growth through extraordinary rates of capital accumulation fell on the middle classes, workers, and ordinary savers. Such a distributional bias was not politically feasible for the Roh Tae-woo or for the Kim Young-sam governments. In this context, the decisions on interest rate and capital account reforms became major points of contention among the economic bureaucracy, the *chaebols*, small and medium-scale enterprises, and NBFIs. The peculiar trajectory of Korean capital account reforms was a direct outcome of these distributional struggles in which the *chaebols* had the upper hand.

The Kim Young-sam government was the first civilian government since the brief Chang Myon government in 1960. As such, the Kim government was under pressure for continuing the democratic reforms of the Roh government and addressing the economic injustices of the previous decades. Furthermore, the distributional pressures were building up from 1987 onwards, as can be seen in the secular increase of the wage share in GDP (Figure 3.1) and the rapid growth of the real wage (Figure 3.2). In addition to the increasing militancy of organized labor, which led to significant gains in average real wage and the wage share in GDP, the Kim Young-sam government was under mounting demands for reduced industrial concentration from small and medium-scale businesses. The intensity of the distributional demands in this period was not surprising,

36 Several measures led to the differential treatment of short-term and long-term capital flows. The Korean authorities liberalized short-term borrowing by banks through a series of measures in the early 1990s (Cho, 2001). In line with these reforms, the Roh government abandoned the pegged exchange rate system (employed since March 1980) and adopted a managed floating system (Johnston et al. 1997; Kim et al. 2001, 26–28). In 1993, the Korean economic bureaucracy abolished the limits on foreign currency loans borrowed by foreign exchange banks (Johnston et al., 1997, 82). Also in 1993, the Korean authorities removed all restrictions pertaining to foreign currency loans by manufacturing industries for imports of production material (Johnston et al., 1997, 83). In 1994, the Kim Young-sam government eased restrictions over resident corporations' and their overseas branches' borrowing from international markets (Johnston et al., 1997, 84). However, long-term borrowing, mainly through foreign investment in domestic bond markets, was subject to significant restrictions and quantitative limits (Cho, 2001, 171–72).

37 In the words of Kang (2000, 90):

> The South Korean state of the 1980s and 1990s was no longer the autonomous creature of the idealized Park era that could rise above particularistic interests. It was instead deeply implicated in the corruption and inefficiencies of self-dealings of an advanced stage of developmental capitalism.

given that the benefits and burdens of the spectacular Korean growth in the previous 25 years were unequally distributed. However, a distributional compromise was not easily within reach in this period. One of the main reasons was that the *chaebols* continued growing at a breakneck pace. As such, ironically, the *chaebols* too voiced public complaints for greater liberalization and reduced bureaucracy (Yoon, 1996, 514–15). In contrast to small and medium-scale enterprises, big businesses demanded liberalization in order to increase their economic autonomy and their already formidable power in the Korean economy (Lee et al., 2002).

The Kim Young-sam government responded to the distributional pressures and the economic reform demands by adopting the rhetoric of wide-ranging—but highly vague—liberalization and globalization reforms, the *segyehwa* program (Hundt, 2009, 75).[38] Not surprising in the context of export-dependent Korean development, the main motivation for the *segyehwa* plan was "to increase national competitiveness in a rapidly globalizing world" (Shin, 2003, 10). The *segyehwa* program was the embodiment of a positive orientation toward deregulation and liberalization in the Kim Young-sam government. However, the Korean economic bureaucracy did not necessarily share this positive orientation toward liberal reforms. On the contrary, there were schisms among the Ministry of Finance, Economic Planning Board, and the Bank of Korea as to how to structure economic liberalization reforms. The fact that Kim Young-sam was inexperienced on economic policies and chose to delegate authority on an *ad hoc* basis exacerbated the disagreements among various parts of the economic bureaucracy (Mo, 2001, 470).

The lack of coherence and the susceptibility to domestic pressures made an impact first on the issue of interest rate liberalization. As argued previously, *chaebols* opposed the liberalization of interest rates during the 1980s under the Chun Doo-hwan government, while simultaneously demanding financial liberalization. This mixed attitude toward financial liberalization did not change in the 1990s (Mo, 2001), for reasons outlined in the previous sections. NBFIs, now the source of dynamism in the financial sector, lobbied heavily for the deregulation of interest rates on instruments such as short-term commercial paper (Cho, 2003). It should be remembered that the NBFIs grew by replacing, to a certain extent, the informal curb market for short-term financing. Thus, their main business was in short-term financial instruments (Lee et al., 2005). Small and medium-scale enterprises, on the other hand, were against interest rate liberalization. These enterprises' access to financial markets was limited, and they relied on commercial bank loans much more than big businesses (Nam, 1994). A surge in interest rates would have devastating consequences for these firms, which faced a hostile economic environment because of *chaebol* expansionism.

The result of these conflicting interests and political pressures was a curious course of financial liberalization (Lee et al., 2002). The Korean authorities announced a blueprint of interest rate deregulation in 1991, under the Roh government (Cho, 2003). This liberalization blueprint involved an

38 Interview with Park Se-il (Seoul, February 7, 2007).

orderly, sequential, and cautious approach to interest rate deregulation (Dalla and Khatkhate, 1995). One of the elements of this blueprint was the liberalization of long-term rates ahead of short-term interest rates. However, the actual implementation of the plan followed a different course. The Korean economic bureaucracy viewed interest rate liberalization with greater suspicion. In some cases, the economic bureaucracy exercised control over the interest rates through various means even after the liberalization measures became legally effective (Lee et al., 2002). One notable example was the corporate bond rates, where informal and indirect controls, including moral suasion, prevented the actual deregulation of interest rates (Cho, 2003, 86).[39] The Korean economic bureaucracy followed such a course of action in order to avoid a surge in interest rates after deregulation.[40]

However, the cautious approach was not uniform. Most importantly, under pressure from NBFIs, the Korean authorities swiftly liberalized interest rates on short-term commercial papers (Choi, 2002; Cho, 2001, 2002; Lee et al., 2005, 2002). The outcome of these policies was an anomaly in the term structure of the domestic interest rates. As Cho (2003, 86) remarks, "Interest rates on three-month CPs [commercial papers] exceeded those on three-year corporate bonds for most of 1994–97." Since there was already an excess demand for short-term finance, the fact that the NBFIs enjoyed greater freedom in setting interest rates made this branch of the Korean financial industry quite lucrative (Lee et al., 2002). One segment of the NBFIs held an even greater promise. Merchant banks, which have been in existence since 1976 by occupying a marginal role in the Korean economy (Bank of Korea, 1996), were subject to minimal foreign borrowing restrictions compared to other bank and NBFIs.

The *chaebols* were eager to acquire and establish NBFIs in general and merchant banks in particular, given the fact that merchant banks faced few restrictions on foreign borrowing (Lee et al., 2002, 26). The Kim Young-sam government accommodated the *chaebols*' expansion into finance by licensing nine merchant banks in 1994, increasing the number of merchant banks from six to fifteen. Political considerations played a considerable role in the lax issuance of merchant bank licenses, as the majority of new merchant banks were based in the region where Kim Young-sam enjoyed strong electoral support (Choi, 2002, 260). The number of merchant banks increased to 30 by 1996 (Cho, 2001, 174). Thus, the Korean state's control over the finance industry became ineffective by 1996, as the *chaebols* and their affiliates owned a significant share of the most lucrative areas of the financial industry, merchant banks and other NBFIs.

39 As Cho (2003, 86) argues: "Corporate bond rates were likewise officially deregulated in 1991 but were, nevertheless, indirectly controlled until mid-1997 with restrictions imposed on the volume to be issued."

40 This interpretation of the causes of delayed liberalization of domestic interest rates is common in the literature. See Choi (2002), Dalla and Khatkhate (1995), and Nam (1994). For example, Nam (1994, 210) advances the following argument with respect to the delayed liberalization of domestic interest rates: "The major motivation of still regulating most interest rates in Korea is to keep lending rates from rising too high and to avoid any financial panic for business firms whose capital structure is generally very weak."

The remaining restrictions on the foreign borrowing of merchant banks faced severe criticism from the *chaebols*, which controlled several non-bank financial institutions by the mid-1990s (Choi, 2002). The *chaebols* had an interest in using international capital to finance their expansion, even in the presence of astronomic indebtedness levels. Expansionism was a dominant strategy and an entrenched institutional practice for large Korean firms. Another contributing factor to the *chaebol* preference for cheap international finance was the low value of the Korean *won* vis-à-vis the Japanese *yen* and the U.S. dollar. The depreciation of the Korean *won* can be seen in Figure 3.7. The decline in the real effective exchange rate was sharper. The cause of the depreciation was the strong appreciation in the Japanese *yen* from 1992 onwards (Park, 1996, 206). Thus, although Korea was receiving large amounts of capital inflows, there was no adverse effect on the exchange rate. To the contrary, Korean products were becoming more and more competitive in global markets as a result of the *won* losing value.

The finance industry, which was increasingly under the control of the *chaebols*, also exercised political pressure for further liberalization. This stemmed from the opportunity created by the liberalization of short-term money market rates. Another factor was the changing structure of corporate finance among the top 30 *chaebols*. Thanks to portfolio investment liberalization measures in the early 1990s, the bigger *chaebols*—Samsung, Hyundai, Sunkyung, Daewoo, and LG—shifted the source of their funds to international capital markets (Cho, 2001, 176). This structural change presented both a challenge and an opportunity for Korean banks. On one hand, the vacuum left by the bigger *chaebols* meant loss of business. On the other hand, capital account liberalization provided the possibility of funding smaller *chaebols* through foreign borrowing (Cho, 2001). The Kim

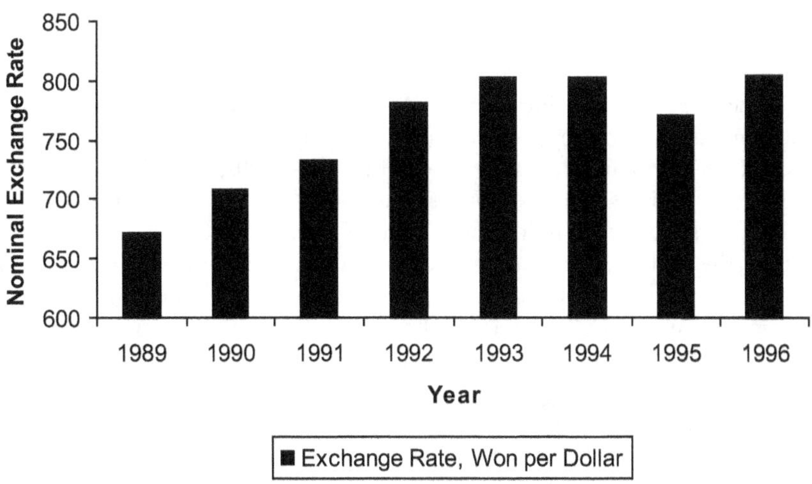

Figure 3.7 Nominal Exchange Rate, 1989–96.
Note: A higher value means depreciation.
Source: IMF, *International Statistics*.

Young-sam government accommodated the demands of the finance industry by removing several of the restrictions on banks' foreign borrowing.[41]

The sum total of these measures under the Kim Young-sam government was the liberalization of the Korean capital account in a way that was highly conducive to the *chaebols*' thirst for finance capital and the desire to tap into international capital markets (Choi, 2002; Agosin, 2001; Thurbon, 2001; Cho, 2002). Park (1998, 39) argues this point succinctly:

> Although the deterioration in the quality of assets and prevalence of short-term external financing were clearly visible, the supervisory authorities did not order the financial institutions to take corrective measures. They did not do so, because nurtured in the old tradition of direct control and bank examination, they had neither the resources nor experience in monitoring and exercising regulatory power to maintain overall soundness and profitability of financial institutions. Long relegated to the role of supporting manufacturing industries under the control of government, banks and other financial institutions had become accustomed to accommodating much of the credit needs of the industrial conglomerates without necessarily checking their creditworthiness.

The result was "a rapid accumulation of foreign debt, particularly short-term debt, and a growing list of highly risky financial investments" (You and Lee, 2001, 290), the majority of which was short-term (Chung, 2004, 26–28). Thus, this was how a major financial and economic vulnerability—what Kang (2000, 93) fittingly calls "the Achilles heel of the South Korean developmental state"—came to be.

The competing explanations on the Korean capital account liberalization are at odds with the evidence. For instance, the Korean capital account reforms cannot be explained by the increasing preponderance of liberalism within the Korean economic decision-making. Likewise, they cannot be accounted for by technocratic ignorance. The secondary literature on the reforms as well as interviews and public statements by various high-level technocrats suggest that the Korean economic bureaucracy and political class were, in the early 1990s, still divided between moderate liberalizers and traditionalists, although the developmentalism of the traditionalists was increasingly at odds with the realities of Korean economy.[42] In contrast, the evidence suggests that the Korean economic bureaucracy was at best lukewarm to the idea of capital account liberalization, as illustrated by the following quote from an OECD report on the *reservations* of the Korean government on the liberalization of capital movements (quoted in Kim et al. 2001, 36):

41 Various measures enabled such foreign borrowing, including the reform of the foreign exchange regulatory system beginning in 1994. As Kim et al. (2001, 35) argue: "Domestic firms, particularly large business companies (the so-called chaebol), were severely critical of remaining restrictions and thus claimed that the rigid control on capital inflows undermined the international competitiveness of domestic firms in the world market due to high financial costs. Amidst these complaints and the foreign pressure for further deregulation, the Korean government unveiled the new Foreign Exchange System Reform Plan in December 1994."

42 Interviews with Kwon Tae-kyun (March 2, 2007) and Kim Tae-dong (March 7, 2007).

> Given the large spread between international and domestic interest rates, the Korean authorities have maintained a progressive approach to the liberalization of capital inflows and short-term operations, as rapid capital inflows may hamper macroeconomic and financial market stability. A surge in capital inflows will boost domestic liquidity, leading to inflationary pressure beyond the level that can be handled by an appropriate policy mix.

The above passage illustrates that the Korean economic bureaucracy was aware of the macroeconomic dangers of capital inflows. Similarly, there was also the recognition of the volatility of capital flows, viewed as particularly worrisome given the geopolitical situation of the Korean peninsula (quoted in Kim et al. 2001, 36):

> As one of the remaining cold war areas, the Korean peninsula is still vulnerable to political and military developments in the region, despite the constant peace efforts. Accordingly, a slight geopolitical event in the peninsula might lead to a big swing in capital flows.

In addition, the Korean economic bureaucracy was well aware of the loss of policy-making autonomy that results from capital account liberalization. For example, the Minister of Finance, Hong Jae-hyong, raised his concerns over the decreasing effectiveness of monetary policy at an early stage of capital account liberalization, in September 1993. His statement was noteworthy because it indicated a cautious stance toward liberalization:

> An acceleration of capital inflow has made it more difficult to administer monetary policy. . . . This amount already exceeded last year's total of US$2.1 billion and represented 30% of the nation's monetary supply during the first half. Thus, we are cautiously considering the raising of foreign ownership ceiling based on a comprehensive evaluation of the capital market, foreign capital inflows and the money supply.[43]

The concerns discussed above and the significant difference of domestic and foreign interest rates led the Korean authorities to take a cautionary approach to the liberalization of foreign investor entry into the domestic securities market. The Korean economic bureaucracy anticipated large inflows as a result of such liberalization, and they wanted to avoid the adverse macroeconomic consequences of such inflows (Dalla, 2002). This policy stance amounted to imposing controls over long-term capital flows, since the domestic securities market involved corporate bonds and public debentures with long-term maturities.

Similarly, it is a mistake to interpret the Korean capital account reforms as the culmination of the diminished state capacity to monitor and control the finance industry and the *chaebols*, as some authors are prone to do (Cho, 2001; Thurbon, 2001). That is because the diminished capacity of the Korean state did not happen in a vacuum. It was rather the outcome of a new balance of power between the Korean state and the *chaebols*. As shown above, the Kim Young-sam

43 *Business Korea*, September 1993: 29–30.

government and the Korean economic bureaucracy did not simply fail to oversee the dangerous foray of the *chaebols* into world capital markets through merchant banks and other NBFIs. They rather willingly accommodated it.

Playing with fire and the crisis

The effect of the domestic financial and capital account liberalization measures can be seen by examining capital inflows and outflows between 1990 and 1997 (Table 3.4). Credit inflows to banks exploded in 1994, increasing from 0.72 to 7.37 billion dollars. This increase was sustained in 1995 and 1996, where credit inflows were 11.39 and 9.95 billion dollars. However, banks were not the only recipients of large credit inflows during this period. Other private actors (such as the *chaebols*) registered large credit inflows: 6.6 billion dollars in 1994, 10.66 billion in 1995, and 15.14 billion in 1996.[44] Since the outflows did not match the increase in credit inflows, Korea received large amounts of foreign capital through the credit channel. Furthermore, the majority of these flows were short-term credits.

Similarly, debt and equity inflows showed large increases between 1992 and 1997. For example, while debt inflows were in the magnitude of 2.71 billion in 1991, they reached 10.4 and 15.56 billion dollars in 1995 and 1996. Equity inflows were worth 0.2 billion dollars in 1991. In 1992, this figure was 2.48 billion of dollars. In 1996, the year before the Asian financial crisis, equity inflows were around 6 billion dollars. The surge in equity and debt inflows was much greater than the increase in outflows, which again shows that Korea was a net recipient of large amounts of capital inflows.

The large influx of capital financed a boom in fixed investment by resident corporations in Korea and by their overseas branches (outward FDI). After a negative rate of growth in 1992 (−0.8 percent), fixed investment grew 5.2 percent in 1993. As restrictions on short-term borrowing for capital goods were lifted, the fixed investment growth rate rose to 11.8 percent in 1994 and to 11.7 percent in 1995. The growth rates of equipment investment in 1994 and 1995 were 23.6 and 15.8 percent, respectively (Park and Choi, 2004, 51). FDI outflows grew remarkably from 1992 onwards, reaching 2.46 billion in 1994, 3.55 billion in 1995, and 4.6 billion dollars in 1996 (Table 3.4).

The magnitude of the increase in corporate leverage can be better understood by comparing average levels of corporate leverage—defined as the ratio of total debt to total equity—in Germany, Japan, Korea and the United States between 1988 and 1996 (Claessens et al., 1998, Table A5). One discernible pattern is the high leverage of Japanese and Korean companies compared to their American and German counterparts. In this period, average corporate leverage figures for U.S. companies oscillated between 0.8 and 1.12. For German companies, the average corporate leverage stayed firmly around 1.5 throughout the whole period. The Japanese corporate indebtedness decreased from 3 to 2.4. The indebtedness

44 It should be noted that credit inflows to sectors other than public and financial transactions (which is covered in the *other* category) was greater than bank credits.

Table 3.4 Capital Inflows and Outflows, 1990–97†

Item	*1990*	*1991*	*1992*	*1993*	*1994*	*1995*	*1996*	*1997*
FDI								
Inflows	0.79	1.18	0.73	0.59	0.81	1.78	2.33	2.84
Outflows	−1.05	−1.49	−1.16	−1.34	−2.46	−3.55	−4.59	−4.4
Equity								
Inflows	0.38	0.20	2.48	6.62	3.61	4.22	5.95	2.53
Outflows	−0.05	0.01	0.01	−0.20	−0.38	−0.24	−0.65	−0.32
Debt								
Inflows	0.28	2.71	3.39	4.47	5.10	10.4	15.56	10.78
Outflows	−0.45	0.19	0.07	−0.78	−2.10	−2.67	−5.76	1.40
Derivatives								
Inflows	−0.44	−0.57	−0.92	−0.54	−0.56	−0.74	−0.33	−1.02
Outflows	0.37	0.52	0.77	0.45	0.45	0.62	0.41	0.93
Credit Inflows[a]								
Banks	1.94	4.25	1.82	0.72	7.37	11.39	9.95	−9.78
Others	4.35	3.46	3.80	−0.35	6.60	10.66	15.14	−3.23
Credit Outflows[a]								
Banks	−2.24	−1.81	−3.29	−3.99	−5.06	−9.20	−8.17	−8.34
Others	−0.20	−0.82	0.23	0.07	−1.94	−4.60	−4.77	−5.00

† Billions of U.S. dollars. Source: IMF, *International Financial Statistics.*
a This category comprises various financial transactions and is labeled as "other investments" in the *International Financial Statistics* database, including transactions in currency and deposits. Following common practice, it is assumed here that loans and trade credits constitute the majority of transactions in this category.

levels of Korean firms stood in contrast to the Japanese downward pattern. In 1988, Japan and Korea had roughly similar levels of corporate indebtedness (2.99 and 2.82). However, by 1996, Korean corporate indebtedness jumped to 3.545 (Claessens et al., 1998, Table A5).

Not only did Korean corporations become more indebted during this period, but the maturity structure of their debts became riskier. The share of long-term debt in total debt was around 50 percent between 1988 and 1991. The share of long-term debt decreased to 41 percent in 1992 and stayed around that level between 1992 and 1996 (Claessens et al., 1998, Table A5).

In addition, inexperienced financial institutions (mostly merchant banks) engaged in borrowing and lending in markets abroad with maturity mismatches between their assets and liabilities (Chung, 2004, 32). The growing foreign exchange liabilities of Korean banks between 1992 and 1997 are presented in Figure 3.8. The total amount of foreign exchange liabilities increased from 35.8 to 103.6 billion dollars between 1992 and 1996. Concomitantly, bank credit to private sector rose dramatically between 1992 and 1997, as can be seen in Figure 3.9.

The increasing debt of the *chaebols* and foreign exchange liabilities of Korean banks (with heavy currency mismatches) were important factors in the emergence of the 1997 financial crisis. As is common to the financial crises in the

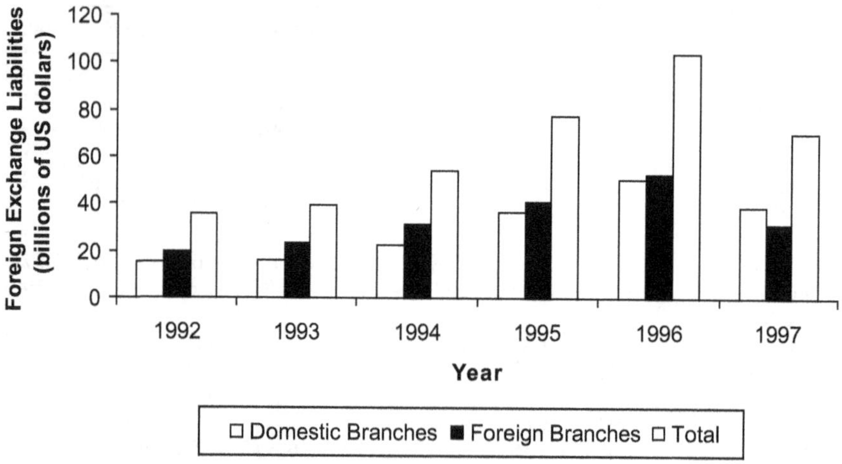

Figure 3.8 Korean Banks' Foreign Exchange Liabilities, 1992–97.
Source: Kim et al. (2001, 41).

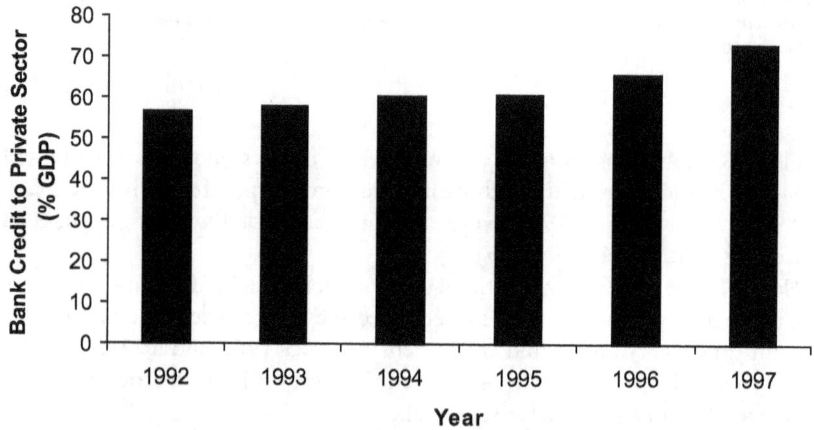

Figure 3.9 Bank Credit to Private Sector (% GDP), 1992–97.
Source: Haggard (2000, 17).

developing world, the stage for the crisis was prepared with shocks such as high-profile bankruptcies in 1997 that led to a sharp drop in investor confidence (Park and Choi, 2004, 51). The crisis erupted as panicking investors attacked the *won* and depleted the South Korean foreign reserves (Chung, 2004, 33).

It should be noted that high corporate leverages were normal practice in South Korea and seeing them as the primary culprit of the crisis is not a tenable view

(Chang et al., 1998, 738). High corporate indebtedness was risky, but it was an undeniable—and successful—aspect of the Korean development model. What proved to be poisonous was high corporate indebtedness funded through an inexperienced financial sector that took significant currency mismatch risk, which resulted from Korea's uneven opening to international capital flows.

Conclusion

This chapter presented an account of the perilous manner in which Korea adopted capital mobility across national boundaries. The fundamental causes of such risky policies lay in the breakdown of the developmental alliance between the state and the *chaebols*. The state's control over credit, and thus finance capital, was the brick that held together the coalition between the Korean state and the *chaebols*. Once the Korean state began the long process of relinquishing its control over credit, it shattered the developmental alliance that powered the rapid Korean industrialization. The gradual collapse of the developmental alliance inevitably led to a change in the capacities of political actors to shape economic policies. While the *chaebols* gained tactical power in the articulation of their interests, the Korean state actors lost the resources that had enabled it to discipline big business. Such a fundamental transformation occurred in the context where the *chaebols* continued and enlarged their institutional practice—itself a relic of the past—of high leverage and high investment to expand their productive capacity and increase their footprint in the Korean economy.

The Korean economic bureaucracy resisted the calls for greater liberalization only partially and was to a certain extent complicit in allowing big business to tap into cheap—but risky—external funds. Had the Korean state retained tighter control over credit allocation, the financial opening of the Korean markets would have been much more cautious and gradual. Yet, the political developments under Chun Doo-hwan and Roh Tae-woo made such a cautious opening formidably difficult to manage for the Korean state. By the time Kim Young-sam came to power, the distribution relations that enabled the Korean development model—repressing the organized labor, the middle classes, and the domestic savers to provide funds for the *chaebols*—were not socially and politically feasible. As a result, the balance of power between the *chaebols* and the state was decidedly in favor of the *chaebols* by the 1990s. Eager to tap into world financial markets, the *chaebols* pressured for a particularly perilous course of external liberalization. As Eichengreen (2003a, 10) puts it:

> When in the first half of the 1990s capital accounts were liberalized (often in the worst possible way, by permitting banks to borrow offshore while still limiting foreign investment in domestic bond and equity markets, and providing artificial incentives for short-term rather than long-term flows), this volatile mixture combusted. But it is not enough to argue that these policies were ill advised and that future governments should avoid them. It is important to understand that the policies in question were integral to the Asian development model.

The capital account liberalization policies pursued by the Korean state in the 1990s conformed to the Korean development model, as Eichengreen (2003a, 10) argues. However, such conformity came at a great cost. The marriage between capital account liberalization and the Korean development model was a happy marriage only for a short while, because it contained great contradictions. This chapter highlighted such contradictions and showed how they culminated in the 1997 financial crisis.

4 Premature financial opening and boom-bust cycles in Turkey

In 1989, Turkey became one of the first—and few—emerging economies to fully liberalize its capital account. This was an unexpected policy decision. Prior to capital account liberalization, the Turkish economy ran persistent trade deficits with the rest of the world. The public sector could continue its operations only by borrowing at increasing rates. The inflation rate was on the rise toward 100 percent. Domestic interest rates were much higher than interest rates in global markets. Furthermore, capital accumulation in Turkey prior to financial opening relied on public infrastructure investment, and the private sector's share in fixed capital investment was in decline. It was doubtful that the liberalization of capital movements across borders would stimulate growth. Under pressure from widespread protests by organized labor, the political party in government, the Motherland Party, did not hesitate to use inflationary policies to postpone distributional demands. There was the risk that funds from the rest of the world would finance public sector borrowing and consumption, rather than productive investment.

This chapter analyzes the 1989 capital account liberalization reforms in Turkey. The Turkish case illustrates how mounting distributional pressures from worker mobilization, after years of wage repression, paved the way for a highly consequential institutional change. The Motherland Party government at the time responded to increasing political competition, the risk of stagflation, and high public sector borrowing requirements by liberalizing the movement of capital across the Turkish borders. In retrospect, the 1989 capital account liberalization was premature. Since then, the Turkish economy sank deeper into a vicious cycle, where short-term capital flows from the rest of the world fed economic booms that periodically ended in crises. The Turkish economy had two major financial crises, in 1994 and 2001, and a serious recession between 1998 and 1999. In 1994 and 2001, short-term capital flows were directly responsible for triggering the collapse of the Turkish financial markets.

In what follows, I begin by examining the recurring balance of payments problems in Turkish history. The recurring balance of payments problems followed from a pattern of consuming more than what could be financed through domestic production and exports. The capital account liberalization in the 1980s should be examined with this history in mind. Thus, this chapter begins with an overview of the Turkish economic history. I show that distributional conflict was the rule rather than the exception in Turkish economic history. Periodic booms, mostly financed by debt, were critical for electoral success in a country where capital accumulation and growth were not sufficiently strong to finance the high levels of imports and consumption. Although the Turkish economic growth between the 1950s and 1970s was faster than growth in a country with more endemic distributional conflict, such as Chile, the conflictual distribution relations and recurring balance of payments problems made economic policy decisions subject to acrimonious political struggles.[1]

Background: distribution relations and recurring balance of payments problems

The Republic of Turkey was founded in 1923 by the bureaucratic, intellectual, and military elite of the Ottoman Empire after a nationalist mobilization and war (War of Independence) fought against various Allied forces and their proxies. Several high-ranking military officials of the empire, organized around Mustafa Kemal Atatürk, formed the key executive group of the new republic (Eisenstadt, 1981). Driven by a strong modernist and secular ideology, the group that founded the republic viewed westernization and economic development of the country as their main objectives. However, the newly founded republic inherited a country without industry (Boratav, 1981). A weak bourgeoisie consisted mostly of the large merchants of the Ottoman Empire. Furthermore, production was artisanal (Hale, 1980). In its economic outlook, the core founding group was broadly liberal (Okyar, 1965). After a brief period of open economy in the 1920s—partly forced by the Treaty of Lausanne that terminated the War of Independence and partly a natural outcome of the founding elite's liberalism—the republic adopted protectionism and statism as its economic strategy (Arnold, 2012; Birtek, 1985; Boratav, 1981; Okyar, 1979). The most proximate causes of the fundamental change in economic policy were the Great Depression and the influence of Russia's industrialization through central planning (Okyar, 1965). Statism also found support in the intellectual currents of the newly established republic, particularly in the Kadro movement, a short-lived but influential leftist publication. This was not entirely surprising. After all, state-driven development through protectionist trade policies—inspired by the German historical school—had adherents among the prominent thinkers of the Ottoman Empire in the second half of the nineteenth century (Toprak, 2012). The new policy direction implied that the state was to play the chief role in capital accumulation by directly investing into manufacturing and intermediate goods industries. The Kadro movement offered a bold socio-economic transformation project, but the movement got

1 The argument presented in this chapter is inspired and anticipated by authors such as Boratav (2003), Demir (2004), Ersel (1996), and Yeldan (2001). The following analysis complements the existing literature by closely analyzing the political dynamics in the 1989 capital account liberalization.

suppressed after a few years.[2] The shutdown of the intellectual movement was partially due to the increasing authoritarianism of the Turkish state as Mustafa Kemal Atatürk consolidated a one-party regime under the rule of the Republican People's Party (RPP). The more radical agenda of the Kadro movement was not entirely in line with the outlook of the elite group around Mustafa Kemal Atatürk (Türkeş, 2001). The elites around Mustafa Kemal Atatürk rejected the notion of class conflict because they prioritized national unity, and they aimed the establishment of a "home-grown" bourgeoisie (Boratav, 2003, 40). Furthermore, the influence of "liberals" with important connections to the emerging urban bourgeoisie and provincial notables (consisting mostly of landlords and merchants) also played a role in the suppression of the Kadro movement.[3]

Thus, Turkey initiated its industrialization drive in the 1930s, under one-party rule and statism (Boratav, 1981). The practice of economic planning through five-year development plans also started in this period (Hershlag, 1988, 7). The statist period was a considerable success in terms of economic growth; the annual per capita GNP growth rate between 1933 and 1939 was 5 percent. The annual GNP growth rate was 7.1 percent. The rapid industrialization between 1933 and 1939 under protectionism benefited the newly emerging Turkish industrialists. The state investment was the main engine of capital accumulation; accumulation in the private sector was complementary and limited mostly to construction and light industries. Although the national income data for this period do not enable a precise analysis of distribution relations, the working class enjoyed significant improvements in living standards, despite a fall in the wage share. The peasantry, in contrast, suffered from the state-driven industrialization drive, although the high levels of accumulation and growth absorbed a portion of the surplus labor in the agricultural sector (Boratav, 2003, 75–79). More importantly, the one-party regime of the RPP followed an ambitious program of cultural modernization, implemented in an authoritarian fashion in an overwhelmingly agrarian country (Sunar, 1990). Without a commensurate transformation of social relations and institutions, particularly in the countryside, the wholesale cultural modernization project did not have much support outside urban centers. As a result, the inability of the one-party regime to establish a firm basis among the peasants diminished the legitimacy and the durability of the RPP rule.

The economy registered negative growth during World War II: the annual per capita GNP growth rate was −7.5 percent between 1939 and 1945 (Hershlag,

2 While the Soviet Russia's experience with industrialization and socialism was a major influence on the Kadro movement, the movement yearned for an alternative to both capitalism and socialism. The leading voices in the Kadro movement aimed for a society without class conflict, although they were vague on their nationalist alternative to capitalism and socialism (Bayar 1996, 776; Tekeli and İlkin 2003).

3 This group of "liberals," which coalesced around Celal Bayar (a former banker and a key member of the group that founded the new republic), did not have a strong economic ideology. Rather, the group espoused a pragmatic and nationalist pro-business program, even if such a program implied protectionism (Bayar 1996, 93; Yiğit 2013). Bayar, like many members of the elite group that founded the republic, did not have much sympathy for leftist views and for the idea of social classes. The majority of the founding elite perceived notions such as social class as antithetical to their aspirations for national unification and territorial integrity (Yiğit, 2013, 94).

1968). During World War II, the Turkish statism took an increasingly interventionist and authoritarian character. Price controls as well as measures to repress the Turkish organized labor were among the autocratic policies implemented by the RPP governments (Boratav, 2003, 90–91). Furthermore, the RPP regime used two extraordinary measures, a one-off wealth tax (the Capital Tax Law, in effect between 1942 and 1944) and an onerous agricultural product tax (the Tax on Soil Products, in effect between 1944 and 1946). The Turkish state heavily discriminated against the minorities in the application of the wealth tax, which destroyed the livelihoods of a significant number of Armenian, Greek, and Jewish citizens. Furthermore, the wealth tax led to the transfer of property and capital from the minorities to the Muslim commercial bourgeoisie, particularly outside İstanbul. The Tax on Soil Products did not take into account the ability of the peasants—many of whom produced for their own consumption and exploited family labor in small plots of land (Aktan, 1966)—to pay heavy taxes. Many peasant families, especially the ones who cultivated small plots of land, lacked the means to pay such heavy taxes. Hence, the consequences of the Tax on Soil Products were perverse, as this measure led to greater concentration of land in the hands of wealthy landlords (Boratav 2003, 83–90; Karpat 1959, 100–04). In addition, a land reform passed at the end of the war faced strong opposition by the wealthy landlords and their political representatives. As a result, the land reform was ineffective. In this regard, the social-structural changes in Turkey contrasted sharply with South Korea, where a successful land reform diminished the power of the landlord class and prepared the ground for successful industrialization and urbanization (Chapter 3).

The recession during World War II created significant disappointment with the one-party rule and paved the way for multi-party politics. Not only the recession, but also the harsh distributional consequences of the Tax on Soil Products were the catalysts for a major political change. The RPP regime under İsmet İnönü—a war hero, a key member of Mustafa Kemal Atatürk's inner circle, and the second President of Turkey—oversaw the transition to multi-party politics. As Sunar (1990, 748) observes, multiple factors underlay the transition to multi-party politics, but two factors should be singled out. First, the RPP government under İnönü wanted a secure place in the emerging world order under the U.S. hegemony, where capitalism, greater integration with world markets, and pluralist democracy were the norms. Second, the regime established by the modernizing elite had confidence that the strong bureaucracy and institutions of the new republic—supported by a coalition of middle-class professionals employed by the Turkish state, certain segments of the capitalists, and provincial notables—would be able to control the gradual transition to pluralist democracy. As it turned out, this was a misplaced confidence.

The main opposition to the RPP came from the Democrat Party (DP); and, the class background of the DP holds the key to understanding the party's electoral success. As argued above, Turkey under the RPP rule was a republic where a secular elite composed of bureaucrats, intellectuals, and military officers controlled state institutions. The top-down, ambitious, and secular modernization agenda of the Turkish state under the RPP rule found opposition in many segments of the Turkish society, including the peasants that constituted the majority of the Turkish society in 1950. In addition, a nascent commercial bourgeoisie as well as agricultural landlords did not have a favorable view of the statist turn in the previous era. The DP—whose leaders included prominent landlords, capitalists, and conservative intellectuals—explicitly distanced itself from the RPP rule by promising greater liberties in the cultural, political, and economic arenas. Furthermore, the DP embraced a conservative and nationalist political discourse with explicit references to religious values (Mert, 2007). Such a political strategy was highly effective in building a broad political coalition (Atılgan, 2015b). The DP had the support of peasants, artisans, merchants, and certain segments of the industrialists that sought less intervention in the economy (Atılgan, 2015b; Weiker, 1981). The DP's populist discourse juxtaposed the will of the "people" against the bureaucratic elite of the Turkish state (Karpat 1970, 1659; Sunar 1990). In this form, the populist discourse proved to be highly successful and has been a mainstay of Turkish politics since the DP era (Heper and Keyman, 1998). Although the DP lost the first and blatantly unfair multi-party elections in 1946, the party came to power in 1950 as a result of free and fair elections.

Hence, the DP had a pronounced opposition to statism and made the replacement of state's economic role by private enterprise as one of its main goals (Hershlag, 1968, 131–38). Such an orientation was possible because the Turkish economy entered into the 1950s with a booming economy, mostly due to an exceptional growth in the agricultural sector (Pamuk, 1984). The strong economic performance was based on a number of factors such as the availability of foreign aid and credit due to the Marshall Plan, favorable climate, mechanization in agriculture, excess demand in world markets for Turkish grain because of the Korean War, and improvement in terms of trade (Kepenek and Yentürk 2000; Pamuk 1984).

Nonetheless, the liberalism of the DP was rather limited to the integration of the Turkish economy to the global capitalist markets (Hershlag, 1968). Private enterprise increased its share in economic activities, but not at the expense of the state's role in economy. Instead, private entrepreneurs were investing mainly in economic activities such as trade, finance, and light import substitution industries such as textiles, leaving intermediate and capital goods production to the state (Hale 1981, 89; Hershlag 1968, 176). With agriculture-based growth coming to a sharp end in 1954, the government invested in state economic enterprises (SEEs) to maintain the same economic activity level and to replace consumer good imports with domestic production (Hale, 1981, 91). Thus, instead of a gradual movement toward a liberal regime where private enterprises were increasingly replacing state capital in capital accumulation, Turkey grew with continuing state involvement. Furthermore, the economic growth in this period did not occur in sectors that would lead to productivity gains in the long-run (Temel, 1998).

Accordingly, economic change under the DP rule was rapid but it contained many contradictions. First, the DP government did not have an allocation and investment strategy, despite the fact that the state's presence in the economy was substantial.[4] Second, the domestic industrialization in the 1950s was not sufficient to meet the demand created by fast urbanization. One of the main reasons for the mismatch between the rates of industrialization and urbanization was the slowdown in industrial capital accumulation (Boratav, 2003, 101). In the DP era, particularly between 1950 and 1954, the expansion of agriculture was much faster than the expansion of industrial production capacity (Atılgan, 2015b; Zürcher, 2017). As a result, Turkey had to rely on imports to satisfy changing consumption patterns and private enterprise's needs of capital and intermediate goods (Kepenek and Yentürk, 2000). The high level of imports combined with the poor performance of exports contributed to the deterioration in the balance of payments in the second half of the 1950s (Singer, 1977). During the same time, the government undertook large infrastructural investments such as roads and dams. In addition, the DP government adopted expansionary policies by channeling substantial amounts of subsidies to the agricultural sector (Keyder, 1987). Such an orientation reflected an agrarian-capitalist accumulation model, which was in line with the class alliance that underpinned the DP's success as a political party. However, the agrarian-capitalist accumulation model was sustainable to the extent that the terms of trade for low value-added agricultural produce was favorable and the demand for high value-added manufactured goods from the rest of the world was muted. As it turned out, neither one of these conditions materialized after 1954. Hence, the accumulation dynamics under the DP rule resulted in trade deficits and balance of payments problems after 1954, the year when the rapid economic growth driven by the agricultural sector vanished.

The developments in the financial arena reflected the DP government's predilection for pursuing economic expansion without much regard for long-term consequences. For instance, with the establishment of four major private banks and the government's policy of reducing the interest rates on loans, credits to the private and public sectors increased considerably in the 1950s (Kepenek and Yentürk, 2000, 97). However, the increase in credits did not translate to the allocation of funds into production in this period. Economic activities such as construction, trade, and agriculture took the lion's share of bank credits. In this period, Turkey financed its increasing current account deficit through a combination of foreign aid (mostly from the United States), foreign debt, and short-term supplier and commercial credits (Bulutoğlu 1970, 118–19; Hale 1981, 104; Singer 1977, 392). The government also resorted to printing money to finance deficits. As a result, the second half of the 1950s was a period of increasing inflation, overvalued national currency, increasing national debt, bottlenecks in industrial production, and decreasing growth (Hale, 1981; Hershlag, 1968). Despite massive foreign aid at the beginning of the 1950s, the balance of payments collapsed in 1958, which led to a heavy devaluation (220 percent) of the Turkish lira (Bulutoğlu, 1970, 123).

4 The haphazard character of the economic governance in this period was best exemplified by rather partisan investments in the SEEs and arbitrary pricing of their products.

The worsening economic depression was partially responsible for a military coup d'état in May 1960 that ended the DP government in a most disgraceful manner (Ahmad, 1977; Weiker, 1963). Three of the leading cabinet members of the DP government, including Prime Minister Adnan Menderes, were executed by hanging by the military junta that staged the coup. The root causes of the military coup d'état lay in the DP government's use of heavy political repression under economic stagnation and severe hardship for various social classes, including the peasants that constituted the DP's core base. The economic policies of the DP mostly benefited a small segment of merchants, capitalists in light industries and construction sector, and big landlords (Atılgan, 2015b; Boratav, 2003). The DP governments after 1954 targeted all opposition, including parliamentary opposition and the print media, as threats to the "national will" (Atılgan, 2015b, 428). In April 1960, the DP government's attempts to eliminate opposition voices by further repression led to student mobilizations on leading university campuses, in ways that echoed the student-led mobilizations in South Korea that toppled the Rhee regime (see Chapter 3). The DP government's response to student mobilizations was heavy-handed, which further deepened the rift between the government and students. The DP government also encountered significant opposition from academic personnel in leading universities, journalists, and prominent Turkish writers. Although these intellectuals formed a heterogeneous group, they were unified in their aspirations for a much more liberal and democratic country. On the economic front, the mismanagement and partisanship of the DP government led to declining standards of living for the salaried professionals such as public employees and military officers. Most notably, the emerging industrialists were weary of the political pressures and increasing interventionism under the DP rule (Atılgan, 2015b, 497–501). By 1960, Turkey was facing crises on economic, political, and social fronts. Such an environment created the power vacuum that prepared the grounds for the 1960 coup d'état.

A group of low-ranking officers spearheaded the military coup outside the chain of command (Esin, 2005; Özdağ, 2004). The military junta established the National Union Committee after the coup and avowed a return to democracy as one of the immediate goals of the military regime. Ironically, the National Union Committee (NUC) was itself composed of officers with sharply divergent views (Ahmad, 1977). After an internal struggle, Cemal Gürsel, the head of the NUC, sidelined the officers who envisioned a radical reordering of Turkish politics and the state (Doğru, 1998; Özdağ, 2004).[5] The upheaval within the military junta led to the reconstitution of the NUC. A massive and widely indiscriminate purge in the military, state bureaucracy, and universities accompanied the internal struggles at the top echelons of the military junta. However, despite such purges, the authority of the NUC was not firm, as military officers within the army itself organized an informal committee and continued to interfere with the political developments in 1961. Nonetheless, by the end of 1960, the reconstituted

5 The group of officers with such tendencies, the "radicals," coalesced around Alparslan Türkeş, a colonel with a fascist agenda and one of the key instigators of the 1960 coup. Türkeş would later become the leading politician in the Turkish ultra-nationalist movement.

NUC initiated the formation of a Constituent Assembly, which was tasked with preparing a new constitution. In drafting the constitution, the NUC appointed prominent law professors and the final version of the 1961 Constitution was approved by the Constituent Assembly (Hale, 1981; Zürcher, 2017).

The 1960 coup and the 1961 Constitution ushered a new phase in Turkey's class relations and political regime (Atılgan, 2015a, 523–26). The leading figures of the NUC such as Cemal Gürsel were much closer in outlook to the urban bourgeoisie and the industrial capitalists than to the landed classes. The Constituent Assembly were dominated by urban professionals, academics, and the elite cadres of the Turkish bureaucracy—groups that championed capitalist development, cultural modernization, and pluralist democracy (Atılgan, 2015a; Soysal, 1969; Tanör, 1969). The 1961 Constitution reflected these ideals. The constitution contained provisions on civil, social, and economic rights. It also offered a forward-looking framework on judiciary independence and the balance of power between legislative and executive branches of the state. Hence, Turkey entered the 1960s with the rising clout of educated urban professionals and the capitalist class, classes whose aspirations were enshrined in a progressive constitution (Atılgan, 2015b, 566–69). Furthermore, the 1961 Constitution also provided the legal grounds for the working class to organize and vie for collective bargaining rights. However, contrary to the spirit of the new constitution, the Turkish military took a much more active role in the new political regime. The 1961 Constitution established the National Security Council (NSC), where the top brass of the military occupied key positions (Tanör and Yüzbaşıoğlu, 2001, 339–47). This committee would act as a shadow government in the coming decades. In addition, informal organizations and secret cabals who were eager to reorder Turkish politics continued to flourish in the military itself (Akyaz, 2002; Zürcher, 2017).

The transformation of power relations and politics in the aftermath of the 1960 coup also led Turkey to adopt a new development strategy, import substitution industrialization (ISI). In Turkey, import substitution was a *de facto* necessity imposed by the shortage of foreign exchange since the 1930s (Boratav, 2003, 118). However, a development strategy that aimed to foster domestic capital accumulation through targeted investment in select import substitution industries did not exist until the early 1960s (Bruton, 1998; Hirschman, 1968; Pamuk, 1984; Toye, 2003). That changed with the establishment of the State Planning Organization (SPO) in 1960 (Kansu, 2004, 57). Unlike the economic plans of the 1930s, the five-year plans starting in 1963 were designed to achieve comprehensive economic and social transformation in the long-run (Akçay 2007; Kepenek and Yentürk 2000, 143).[6]

Overall, the Turkish economy went through a significant industrialization process in the 1960s and 1970s. The social consequences of the rapid industrialization were profound. First, a particular segment of the capitalist

6 These plans were inspired by the Harrod-Domar growth model (Kepenek and Yentürk, 2000, 144). Hence, there was an emphasis on capital formation based on the assumption that high growth with a high level of investment would bring economic development (Bruton, 1998).

class—the segment that controlled the manufacturing of light and durable consumer goods—increased its preponderance in the Turkish economy (Boratav, 2003, 120–26). Concomitantly, the large Turkish capitalists started pursuing horizontal expansion and became conglomerates with sizable presence in multiple domestic markets. The protection of domestic markets under the ISI was the key to the conglomerates' growth. Furthermore, this segment of the capitalist class also began establishing organizations to represent its interests. Second, the working class emerged as a significant economic, political and social actor in this period. The framework provided by the 1961 Constitution was a crucial factor that enabled the workers to organize without facing state repression (Atılgan, 2015a, 530–35).

The rising power of capitalists and workers was not entirely surprising in the context of rapid industrialization, since the advance of mechanized industry under capitalist accumulation has been shown to generate the structural conditions for new classes to emerge as preponderant collective actors (Silver, 2003). However, such a structural change in Turkey did not entirely curtail the power of the agrarian classes. Nor did it lead to widespread proletarianization. The continuing clout of the Turkish agrarian classes followed from the fact that, despite the march of industrialization since the 1930s, Turkey was still an economy with a large proportion of its population earning their living in the agrarian sector (Boratav, 2003). The partial proletarianization was, in turn, related to the continuing importance of the agrarian economy in the context of rapid urbanization. As Boratav (2003, 132) notes, the agrarian economy and the growing service sectors in the context of rapid urbanization prevented widespread proletarianization in Turkey. Instead, Turkey in the 1960s and 1970s featured a flexible accumulation model where agrarian and service sectors characterized by low productivity continued to exist and flourish (in the case of service sectors) alongside high-productivity manufacturing sectors.

Consequently, the Turkish politics between 1960 and 1980 was characterized by a competitive party system, military tutelage, and increasing distributional conflict. The military's role did not remain limited to its presence in the NSC. Under the leadership of the Chief of the General Staff Memduh Tağmaç, the military forces staged a coup in March 1971. However, unlike the 1960 coup, the 1971 coup did not usher significant social changes. Hence, the distributional conflicts and political polarization that characterized the 1960s lingered in the 1970s. In the 1960s, the acrimonious political struggle between the Justice Party (JP) and the RPP dominated the Turkish party politics. The JP claimed the political heritage of the DP; agrarian classes constituted its core base. However, the JP received also the support of the dominant segment of Turkish capitalists, large conglomerates. By the end of the 1960s, the presence of diverse social groups under one political party led to the declining power of the JP and further fragmentation among Turkish right-wing political parties (Atılgan, 2015a, 573–605).

What was novel in this period was the mushrooming of left- and right-wing movements whose ideologies directly challenged the existing social and political order in Turkey. Furthermore, starting in the late 1960s, these movements began to embrace violence as a legitimate tactic in their struggles against each other and against the Turkish state. There is significant evidence linking the rapid rise of political violence by the end of the 1960s to cold war dynamics (Atılgan, 2015a, 596–601). For instance, the security forces within the Turkish state sheltered and supported the right-wing movements, in particular the ultra-nationalist organizations, as the first line of attack against left-wing organizations. The right-wing organizations, in particular the ones with ties to the ultra-nationalist movements spearheaded by Alparslan Türkeş, embraced rabid anti-communism as one of their key ideological principles. The 1971 coup silenced the wave of rising violence in the first half of the 1970s, but that was a short-lived respite. By the end of the 1970s, political assassinations were a daily occurrence, particularly on university campuses (Ozan, 2015).

The increasing economic fragility further exacerbated the political polarization. The economic troubles in this period followed from the particular implementation of the ISI in Turkey. To be sure, the ISI in Turkey delivered rapid economic growth in the 1960s and the first half of the 1970s. In this period, the large conglomerates reaped easy profits by producing consumer goods for domestic markets. The SEEs supported capital accumulation in the private sector by producing intermediate and capital goods (Boratav, 2003, 132–35). The large conglomerates, in contrast, shied away from investing into intermediate and capital goods industries. Nonetheless, the Turkish economy registered strong increases in labor productivity in the 1970s (Figure 4.1). As can be expected in the process of

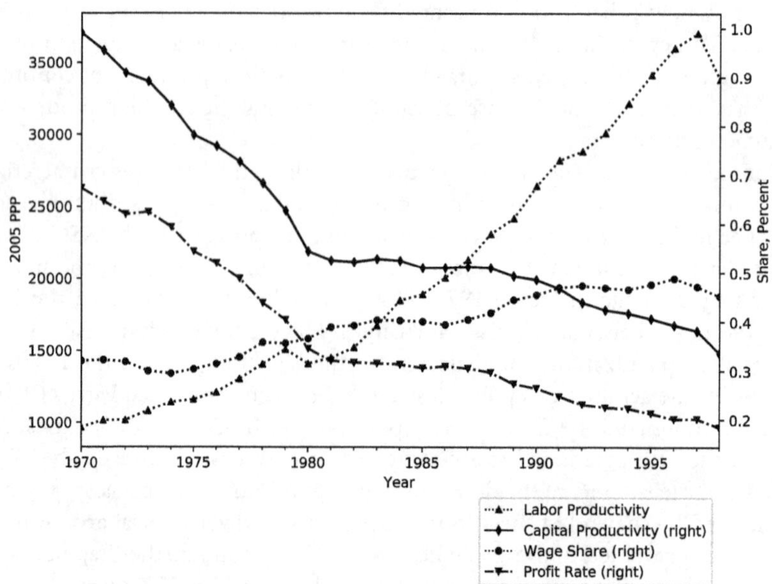

Figure 4.1 Distributional Dynamics, 1970–98.
Note: See Appendix A for the definition of variables and for the explanation of axes in this figure.
Source: Extended Penn World Tables v. 4 (Foley and Michl, 1999; Marquetti, 2003).

rapid industrialization, the capital stock per worker also showed a steady increase (Figure 4.2), which translated into declining capital productivity and decreases in the profit rate (Figure 4.1). Given the industrial consolidation that occurred since the 1960s, such declines in the average profit rate were not particularly biting for the large conglomerates, the most powerful segment of the Turkish capitalist class. However, in spite of the gains in productivity and the rising stock of capital, such an accumulation model was fragile for a few reasons.

First, both private and public production capabilities in Turkey were behind the technological frontier in the rest of the world. Catching up required sustained investment into productive activities and the technological upgrading that would accompany such investment (Kiyota, 2014; Kojima, 2000; Vernon, 1966; Hirschman, 1968). The problem was that it was much more profitable for the Turkish capitalists to produce goods for the protected domestic markets without seeking higher efficiency (Hershlag, 1988, 7). Second, although Turkey adopted planned development in the 1960s and continued planning in the 1970s (Fry, 1972), the structure of the financial system and credit allocation to private sector were neglected issues. Unlike South Korea (Chapter 3), which made cheap credit allocation to the champions of industry one of the central pillars of its industrialization, the medium to long-term capital resources available to the private sector were insufficient in Turkey (Fry, 1972, 42). As a result, the share of credit to industrial activities remained at low levels in the overall credit allocation in the 1960s and 1970s (Kepenek and Yentürk, 2000, 154–66). Despite an astronomical

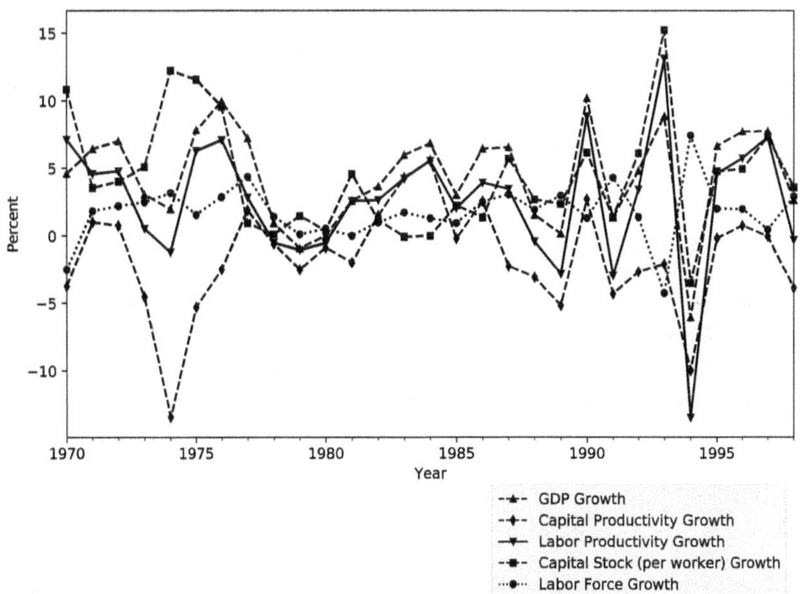

Figure 4.2 Growth Dynamics, 1970–98.
Note: See Appendix A for the definition of variables used in this figure.
Source: Extended Penn World Tables v. 4 (Foley and Michl, 1999; Marquetti, 2003).

expansion of credits, especially between 1973 and 1977, the economic activities related to production continued to receive a small share of total credits (Kepenek and Yentürk, 2000, 155–62). Third, although technological upgrading required a sustained and disciplined investment strategy, the SPO lacked the capacity to implement such a strategy. One of the primary reasons for the SPO's insufficient capacity was its lack of autonomy. The SPO was vulnerable to political demands and pressures from the Turkish capitalist class. The autonomy of the SPO declined further after 1967, the date when Turgut Özal—the future architect of the comprehensive capital account liberalization—took the helm at the organization (Atılgan, 2015a, 587). Again, the comparison with South Korea (Chapter 3), where the Economic Planning Board's autonomy was substantial, is instructive.

The fragilities in the Turkish accumulation process had significant consequences. Turkey had persistent fiscal and current account deficits in the 1960s and 1970s. In the 1970s, these deficits were increasingly financed through monetary expansion and domestic borrowing, which led to inflationary pressures (Hale, 1981, 166). Foreign debt also showed a considerable increase in the 1970s (Kepenek and Yentürk, 2000, 172). With the oil shock and worldwide price increases in the 1970s, inflation entered an upward spiral, reaching 68 percent in 1979 (Hale, 1981, 162). The high inflation in the 1970s exacerbated the low competitiveness of exports and thus contributed to a severe balance of payments crisis between 1978 and 1980 (Hale, 1981, 172).

The reason why Turkey could continue its industrialization process despite increasing balance of payments problems in the 1970s was the availability of foreign exchange resources (Pamuk, 1984). One exceptional source of foreign exchange for Turkey was the remittances of Turkish guest workers in Germany. Combined with rising levels of foreign debt, the Turkish economy could escape the foreign exchange shortage that is endemic to ISI. As a result, the Turkish industry achieved an impressive 10.1 percent growth between 1971 and 1977 despite worsening economic conditions (Pamuk, 1984, Table 1). The Turkish real GDP grew, annually, on average by 6.2 percent in the same period (Figure 4.2).[7] Such growth did not lead to gains in the wage share, as can be seen in Figure 4.1. In other words, the salaried workers in Turkey did not benefit from the gains in labor productivity, although their living standards improved in absolute terms in the 1970s (Boratav, 2003). Furthermore, the economic growth in Turkey came to a halt with an economic depression at the end of the 1970s. The balance of payments problems and foreign exchange shortage were the main causes of the country's economic problems. Given that workers were much better organized and politically active, the distributional conflict in Turkey intensified during the second half of the 1970s.

The intensifying economic crisis after 1978 exhibited, in unmistakable terms, the endemic problem of the Turkish economy: the provision of foreign exchange. By 1979, foreign exchange shortage was so severe that the main task the economic bureaucracy faced was to find sufficient foreign exchange for importing

7 Wage growth is omitted in this graph, as it will be analyzed in greater detail below.

basic goods, and most importantly fuel-oil. Such a task shortened the economic policy horizon in Turkey to remarkable levels.

The severe economic depression and the balance of payments crisis were accompanied by acute political polarization and violence. The economic and political conditions provided an environment conducive to radical change in the government policies. Such a new orientation occurred in 1980: the Demirel government initiated a comprehensive neoliberal transformation in the economy, from inward-oriented industrialization to market-driven economic development.

External liberalization

There were two crucial events that marked the beginning of the neoliberal era in Turkey. On January 24, 1980, the Demirel government introduced an ambitious liberalization program, after a long period of import substitution industrialization. On September 12, 1980, about eight months after the government's announcement of the liberalization program, the military intervened. The period that followed was characterized by center-right governments that liberalized the country's trade regime, implemented domestic liberalization reforms, and encouraged export-oriented growth.

The following analysis is concerned with the external liberalization during the 1980s. First, the January 24 economic reform package is analyzed. Second, the period between 1980 and 1983 is traced out. During this time, the military regime enabled the effective implementation of the liberalization reforms. Then the investigation focuses on the rise of Turgut Özal from the position of economic czar under Demirel and the military regime to the center stage of Turkish politics in the 1983 elections.

The 24 January 1980 economic package and liberalization reforms

As argued previously, the Turkish economy was in a severe balance of payments crisis in 1979. The acute shortage of foreign exchange rendered the importation of basic necessities (for consumption as well as production of goods) exceedingly difficult. In addition, the government of Süleyman Demirel was under mounting pressure on the political front, as the conflict between left and right-wing organizations became more violent. The political rise of Turgut Özal began in this environment. Özal, an engineer by training but an economist in practice, had been employed in various branches of the state economic bureaucracy in the 1950s and 1960s. He subsequently headed the SPO between 1967 and 1971. He was employed in the World Bank between 1970 and 1973 and then took important positions in the private sector. Özal was a long-time acquaintance of Prime Minister Demirel, and had strong support from the most powerful conglomerates. He became the undersecretary to the Prime Minister in 1979. Demirel expected Turgut Özal to address the intensifying economic crisis.

Özal had advocated a greater role for the private sector during the period he was the head of the SPO. As a result of his tenure at the World Bank and his employment in the private sector, Özal's economic vision and ideology diverged further from the views that were then prevalent in the SPO. Although his economic vision was not particularly well-formed, he believed in deregulation, limiting the role of government, and constituting a free-market economy in Turkey (Ulagay, 1988). Virtually unchallenged in office, he gradually began to implement this vision.[8]

Market-oriented liberalization policies were also actively sought by big businesses (Kazgan, 2005). The 1970s was the decade when industrialists, who flourished under state tutelage in the previous decades, consolidated their horizontal expansion and market share in the domestic market. For this class, the state-controlled economy became a major impediment to their growth. Furthermore, the increasing power of unions in the 1970s put upward pressure on wages, although the wage share in the economy was flat due to rising labor productivity (Figure 4.1). The upward wage pressure was nonetheless a concern for individual capitalists, particularly if they operated in sectors where labor productivity gains were minimal (Foley and Michl, 1999).

In addition, international financial and economic organizations—the IMF, the OECD, and the World Bank—were pushing for stabilization and liberalization reforms. The IMF pressure came at the end of a prolonged crisis of ISI. Import substitution industrialization in Turkey was not viable because of foreign exchange shortages. As external finance became more precious, the influence of international financial institutions grew. In an economy like Turkey's, which was weakened by severe foreign exchange shortage and heavy debt, the political administration was vulnerable to pressures for market-oriented reforms. Thus, the IMF pressures for a structural adjustment program that would involve major liberalization reforms were important in 1980. As will be seen in the analysis that follows, the IMF and the OECD did not carry such an influence in the 1989 capital account liberalization episode.

On January 24, 1980, the government announced a comprehensive economic reform package, which was designed primarily by Turgut Özal. An IMF standby agreement subsequently accompanied the reform package, resulting in substantial financial support from the OECD and the World Bank in addition to the IMF line of credit (Taylor, 1990; Arıcanlı, 1990; Kıray, 1990). As observed by Boratav (2003, 148–49), the reform package was a combination of stabilization and structural adjustment measures. The stabilization measures included fiscal and monetary contraction, price increases on SEE products, a very large devaluation,[9] and restrictions on domestic credit supply (Boratav 2003, 147–52; Öniş 1986). The Price Control Committee, which had the power to determine private sector prices, was abolished. As a result, price controls for various categories of goods produced by the private sector were removed (Kazdağlı, 2001, 457). Özal and his economic team assumed that contractionary policies, combined with

8 One of the first steps in a sweeping change in economic management and orientation was to decrease the influence of the SPO, by slashing its staff (ANKA, January 16, 21, 1980).

9 The exchange rate (Turkish lira per dollar) was devalued from 47 to 70.

a substantially weaker Turkish lira, would ease inflationary pressures (Kazgan, 2005).

Structural adjustment measures involved the liberalization of the trade regime, lifting price controls, and removing subsidies from specific products and sectors. Another crucial aspect of the economic reform package was the measures taken to encourage exports. Indeed, as noted by various scholars, the model of export-oriented industrialization and growth was the guiding spirit for the reform package. The economic bureaucracy under Özal assumed that the orientation toward exports would ease the pressure on the balance of payments (Kazgan, 2005, 199).

Abandoning import tariffs and quotas while implementing export-oriented measures signaled the end of ISI in Turkey. Thus, Turgut Özal intended nothing less than a fundamental transformation of the Turkish economic structure. This is evidenced in the following quote by Özal, where the objective of establishing free-market principles in Turkey is clearly emphasized (ANKA, June 3, 1980):

> The new economic programme is not a short-termed one. . . . It is a fact that, the closest economic system to that implemented by the advanced western nations for centuries is the free-market system. Turkey on the other hand, had been implementing instead, an economic system resembling the socialist economies of the Eastern Bloc. The basic philosophy of our new economic programme is to revert the economy rapidly back to the free-market system.

It should be noted that the economic reform package was particularly hostile to workers and peasants, and to all fixed-income social groups in general (Boratav, 2003). The price increases in SEE products, which constituted a large share of an ordinary spending basket, ranged from 50 percent to 400 percent (Kazdağlı, 2001, 457). Such price increases inevitably created animosity toward the economic reform package. In addition, various agencies within the Turkish state, including SEEs, also showed reluctance in the implementation of the reforms as the power of state bureaucracy over the economy, such as setting prices, was being curtailed drastically.[10]

The fact that the package could be announced is a testimony (1) to the severity of the balance of payments crisis and the economic depression since 1978, and (2) to the political bottleneck that characterized the country. However, the Demirel government was not particularly consistent in implementing the reform measures. In fact, the effective implementation of the January 24 radical liberalization reforms would be carried by a force that would not bow to political and electoral pressures: the Turkish Armed Forces.

The military forces, under the leadership of Kenan Evren, terminated democratic politics on September 12, 1980, by lifting the 1961 Constitution and banning all types of political activities. The right to form associations and organizations as well as the right of peaceful protest were suspended. The NSC, constituted by five generals, assumed supreme power and authority. Unlike the military

10 ANKA June 3, 1980.

takeovers in 1960 and 1971, the coup d'état was thoroughly planned and executed in the existing hierarchy of the military. Although some forces advocated for an extensive role of the army after the takeover, the "minimalists" were more influential in setting the course of the coup d'état: the military junta's goal was to stop violence, implement a drastic reordering of the political system, reconstitute some form of democracy, and then return to their barracks (Hale, 1988).

Initially, the NSC planned to form a new government with participation from the existing political parties. However, after an early attempt to form such a government failed, the NSC established an interim government headed by Bülend Ulusu, a former admiral. The political parties that existed before September 12, 1980, were dissolved in October 1981. The NSC formed a consultative assembly. A new constitution was drafted in 1982 and approved through a referendum in 1982. The support for the new constitution and the military rule was overwhelming; the voter participation was above 90 percent and 91.37 percent of those who voted affirmed the new constitution, proving the popularity of the military rule (Karpat, 1988, 154).

The 1982 Constitution included an article banning the leading political cadres of the past—including Prime Minister Demirel and opposition leader Ecevit—from entering into politics for an extended period of time (Hale, 1988, 171–72). This ban meant a significant break with the political past (Karpat, 1988). It also created a political vacuum, which would play an important role in the ensuing rise of Turgut Özal as the most powerful politician during the 1980s.

Two actions of the military junta were consequential for the subsequent course of economic management in Turkey. First, the military junta put Turgut Özal and his economic team in charge. This essentially was a green light for further liberalization of the economy. Second, political repression, widespread detention and arrest, outright torture, and the abolition of various civil rights stifled opposition to any economic reforms. The government under the military regime, with Özal as the Vice Prime Minister, continued a gradual but bold liberalization plan.

One of the first decisions of the military junta was to ensure that Turkey continued with the IMF program (Çölaşan, 1984, 263). In other words, the military regime opted to continue with the liberalization reforms and with Özal in particular. This was a natural choice, from the viewpoint of the NSC. The immediate and most important concern of the generals was to establish order and cease political violence (Karpat, 1988), but one of their priorities was also to foster economic growth and stability (Hale, 1988, 166). The Turkish economy was heavily dependent on foreign credit at the time. Thus, there was no easy alternative to the IMF and its financial support, as long as the Turkish economy remained integrated into the global economic system. This fact made Özal indispensable. After all, Özal had the most extensive relations with the IMF and the World Bank. He had also been the chief designer of liberalization reforms heavily sanctioned by these organizations. The failure of establishing a government with politicians from old political parties created a power vacuum, which contributed to the rise of Turgut Özal and his team. Furthermore, Özal had the support of the big business groups. In fact, Vehbi Koç, then perhaps the wealthiest person in Turkey,

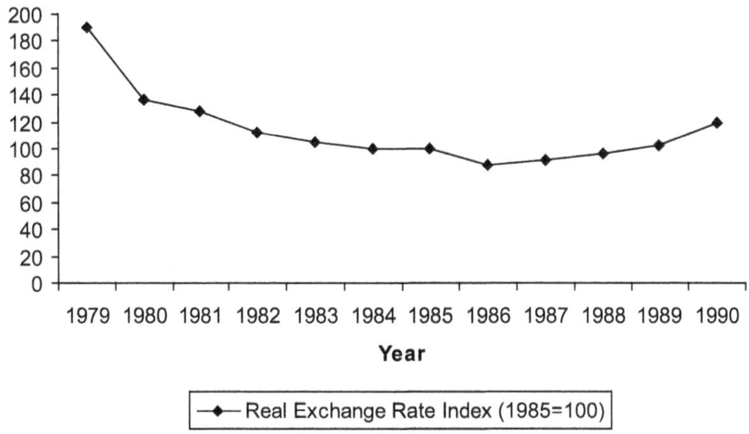

Figure 4.3 Real Exchange Rate, 1979–90.
Note: 1985 = 100. Lower values mean depreciation of the Turkish lira.
Source: Öniş (1993, Table 1).

sent a letter urging the NSC to ensure the reign of Turgut Özal as the head of the Turkish economy (Çölaşan, 1984).

Overall, the policies between 1980 and 1983 aimed at increasing exports and thus at overcoming the balance of payments problems of the late 1970s. In 1981, the export orientation of the January 1980 economic reform package received further support from a World Bank economic mission visit to Turkey. This mission, headed by the influential economist Bela Balassa, encouraged the continuation of the reform package and export-led growth strategy.[11] A number of factors prepared the ground for the surge of exports. The most important of them was the large nominal devaluation in January 1980, which was followed by periodic adjustments. The goal of the periodic adjustments was to maintain a competitive exchange rate, when the nominal exchange rate showed a continuing tendency to appreciate because of high domestic inflation (Öniş, 1993). The effectiveness of exchange rate policies can be observed in Figure 4.3. As can be seen, the real exchange rate showed a steady trend of decline starting in 1980.

One of the most important factors that enabled the stabilization and structural adjustment reforms was the repression of real wages. Real wages showed negative growth after the 1980 coup. On average, the real wages in 1980 declined by 13.2 in the public sector and 24.7 in the private sector (Boratav, 1990, 208). Although the real wages recovered modestly in 1981, their decline continued in 1982 through 1984 (Boratav, 1990). The decrease in real wages was even sharper in the public sector between 1982 and 1984 (Boratav, 1990, 208). Consequently, the wage share in the Turkish economy plunged as well, as can be seen

11 Interview with Gazi Erçel, former Governor of the Central Bank, July 3, 2006. This report was published in 1982 under the title *Turkey: Industrialization and Trade Strategy.*

in Figure 4.1. Overall, the working class lost significant purchasing power and did not have any means to counter the increasing income inequality in the country.

The government also supported the export industries through a number of incentives. These incentives included income tax reduction schemes, a foreign exchange allocation scheme, export credits, reduction in interests on export-oriented investment credits, and duty exemptions for inputs that would be used in the production of export goods (The World Bank, 1982). Given the dominance of large conglomerates in the Turkish economy, such incentives amounted to a direct support for the most powerful segment of the Turkish capitalist class.

Strong exports contributed to the recovery of the economy. The exports constituted only 4.3 percent of the GNP in 1980. The share of exports rose to 6.6 percent in 1981, to 8.9 percent in 1982, and to 9.5 percent in 1983 (Figure 4.4). Imports grew at a slower pace during the same period. Thus, the ratio of exports to imports—an important gauge of the balance of payments sustainability—improved from 36.8 percent in 1980 to 65 percent in 1982 and to 62 percent in 1983.

The Ulusu government under the military regime also began implementing stepwise financial liberalization measures. The first financial liberalization policy removed the ceilings on personal time deposit rates (Akyüz, 1990, 99). This first liberalization reform was implemented with no adequate regulatory institutions. After a period of restraint by major banks, smaller banks and brokers began offering certificates of deposit with spectacularly high interest rates (Akyüz, 1990). Quite naturally, no institution in Turkey could pay such high interest rates and the entire growth of the financial brokerage industry was based on selling increasing amounts of financial papers. The financial bonanza and the Ponzi scheme burst spectacularly in 1982. Özal left the government after the financial crisis.

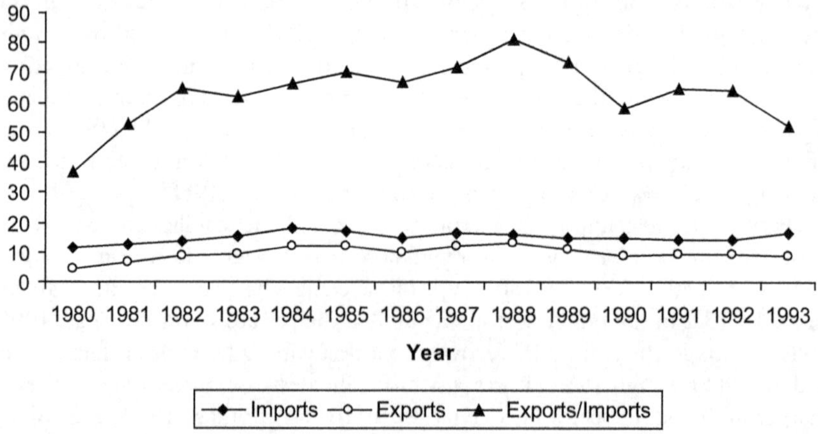

Figure 4.4 Exports and Imports, 1980–93.
Note: Exports and imports are in percentages of GNP.
Source: Turkish Statistical Institute (2003, Table 17.2).

The 1982 banking crisis illustrates a pattern in Özal's policy-making in economic affairs. This pattern can be summarized as "liberalize first, think later." Furthermore, not only Özal but even his most sophisticated technocrats were often vague on the content and the nature of the liberalization reforms, including the export-oriented development strategy.[12] Since there was no political opposition, Özal and his team had to struggle only against bureaucracy, most notably the Ministry of Finance.[13] However, Turgut Özal was often dismissive of the economic bureaucracy's cautionary recommendations (Çölaşan, 1984).[14]

Finally, the military rule between 1980 and 1983 also determined an important feature of Turkish politics in the following years: the insulation of politics from social groups (Cizre-Sakallıoğlu and Yeldan, 2000, 494). This was achieved through a number of legal means. The most crippling legal instrument was to ban all trade unions, voluntary associations, and public professional organizations from engaging in political activities (Özbudun, 1991, 42). Thus, the legal changes enacted by the NSC and by the Consultative Assembly amounted to restricting the political sphere to parties and to severing the link between civil society and political parties (Özbudun, 1991, 43).

This political structure guaranteed that, with the exception of protest voting, there was no mechanism that allowed popular classes to participate in politics. This, in turn, brought forth a dire consequence: the overwhelming power of two groups of people. One of these was the technocratic and political elite that coalesced around the figure of Turgut Özal. The other one was the capitalists, especially big businesses, who could have access to and therefore influence powerful politicians. As such, it was not surprising that the period after 1980 was characterized by the alliance between capitalists and privileged political actors (Boratav, 2003; Cizre-Sakallıoğlu and Yeldan, 2000). However, even in such an alliance, the balance of power was tilted toward the political actors around Özal. Heper (1991) calls this imbalance a sort of monism on the part of the Turkish state. As analyzed below, the imbalance and the disconnect between the political actors and the civil society were amplified further by the strengthening of the executive and the prime minister after 1983 (Öniş, 1991; Heper, 1991).

The Motherland Party government

The NSC scheduled the elections for October 1983. The military junta severely restricted political competition. Various parties that had links to the old political structure and cleavages were prevented from participating in the elections. Furthermore, the candidates running for the office were individually screened by the junta. As a result, only three parties could compete in the 1983 elections (Karpat, 1988, 154–55). One of these parties, the National Democracy Party

12 Interview with Kaya Erdem, former Minister of Finance, July 6, 2006.

13 Interview with Ekrem Pakdemirli, former Minister of Finance, July 13, 2006.

14 Various interviewees reiterated this point. For example, Osman Şıklar, the Governor of the Central Bank between 1981 and 1984, argued that Özal and Kaya Erdem—then the Minister of Finance—did not pay sufficient attention to his warnings on the bankers' interest rate competition to attract time deposits. Interview, June 5, 2006.

was headed by a former military officer and more or less represented the NSC's views. The other positively-sanctioned party (the Populist Party) represented the statist "political left" tradition in Turkey (Hale, 1988, 171). The NSC reluctantly agreed to allow Turgut Özal to found a party (Evin, 1994, 24–25).

As Karpat (1988, 155) observes, the Motherland Party (MP), established by Özal, was the only "genuine political organization" in the elections. This party was "a conglomeration of social groups from the middle classes, ranging from small entrepreneurs to capitalists and from moderate traditionalists to activist nationalists and Islamists" (Karpat, 1988, 155). Such a broad coalition was possible because of the political vacuum the military intervention created. Thus, the MP was a new breed of political right in Turkey, which had been more powerful than the left since the end of the one-party period. Unlike the old center of the right, the Justice Party of Demirel, the MP openly embraced liberalism and broke away from the statist tradition (Ergüder, 1991). The MP was also decisively more urban than the Justice Party. It was the embodiment of a new rising bourgeoisie (Keyder, 1987), with a strong conservative appeal because of its espousal of traditional and Islamist values.

The 1983 elections were a victory for Özal and his center-right party. The MP obtained 45.1 percent of the votes and 52.8 percent of the seats in the parliament (Ergüder, 1991, 159). Ironically, it was the NSC who prepared the grounds for this electoral victory. Buoyed by the perceived popularity of the military intervention (Hale, 1988; Karpat, 1988), the NSC allowed Özal's party to participate in the elections partly based on the assumption that it would not obtain sufficient support (Sayarı, 2002, 16). That proved to be erroneous. The MP had a popular and ideological appeal, which the other parties ostensibly lacked. Furthermore, it promised economic and political change after a tumultuous past. These factors, combined with the restricted political competition in the 1983 elections and the ban on the old political elite, enabled the MP to emerge as the dominant party in the repressed multiparty system of the 1980s (Sayarı, 2002).

Unorthodox liberalization, uneven growth, and the restructuring of the state

The MP's unrivaled power in Turkish politics emboldened a bold agenda of liberal economic reforms. However, the market-oriented reforms of the MP comprised various orthodox and unorthodox elements. As such, the liberalization reforms that the MP implemented led to some results that were contradictory to the liberalism rhetoric the party purported.

The orthodox elements of the reforms can be summarized as regressive income distribution, a decrease in the level of domestic demand, steady devaluation, deregulation in key markets and products, the liberalization of the trade regime, increased incentives for foreign direct investment, wage flexibility, and finally, a drive toward privatization. These policies created the conditions for higher profitability for the individual capitalists and significant distributional gains for the Turkish capitalist class as a whole, as can be seen in the rising profit share during the 1980s (Figure 4.1). Given the economic stagnation of the late 1970s, the market-friendly policies supported by international financial institutions yielded rapid economic growth between 1983 and 1987 (Table 4.1). The recovery from the crisis following the January 1980 reform package continued in 1983 and 1984, where the real GDP growth rate was 5.9 and 6.8 percent. The high growth reached its peak in 1986 and 1987, where the real GDP grew by 6.4 and 6.5 percent.

However, the economic growth in Turkey exhibited features that contradicted the liberal rhetoric of the MP government (Öniş, 1991, 31). First, capital accumulation materialized mostly through public investment rather than private investment. In fact, as can be seen in Table 4.1, the share of manufacturing in private investment fell steadily between 1981 and 1987. This was a period of rapid export growth (Figure 4.4) and high profitability for the Turkish private sector. Yet, such profits were not channeled into manufacturing investment. Second, although the Turkish economy was experiencing an increasing integration with the world economy, especially in the financial markets, the financial system itself grew more dominated by state institutions such as public banks. Third, the impressive growth of the export sector, which was the basis of Turkey's creditworthiness after the troubled 1970s, was dependent on the unused reserve capacity of the import substitution industrialization period and on the state-orchestrated special incentives allocated to large family-owned conglomerates (Öniş, 1993).

Furthermore, a rapid expansion of domestic and foreign debt stock provided significant fuel for economic growth. In 1980, the sum of government bonds and treasury bills amounted to 3.6 percent of GNP (Figure 4.5). This ratio fell between 1981 and 1983. It increased to 4.3 percent in 1985 and to 5.8 percent in 1987. While the public sector was relying increasingly on domestic debt for financing its infrastructure investment, it was also accumulating a large amount of foreign debt. The external debt to GNP ratio increased from 31.8 percent in 1983 to 46.79 percent in 1987 (Turkish Statistical Institute, 2003, Table 20.8).

Table 4.1 Economic Growth, 1981–87†

Period	*Real GDP Growth*[a]	*Investment*	
		Private Manufacturing[b]	*Public Infrastructure*[c]
1981	2.6	37.8	65.9
1982	3.6	36.3	71.1
1983	5.9	34.9	73.5
1984	6.8	34.1	74.3
1985	3.0	33.4	74.9
1986	6.4	32.7	81.4
1987	6.5	26.4	87.9

† All numbers are in percentage terms.
a Annual. Source: Extended Penn World Tables v. 4 (Foley and Michl, 1999; Marquetti, 2003).
b Share of manufacturing in total private investment. Source: Öniş (1993, Table 4).
c Share of Infrastructure in Total Public Investment. Source: Öniş (1993, Table 4).

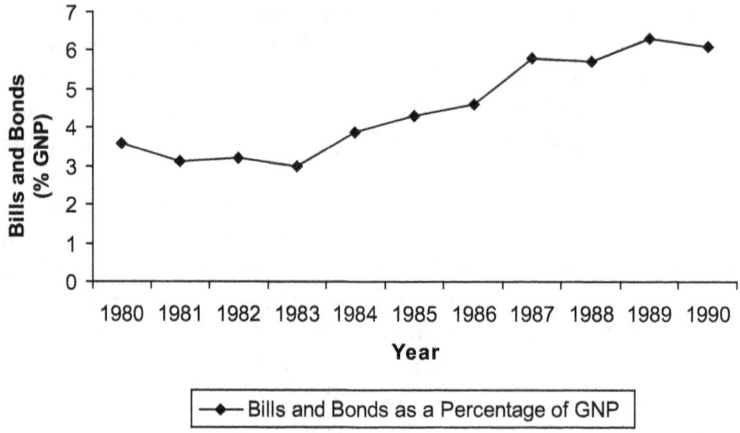

Figure 4.5 Treasury Bills and Government Bonds as a Percentage of GNP, 1980–90.
Source: Turkish Statistical Institute (2003, Table 20.9).

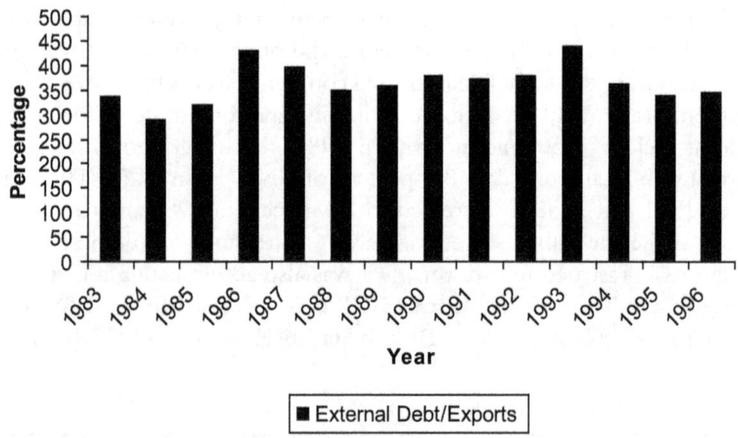

Figure 4.6 External Debt–Exports Ratio, 1983–96.
Source: Turkish Statistical Institute (2003, Table 20.8).

In other words, the Turkish economy grew in the 1980s, but it grew by accumulating large amounts of debt (see Table 4.1 and Figure 4.6).

Such an increase in the domestic and foreign debt came at a great cost. First, the increased financing of the public sector through government bonds and treasury bills crowded out private investment. Second, it led to an increase in interest rates. Third, foreign debt interest payments became more onerous with the accumulation of further debt (Öniş, 1993). Since the Turkish economy did not run trade surpluses during this period, this meant that the increasing debt was possible only as long as the economy could attract more foreign capital. That is to say, the Turkish economy entered into a debt trap in the 1980s.

In terms of social dynamics, the increasing domestic debt constituted a regressive income transfer mechanism. The public sector borrowing requirement showed a continuous increase under the MP. The financing of the public sector through domestic debt enabled the social classes that could buy and sell government bonds and treasury bills to enjoy high interest revenues. In addition, the most profitable sector during the 1980s, and especially during the MP governments, was the banking and finance sector. Such policies amounted to net income transfers from workers and peasants to the capitalist class, since it was the limited tax income of the public sector that enabled the interest payments on mounting domestic debt.[15] Furthermore, it was also net income transfers to the big business groups, since they were the ones who had control over the banking and finance sector.[16]

Thus, as Öniş (1991, 34–35) underlines, wage earners, fixed-income groups, and farmers were the main victims of the Turkish liberalization in the 1980s. Policies such as reduction in the level of domestic demand, continuous devaluation, and the repression of real wages had immediate deteriorating effects on the living standards of the middle and lower classes. Under normal political conditions, these policies would cause opposition and would be difficult to implement due to electoral pressures. But despite the hostility of MP's policies toward fixed-income groups, wage earners, and farmers, these policies did not face real opposition until 1987. This was partly a result of the 1980 military intervention, which blocked the channels of political participation for popular social classes, as discussed above. There were two other factors that enabled the MP government's implementation of these policies.

First, the MP mitigated the potential distributional conflicts by forming a political coalition based on strong economic growth and high levels of public investment and spending (Öniş, 1991, 335). As Cizre-Sakallıoğlu and Yeldan (2000, 499) remark, the public spending offset—and thus legitimized—the liberalization and the worsening income distribution. One can add that public employment and public contracts through patron-client relationships also contributed to the legitimacy of the state in this period.

Second, the MP government, under the leadership of Özal, instituted a fundamental restructuring of the Turkish state and its decision-making apparatus. It is argued above that the military regime between 1980 and 1983 blocked the channels of political participation for civil society associations. Turgut Özal, during his tenure as the prime minister, carried the insulation of politicians one step further by limiting the intra-party democracy and by weakening the bureaucracy. In the words of Heper (1991, 173):

> Prime Minister Turgut Özal, along with an inner circle of ministers and technocrat-planner administrators, mostly recruited from among Turks who

15 As Cizre-Sakallıoğlu and Yeldan (2000, 489) put, "Management of fiscal debt may be viewed as an income transfer mechanism, transferring income away from wage-labour and the peasantry, to domestic 'rentiers.'"

16 *Cumhuriyet*, September 12, 1988.

> had been working in the United States, made all the critical economic decisions virtually without consulting the traditional civil bureaucracy, the Parliament and the political parties as well as interest groups.

Özal, by accumulating a large portion of the decision-making power in the office of the prime minister, emerged as a politician with powers that were unusual in a democracy. Through time, the MP government became the vehicle of Özal's charismatic leadership.

Thus, it is possible to delineate three key elements of the Turkish liberalization under the MP governments in the 1980s (Öniş, 1991, 33). These are the concentration of economic power in the hands of big business groups, the market-oriented liberalization reforms, and the centralization of government—both in terms of presence in the economy and in terms of its decision-making structure. As Öniş (1991, 33) puts it:

> What has been happening is a significant restructuring of the State, that is, centralization of government as well as a (state-induced) concentration of private power, parallel to the steps taken in the direction of establishing a market-oriented economy.

The problems with the Turkish state's promotion and orchestration of economic growth in the context of a liberalized, open economy became apparent in the late 1980s. The export boom in the first half of the 1980s was short-lived. The initial strong performance did not lead to further investment by private market actors that would create and sustain internationally competitive industries. Instead, the state's export promotion strategies were subject to corruption and rent-seeking activities (Öniş, 1991, 1993; Kazgan, 2005; Boratav, 2003).

1989: capital account liberalization

In August 1989, the MP government announced an economic reform package including measures on the trade regime and capital account. The package was the most comprehensive set of reforms on the current and capital accounts since the January 24, 1980 program. While the measures on the trade regime were bold, the most surprising element of the reforms was the Decree No. 32 on the Law for the Protection of Turkish Lira, which removed all restrictions—except for some quantitative limits that would be lifted later—on capital movements in and out of Turkey (İstanbul Stock Exchange, 1999, 402–03).[17] In fact, the Decree No. 32 meant that the Turkish lira was practically convertible and that the Turkish capital account was fully open beginning in August 1989.

Since there was no precedent discussion or consultation with the private sector, the package of economic reforms was a great surprise. Furthermore, the reforms did not distinguish between different types of capital movements and did not

17 See ANKA, August 9, 1989. The Decree No. 32 was published on August 11, 1989 in the Official Gazette No. 20249. Its third and fourth article involved the most important changes with regards to capital account liberalization.

plan a gradual opening of the capital account. Given that the Turkish economy featured a very high stock of foreign and domestic debt, astronomical inflation, and persistent trade as well as budget deficits, the decision to liberalize the capital account in a comprehensive fashion did not have much economic justification.

The comprehensive and abrupt capital account liberalization emerged as a policy response to a number of economic and political developments. First, until 1987 the MP enjoyed a dominant position in Turkish politics partially due to the ban on the activities of politicians who were influential before the 1980 military intervention. In 1987, a referendum revoked the rights of these politicians and thus spurred intensified political competition. Second, the rapid growth between 1983 and 1987 came to an end in 1988. Economic slowdown also brought to the surface the contradictory consequences of rapid economic growth under the MP rule: (1) wages were repressed, (2) rapid growth did not stimulate private investment and capital accumulation, (3) the Turkish economy accumulated an increasing stock of debt, and (4) the public sector relied heavily on domestic and foreign debt to finance its operations. Third, the repression of popular social classes that enabled high profitability between 1980 and 1987 lost its viability in 1988 and 1989. As a consequence, distributional conflicts—in the form of greater demands for real wage increases—intensified. Fourth, the 1989 local elections were a failure for the MP. The approaching presidential elections, which provided an opportunity for Özal to become the president of the Turkish Republic, and the electoral failure, made economic growth and meeting distributional demands urgent priorities. These economic and political conditions led Turgut Özal and a small number of politicians and technocrats (1) to recourse into increasingly expansionary policies, and (2) to form positive expectations for capital account liberalization. Özal and his team believed that foreign capital flows would stimulate the Turkish economy. Intent on boosting economic growth, they also did not pay attention to the objections of the Central Bank, the State Planning Organization, and Turkish industrialists.

The 1987 referendum and political opening

Despite the ban on their political activities, the political leaders of the 1960s and 1970s resurfaced in the political scene from 1983 onwards. A number of parties were founded by close associates of old political leaders, which signaled the revival of the parties from the pre-1980 era (Sayarı, 2002, 16). Although there was a ban on his political activities, Demirel was especially successful in engineering a well-organized political party, the True Path Party. Despite increasing political activity by rival parties, the MP obtained 41 percent of the votes in the 1984 municipal elections (Yeşilada, 1988, 367). The MP also initiated a break from the statist and centralist tradition by promising and later instituting increased autonomy for local administrations, which contributed to the continuing appeal of the party (Ergüder, 1991; Yeşilada, 1988).

By 1985, an increasing number of parties, including political parties that ostensibly followed the heritage of parties that dominated Turkish politics before the 1980 military intervention, were established. In 1986, the True Path Party obtained a sufficient number of seats in the National Assembly and began a vocal opposition to the MP government (Yeşilada, 1988, 369). An election in 1986 to fill the vacant seats in the Assembly showed that support for the MP had eroded to 32 percent (Yeşilada, 1988, 370).

The increasing presence of old political cleavages in the Assembly and in the Turkish political scene culminated in a National Assembly vote for removing the ban on restrictions over political activities of the pre-1980 era leaders. Since the ban was written into the 1982 Constitution, it required a national referendum to take effect (Ergüder, 1991, 158). The MP rallied for keeping the restrictions. The referendum showed that the Turkish population was divided closely on this issue: 50.3 percent of the voters approved removing the restrictions, while 49.7 percent voted for keeping them (Ergüder, 1991, 157–58).

Özal announced early elections immediately after the referendum. The MP obtained 36.3 percent of votes in the 1987 elections, which reinforced the party's hold on power in Turkish politics. Thanks to changes in the electoral law, enacted before the election, the MP won 292 seats in the National Assembly. In other words, despite having lost 9 percent of the votes between 1983 and 1987, the MP's seats in the Assembly increased from 52.8 percent to 64.9 percent (Ergüder, 1991, 159). In fact, as Kalaycıoğlu (2002, 63) observes, "The 1987 elections bore the most disproportional results in recent Turkish history."

However, despite the electoral victory, 1987 was also the beginning of a new political era. Until 1985, the MP did not face any significant political competition and opposition. As a result, the MP repressed wages without political backlash (Tachau, 2002). This situation began to change in 1985, with the entry of new parties into political life. The 1987 referendum, which legitimized the return of old politicians and deep-seated political cleavages, marked the end of this era for the MP. In that sense, 1987 marked the return to competitive politics in Turkey. Such political pressures implied that the MP government's repressive policies entailed considerable electoral risks.

The exhaustion of rapid growth

Despite high inflation, a growing fiscal deficit, and the rising stock of debt, the GDP growth rate was 5.8 percent between 1981 and 1988 in Turkey (Ertuğrul and Selçuk, 2001, 8–9). The strong growth came to a halt in 1988 with the appreciation of real wages (Figure 4.1). Turkey faced the risk of stagflation in 1988, with high inflation and low GDP growth (Boratav et al., 2001, 323).

The slowdown in economic activity can be observed in Table 4.2, where quarterly data on the growth rate of real private and public consumption, imports, and GDP are presented. Public consumption began to decrease in the second half of 1988 (by 3 percent in the third quarter and 5.9 percent in the fourth quarter) and its recovery in 1989 was very slow. Similarly, after a slowdown in the second and third quarter of 1988, private consumption shrank by 5.7 percent in the fourth quarter of 1988. The negative growth continued in the first two quarters of 1989, where the private consumption decreased by 7.3 and 2.8 percent. The private consumption recovered only in the second half of 1989, and this recovery

Table 4.2 Economic Slowdown, 1988–89†

Period	*Private Consumption*[a]	*Public Consumption*[b]	*Imports*[c]	*GDP*[d]
1988				
I	5.9	4.0	12.0	10.1
II	3.4	4.1	12.7	4.3
III	2.6	−3.0	−11.1	1.5
IV	−5.7	−5.9	−22.0	−3.8
1989				
I	−7.3	1.9	−13.0	−3.5
II	−2.8	0.6	−4.8	−2.1
III	1.4	−2.0	25.2	2.1
IV	3.1	2.6	21.0	3.3

† All numbers are in percentage terms.
Source: Turkish Statistical Institute online database, June 2013.
a Real final private consumption expenditure growth.
b Real final government consumption expenditure growth.
c Real value of import of goods and services, period growth.
d Real expenditure on GDP, period growth.

was very modest. The biggest collapse was in imports, where the real expenditure on imports declined by 11.1 percent in the third quarter and 22 percent in the fourth quarter. Negative growth continued in the first half of 1989 (−13 percent in the first quarter and −4.8 percent in the second quarter). The imports began to increase, rather strongly, in the third quarter. As a result of the slowdown in the imports, the private consumption, and the public consumption, the real GDP growth in 1988 and 1989 was weak. The real GDP fell 3.8 percent in the fourth quarter of 1988, and it continued to contract in the first half of 1989.

At the same time, the burden of domestic and foreign debt payments became a serious concern for the economic management (Boratav, 2003, 178). Since the tax base deflated under the MP governments, the share of tax income in the government budget declined as well (Oyan, 1989). Given the decreasing tax income, the Turkish macroeconomic policy became focused on finding resources to finance the public borrowing requirements (Boratav, 2003, 178).

The Özal government created the much-needed resources partly by enlarging the money supply in an uncontrolled fashion. This can be seen in Figure 4.7. The annual inflation rate was 29.6 percent in 1986 and 32 percent in 1987. The rate of inflation surged to 68.3 percent in 1988. High inflation continued in 1989, during which the inflation rate was 69.6 percent. In fact, July 1989 was the month with the highest inflation rate in the history of the republic: 6.2 percent.[18] Such policies show the willingness of the MP government to embrace expansionary policies to deliver economic growth and meet the demands of various constituencies such as public sector employees.

18 *Cumhuriyet*, July 7, 1989.

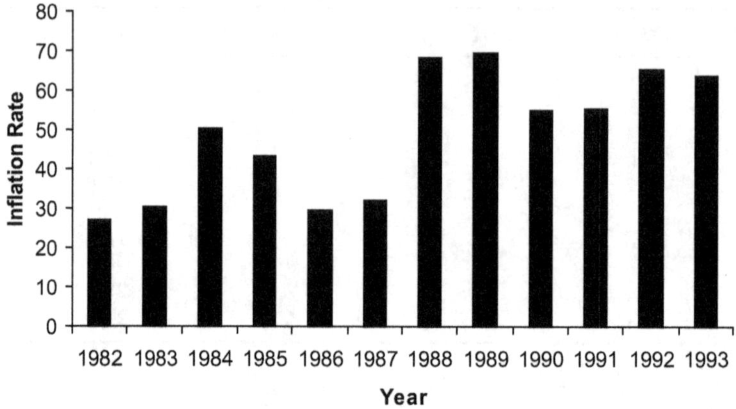

Figure 4.7 Inflation Rate, 1982–93.
Note: Inflation rate is based on the rate of change in wholesale price index.
Source: Turkish Statistical Institute (2003, Table 18.4).

The rush to full convertibility

Thus, the Motherland Party government faced increasing challenges by 1989. The Turkish state was heavily indebted. The growth rate was low, even negative in several quarters of 1988 and 1989. The inflation rate marched toward 100 percent. In such an environment, almost all the government decisions on the economy were motivated by short-term concerns. The main short-term problem was to finance foreign debt service and domestic debt payments. The slowdown in economic activity with persistent high inflation exacerbated the debt trap of the Turkish economy. It also presented the risk of stagflation.

At the same time, 1988 and 1989 were the years in which the long dormant labor sector became increasingly contentious. Hence, the Motherland Party government could no longer maintain low real wages and exercise repression over wage-earners (Boratav, 2003, 175). The widespread social protests by various labor unions in 1988 resulted in significant wage increases. Figure 4.8 illustrates wage growth vis-à-vis GDP, capital productivity, capital stock per worker, labor productivity, and labor force growth. The trajectory of the average real wage following the labor union protests was remarkable. In 1989, the average real wage growth was a staggering 39 percent. In 1990, the growth in average real wage was 21.3 percent. Furthermore, the surge in the real wage was not accompanied by an increase in labor productivity. Such a rise in real wages led to a remarkable recovery in the wage share as well, which can be observed in Figure 4.1. As Cizre-Sakallıoğlu and Yeldan (2000, 488) argue: "The hike in the real wage rate from 1988 signaled that the ongoing structural adjustment based on suppressing of domestic incomes was no longer feasible, politically or economically." Wage repression was one of the pillars of the MP's restructuring of the Turkish economy at the expense of the working class; it undergirded the competitiveness of exports,

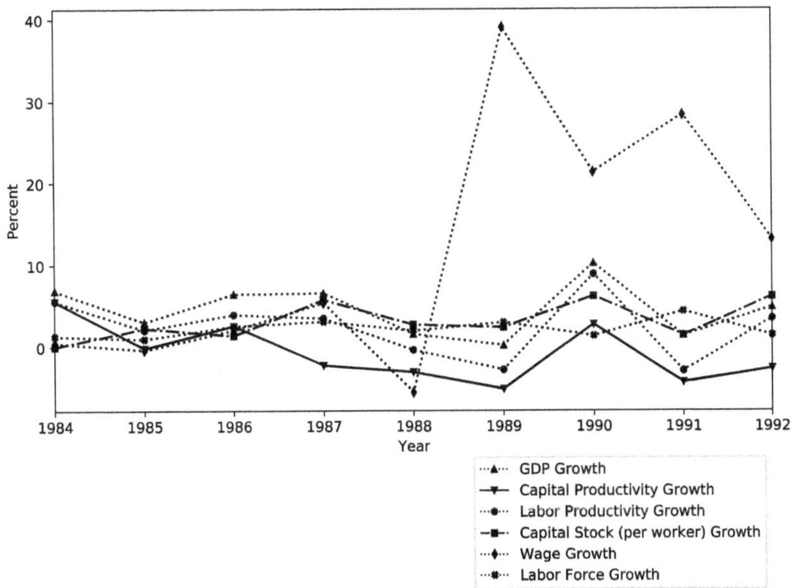

Figure 4.8 Wage Growth, 1984–92.
Note: See Appendix A for the definition of variables used in this figure.
Source: Extended Penn World Tables v. 4 (Foley and Michl, 1999; Marquetti, 2003).

especially in the most dynamic export sectors, such as textiles. In that sense, the increasing power of labor implied the end of rapid growth whose benefits accrued mostly to the capitalist class.

The political pressures on the MP also intensified during this period. The local elections in March 1989 brought defeat and were a heavy blow to the MP government. It became clear that the MP was in the process of losing its dominant position in the Turkish politics. The immediate consequence of the March 1989 electoral defeat was a leap into short-term expansionary policies. The MP government, now instigated by the defeat in the local elections, increased public employee salaries by 56 to 95 percent.[19] Increases in the subsidized purchase prices for agricultural products followed the wage increases (Boratav, 2003, 176). Such increases were not entirely sufficient to reverse the results of wage repression since 1980. However, they constituted a considerable burden on the consolidated public budget. This can be seen in Figure 4.9. While personnel expenditure was 23.6 percent in 1988, it rose to 32.3 percent of the total consolidated budget in 1989.

In addition to electoral pressures, the presidential elections were scheduled for the end of 1989. Since the president was elected by the General Assembly and since the MP held the majority in the Assembly thanks to the disproportionate electoral system, Turgut Özal had a strong chance of being elected as

19 *Cumhuriyet*, July 8, 1989.

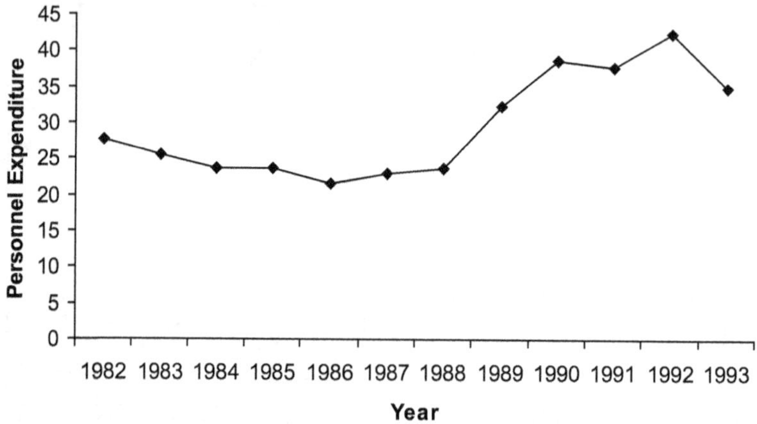

Figure 4.9 Personnel Expenditure's Share in Total Consolidated Budget Expenditures, 1982–93.
Source: Turkish Statistical Institute (2003, Table 20.6).

the president of the republic. In other words, the approaching presidential elections provided an opportunity for Prime Minister Özal to relieve himself from the intensified political competition. Such a prospect created another level of uncertainty in Turkish politics. The MP's economic policies grew increasingly dominated by political concerns. For example, Ekrem Pakdemirli, then the Minister of Finance and one of the closest associates of Turgut Özal, suggested that the primary motivation behind high increases in wages and agricultural prices during 1989 was to build public support for the upcoming presidential elections.[20]

The disorder in the Turkish economy and politics was accompanied by infighting and factionalism in the economic administration. There were at least three cabinet members who held the power to determine macroeconomic policies: Ekrem Pakdemirli, the Minister of Finance; Işın Çelebi, who oversaw the State Planning Organization, the State Institute of Statistics, and Eximbank; and Güneş Taner, who held authority over the Treasury Department and certain public banks. It was no secret that there was a power conflict among these three cabinet members. The Central Bank and the Treasury Department disagreed over several issues, including banking and foreign exchange regulations. Furthermore, Özal himself was not keen on delegating authority when it came to economic matters; he regularly intervened and determined the course of economic policy-making. For instance, Özal directly oversaw the Central Bank operations, even on a daily basis. Thus, the economy administration was incoherent, inconsistent and lacked coordination.[21]

As analyzed below, in such an environment, the administration was eager to revitalize the economy. Foreign capital flows provided such an opportunity. The

20 Interview with Ekrem Pakdemirli.
21 *Cumhuriyet*, August 7, 1989.

timing of Decree No. 32—in the midst of a recession with high inflation and large stock of debt—was curious from a strictly economic viewpoint. It was highly beneficial and opportunistic from a political standpoint. During the 1980s, the MP government could keep a dominant position in Turkish politics by (1) filling the vacuum created by the military intervention, (2) repressing wage-earners and farmers, (3) pursuing high growth, and (4) using public spending and investment in alleviating distributional conflicts. This political and economic regime was no longer sustainable.

Turgut Özal as the Prime Minister had a great role in the decision process leading to Decree No. 32. He expected the capital account liberalization to provide finance and fuel economic growth. It is clear that Turgut Özal perceived full capital account liberalization and currency convertibility as an important step in modernizing the Turkish economy. It can even be speculated that he saw a convertible Turkish lira as an element of a "modern" and "western" economy. Özal's aspirations for the comprehensive liberalization and the integration of the Turkish financial system with the world economy are indeed echoed in several interviews conducted with his close associates.[22] Mahfi Eğilmez, then the Deputy Undersecretary at the Treasury Department, even suggests that Özal viewed full convertibility as the ultimate solution to the foreign exchange shortages Turkey had experienced in the past (2001, 231–33).[23]

Despite Özal's aspirations for the liberalization of the capital account, one should be careful in evaluating such enthusiasm, especially in relation to free-market ideologies. While Özal's ideological orientation was important, it should be remembered that Özal was not consistent in his ideological beliefs and commitment to free markets. He instead espoused liberalism with great fervor when such ideology served his political interests. He also did not hesitate to implement policies that were contradictory to liberalism and stifled the liberalization of markets. The public infrastructure drive, which quickly became corrupt and a vehicle for patron-client relations, was an example. Another example was the enlargement of the public sector in the financial system, which prevented the development of private capital markets in Turkey.

The real reasons for Özal's determination to liberalize the Turkish capital account should be sought in his concrete expectations with regards to the outcome of financial opening. On that front, there is sufficient evidence that Özal had rosy expectations about the consequences of full capital account liberalization. At the time, various economists and the media worried about capital flight and a potential foreign exchange shortage as a result of capital flight. Özal had the opposite view:[24]

22 Interviews with Kaya Erdem, Ekrem Pakdemirli, Hüsnü Doğan, Gazi Erçel, Ali Tiğrel, Güneş Taner, and Işın Çelebi, June-July 2006.

23 Eğilmez further adds that Özal saw a connection between foreign exchange shortages and military interventions. According to this interpretation, Özal envisaged full convertibility as a solution to recurrent problems of the Turkish democracy with the military forces (2001, 231). Such an interpretation is not unlikely, but evidence for it is difficult to find.

24 *Cumhuriyet*, August 12, 1989.

> Tahditlerin kalktığını, herhangi bir yabancı para, örneğin bir Batılı ülkenin parası haline geldiğini açıkça ifade ediyorum. Bu hadisenin meydana gelmesi ile Türk ekonomisi 90'lı yıllarda yeni bir atılıma girecektir. Türkiye'nin dövizleri daha da artacaktır. Türkiye'ye yabancı sermaye girişi artacaktır. Türk müteşebbisleri içeride daha iyi yatırım imkanı bulacak, dış kredi imkanları çok daha rahat gelecektir. Tahditler kaldırılmıştır, bürokrasinin müdahelesi en asgariye indirilmiştir. İhracat bununla beraber daha serbest tarzda yapılacaktır.[25]

The political determination was mainly driven by Özal but also shared by Güneş Taner. Immediately after Decree No. 32, Güneş Taner expressed his expectation that the decision would lead to economic revival in Turkey.[26] The Treasury Department, largely under the control of Özal and Taner, was optimistic about the consequences of capital account liberalization. For example, Selçuk Demiralp, one of the designers of the reform and later the Undersecretary of the Treasury Department, expressed that the Treasury expected the capital account liberalization in 1989 to stimulate foreign savings to flow into Turkey.[27]

Unlike the liberalization reforms in January 24, 1980, the 1989 capital account liberalization was implemented in the absence of the IMF pressure. The Turkish economy did not have a foreign exchange crisis in 1989. Furthermore, it was not in a standby agreement with the IMF. Although the OECD recommended capital account liberalization to high-level bureaucrats, such recommendations did not come as a condition for international credit arrangements. As such, the influence of international economic organization did not go beyond general recommendations.[28]

Not all organizations in the Turkish economic bureaucracy had positive expectations. The hesitant and cautious stance of the economic bureaucracy is exemplified by the following quote from Rüşdü Saraçoğlu, then the Central Bank Governor (quoted in Doğruel and Doğruel 2005, 199):

> İnsanların özgürlükleri açısından çok önemli bir devrim, fakat (...) biz bundan korktuğumuzu Turgut Bey'e daha önce söyledik. Korkmamızın sebebi de, döviz kaçar diye değil, bilakis, fazla döviz gelir diye idi. Ve nitekim öyle oldu. Birdenbire, inanılmaz miktarda, yani Türkiye'nin o dönemler hiç alışık olmadığı bir miktarda döviz gelmeye başladı. Döviz gelince, siz kamuya kredi

25 "I declare without ambiguity, that the restrictions have been removed, and that [the Turkish lira] became another foreign currency; for example the currency of a Western country. With this event, the Turkish economy will be making a leap in the 1990s. Turkey's foreign exchange resources will rise further. The foreign capital entry into Turkey will increase. Turkish entrepreneurs will find better investment opportunities within the country; the opportunities for foreign credit will come much more easily. Restrictions have been removed, bureaucratic interventions have been reduced to a minimum. With this event, exportation will be conducted in a more liberal fashion." (Author's translation.)

26 ANKA, August 11, 1989.

27 Interview, July 20, 2006.

28 Interview with Selçuk Demiralp, former Undersecretary of the Treasury Department.

vermeseniz bile, Merkez Bankası döviz satın alarak para yaratıyor, para yaratılması devam etti.[29]

Saraçoğlu's statement is important because it shows that the Central Bank in 1989 recognized some of the risks associated with capital account liberalization. The Central Bank was not alone in its reluctance. The SPO shared a similar attitude toward capital account liberalization. For example, the head of the SPO at the time, Ali Tiğrel, emphasized that the SPO was not enthusiastic about capital account liberalization.[30]

Both Güneş Taner and Turgut Özal were dismissive of the cautionary approach of the SPO and the Central Bank.[31] Such an approach on the part of Özal and Taner was in line with the history of financial reform in Turkey. Rather than being the outcome of a thorough and careful design, financial reforms in Turkey emerged as patchwork solutions to pressing problems.[32] Hence, the sudden capital account liberalization replicated the pattern observed during the development of the 1982 crisis. In that instance of financial liberalization, Özal and his team adopted the strategy of "liberalize first, think later," with rosy expectations about the growth consequences of financial reforms.

However, the pattern of policy-making driven by short-term fiscal concerns should not obscure the fundamental structural dynamics that led to the comprehensive and sudden capital account reforms in 1989. The intensity of the distributional pressures that the MP faced in 1988 and 1989 was remarkable. Furthermore, the consequences of such distributional pressures in terms of the wage and profit shares were sizeable (Figure 4.1). The revitalized labor unions, which organized effective nation-wide strikes and protests in this period, revealed the unfairness of economic growth under the MP governments in the aftermath of the 1980 military coup d'état. A significant share of the economic growth in the 1980s was directly against the welfare of the working class and groups such as public employees. Furthermore, such hardship did not generate greater growth potential in the future, as investment—the majority of which was public—in productive capital was anemic. The period between 1987 and 1989 was, thus, the end of a capital accumulation model that benefited a narrow segment of the Turkish population.

In stark contrast to the enthusiasm of the government for the reforms, the Turkish industrialists and their interest associations vehemently opposed the decision to fully liberalize the capital account and to further reduce import tariffs.

29 "It is a very important revolution for people's liberty, but (. . .) we had told Mr. Turgut that we were afraid of it. We were afraid not because foreign exchange would leave the country, but because excessive foreign exchange would come. And that is what happened. All of a sudden, foreign exchange started flowing into the country, in quantities Turkey was not used to receiving in those times. When foreign exchange flows in, even if you do not supply credit to the public sector, the Central Bank creates money by buying foreign exchange; the creation of money thus continued." (Author's translation.)

30 Author's interview, July 5, 2006.

31 Interviews with Ali Tiğrel and Zekeriya Yıldırım, June–July 2006.

32 Cizre-Sakallıoğlu and Yeldan (2000, 484) stress the same point, arguing that "financial reforms progressed in leaps and bounds, mostly through pragmatic, *in situ* solutions to emerging problems."

The stance of the Turkish capitalist class, in particular the large conglomerates that were particularly effective in representing their interests through the Turkish Industry and Business Association (TÜSIAD), was not surprising. The conglomerates expanded in the 1980s by entering into export sectors and by acquiring domestic financial intermediaries (Boratav, 2003). A comprehensive capital account liberalization posed the risk of an appreciation in the Turkish lira, which would hurt the competitiveness of Turkish exports. Furthermore, capital account liberalization could attract foreign investment in the domestic financial sector, which meant intensified competition and potential loss of market share for the large conglomerates. Thus, the aftermath of the announcement of the economic reform package was nothing short of open warfare between various chambers of industry, business interest associations, and the MP government.

The most vocal opposition to the capital account liberalization reforms came from Cem Boyner, the president of the TÜSIAD, accusing the government of lacking rationality and credibility in its economic administration.[33] Boyner expressed concerns about the risk of capital flight. Even more importantly, he pointed out that the currency convertibility reforms should be motivated by medium- to long-term consequences and not just short-term concerns.[34] Other important business associations, such as the Union of Chambers and Commodity Exchanges of Turkey (TOBB), also voiced harsh criticism on the timing of the reforms.[35]

Local chambers protested with equal fervor. For example, one of the biggest chambers of industry, the Aegean Region Chamber of Industry, made a declaration on September 3, 1989, deeming the removal of restrictions on capital mobility as "shocking." The declaration emphasized that the decision was premature and surprising in a contracting economy.[36] The reaction of the head of the chamber, Ersin Faralyalı, was especially important, since it shows that the Turkish industrialists were aware of the political calculus that underpinned the capital account reforms. Faralyalı made a declaration a few days after the announcement of the reforms, saying that the government attempted to hide the bankruptcy and indebtedness of the state by giving incentives and opportunities to stimulate consumption.[37] On August 21, 1989, eight prominent business and industry associations, under the leadership of TOBB and TÜSIAD, made a joint declaration. The declaration emphasized that (1) the reform package and the currency convertibility decision were of a political nature rather than an economic one, and (2) building support for Özal's presidency through increased consumption and short-term foreign exchange abundance was the main motivating factor for enacting such reforms.[38]

33 *Cumhuriyet*, August 14, 1989.
34 *Cumhuriyet*, August 10, 1989.
35 *Cumhuriyet*, August 10, 1989.
36 *Cumhuriyet*, September 3, 1989.
37 *Cumhuriyet*, August 10, 1989.
38 *Cumhuriyet*, August 22, 1989.

It should be observed that the government and the economic bureaucracy were equally hostile toward industrialists and their associations. The Treasury Undersecretary Namık Kemal Kılıç gave a declaration on August 27, accusing Turkish businessmen of loving "to weep and whine."[39] Similarly, Prime Minister Özal issued ostensible warnings to business associations on multiple occasions following the criticisms concerning the economic reform package.[40] Such confrontation with the most powerful segments of the Turkish capitalists indicates the government's determination to pursue capital account liberalization, even at the expense of inflicting damage on its relations with the capitalist class.

Epilogue: neoliberal rent distribution

There is a consensus among various scholars that 1989 was a turning point for the Turkish economy (Demir, 2004; Balkan and Yeldan, 1998; Cizre-Sakallıoğlu and Yeldan, 2000; Boratav, 2003; Kazgan, 2005; Boratav et al., 2001; Kepenek and Yentürk, 2000). The central characteristic of this period was the increasing dependence of the Turkish economy on short-term capital flows. This economic dependence can be observed through various statistical indicators.

Throughout the 1990s, the external debt to GNP ratio remained around 40 percent (Figure 4.10). However, the share of short-term debt in total external debt rose from 13.76 percent in 1989 to 25.74 percent in 1996. In the same period, domestic debt stock grew disproportionately (Table 4.3). In 1990, the stock of domestic debt stood at 14.4 percent of GNP. In 1996, it rose to 21 percent of GNP. In 2000, before the massive financial crisis of 2001, the domestic debt stock was at 29 percent of the Turkish GNP.

Increasing debt notwithstanding, the subsequent inflow of foreign capital spurred a rapid growth in the early part of the 1990s. This rapid growth was accompanied by the appreciation of the Turkish lira and increasing balance of payments problems. The economy had a major financial crisis in 1994 as a result of a speculative attack on the Turkish lira. As a result, the GDP per capita decreased by 7.2 percent in 1994.[41]

Turkey recovered from the 1994 crisis through austerity measures and a massive depreciation of the Turkish lira that enabled a subsequent rise in export earnings. This process was facilitated, again, by the repression of real wages (Boratav et al., 2001, 325). Turkey's problems with high inflation (consistently on or above 70–80 percent plateau in this period), a sizeable gap between exports and imports, and increasing domestic and foreign indebtedness continued in the post-1994 period. The growth rate decreased to 3.7 percent between 1988 and 2000 (Ertuğrul and Selçuk, 2001, 8–9).

Thus, a vicious cycle characterized the Turkish economy after the capital account liberalization in 1989. This cycle started with short-term capital inflows that were employed in financing imports and public deficits. It in turn led to a

39 *Cumhuriyet*, August 28, 1989.
40 *Cumhuriyet*, August 15, 17 1989.
41 World Development Indicators, World Bank.

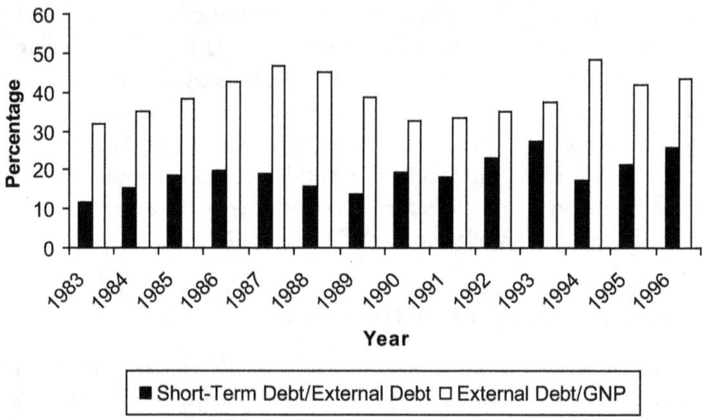

Figure 4.10 Short-Term Debt, 1983–96.
Source: Turkish Statistical Institute (2003, Table 20.8).

Table 4.3 Domestic Debt and Its Components as percentage of GNP, 1990–2000†

Year	*Bonds*[a]	*Bills*[b]	*Domestic Debt Stock*[c]
1990	4.7	1.4	14.4
1991	3.8	2.9	15.4
1992	7.8	3.8	17.6
1993	9.5	3.2	17.9
1994	6.2	7.8	20.6
1995	6.5	8.0	17.3
1996	8.3	10.2	21.0
1997	12.1	8.1	21.4
1998	10.8	10.9	21.7
1999	25.1	4.1	29.3
2000	27.4	1.6	29.0

† Source: Turkish Statistical Institute (2003, Table 20.9).
a Government bonds as share of GNP.
b Treasury bills as share of GNP.
c Domestic debt stock as share of GNP.

rise in interest rates and currency appreciation, which attracted more short-term capital inflows. As a result of this cycle, the economy's stability became vulnerable to market players' expectations about the country's ability to pay its debts. The 1994 financial crisis in Turkey occurred after such a cycle and the ensuing confidence crisis, triggered by the downward revision of Turkey's credit-rating. As summarized by Boratav et al. (2001, 326), the Turkish economy kept on this path in the 1990s:

> High interest rates gave way to inflationary pressures through increased costs of credit; and fed speculative rentier type of accumulation with consequent worsening of income distribution. The limits of this bonanza of 'short-term

> foreign capital-led growth pattern' was the eruption of the financial crisis in 1994 and the continued fragility and severe disequilibria that the domestic markets had to face in the late 1990s.

This vicious cycle also fed the growing indebtedness of the Turkish economy. As a result, the 1990s can be seen as the decade during which the Turkish economy sank into a debt trap (Demir, 2004, 853). The main characteristic of the debt trap was that the creation of domestic and foreign debt became independent of real economic activities. The ostensible sign of this independence was the decoupling of capital account transactions from current account transactions. In other words, capital inflows to and outflows from Turkey reached a volume that could not be explained by the financing of movement of goods and services (Boratav, 2003, 183).

In fact, the freshly created debt during the 1990s carried the purpose of rolling over the existing stock of debt, i.e., the rollover of public debt through short-term private sector borrowing from the rest of the world. In other words, the Turkish economy utilized capital flows from the rest of the world to finance interest and principal payments on its stock of debt (Boratav, 2003; Demir, 2004; Cizre-Sakallıoğlu and Yeldan, 2000).

The private sector (i.e., the banking sector, owned by big conglomerates) acted as the intermediary between the international markets and public sector borrowing. Such an intermediation provided high arbitrage profits (Demir, 2004, 855). Boratav (2003, 194) estimates the real arbitrage revenue to be 25.4 percent in 1998 and 29.8 percent in 1999.

The above-sketched structural transformation in the Turkish economy had two consequences. First, the banking and finance sector emerged as the most profitable and hegemonic sector in the Turkish economy. The Turkish banking and finance sector also stopped carrying the main function of financial intermediation, the mobilization of funds to finance investment and real economic activity. As Cizre-Sakallıoğlu and Yeldan (2000, 486) remark, "Throughout this period, Turkey's banking and financial institutions were disengaging from production to become the dominant forces behind the capital manipulating the economy."

Second, the Turkish industry and commerce began obtaining their net revenues increasingly from financial operations rather than the production of goods and services. This transformation harked back to the 1980s, during which the revenue structure of the big businesses in Turkey moved from real economic activities to financial operations.[42] For the period between 1997 and 2001, the proportion of value-added accruing from interest-bearing financial transactions reached 45 percent of the total value-added of top 500 industrial companies (Boratav, 2003, 197). Accordingly, the industrial production and investment in Turkey plummeted after 1989.

These two aspects—the hegemony of finance capital, the disconnect between real and financial economic activities, and the increasing share of profits obtained

42 *Cumhuriyet*, August 25, 1989.

from financial transactions—can be characterized as the financialization of economic life (Krippner, 2005) after capital account liberalization. However, in an emerging economy like Turkey, a vicious debt trap accompanied the financialization of economic life. As such, the financialization of the economy and growing dependence on short-term capital flows led the Turkish economy to move away from industrialization and sustainable economic growth. Instead, commerce and finance emerged as the dominant and profitable sectors.

As discussed in previous sections, the increasing public sector borrowing under high inflation and high interest rates constitutes a regressive income distribution mechanism. In other words, the state transfers its tax revenue to the business sector through high interest payments. The tax structure of the Turkish economy moved from direct to indirect taxes under the MP governments. This implied that, in the Turkish context, the state took money from wage-earners, farmers, and fixed-income social groups, and transferred it to the big business groups that controlled and owned the banking sector. This mechanism of regressive income transfer through the public sector constituted a form of rent distribution in Turkey. The rents accrued from public sector borrowing enabled the banking sector and the conglomerates that controlled them to become the most powerful economic actors in the Turkish economy. Crucially, the engine of such rent distribution was the uncontrolled movement of capital flows in and out of the country.

Anne Krueger, in her classic article (1974), sees the state-imposed restrictions on economic activity, such as international trade, as the source of rent seeking in society. Curiously, the Turkish capital account liberalization shows how liberalization under unfavorable conditions could lead to rent distribution in society. The rent distribution illustrated above is different from the rent-seeking that Krueger (1974) describes, because the primary allocation mechanism is the market and not the state. However, the movement from the state to the market does not change the injustice involved in the allocation of rents in society. The Turkish case is a poignant example of how uncontrolled capital account liberalization could lead to such rent distribution.

Conclusion

This chapter analyzed the 1989 capital account reforms in Turkey; it outlined how distributional pressures between 1987 and 1989 were the most important determinants of the MP's decision to liberalize cross-border capital flows. A clear political calculus, as highlighted in the previous pages, underlay the institutional change that culminated in the 1989 capital account reforms. However, the political dynamics that led to the reforms were a continuation of the distributional struggles that took shape under the import substitution industrialization of the 1960s and 1970s.

1980 was a crucial turning point in these distributional struggles, as the liberalization reforms that the Demirel government implemented under a severe balance of payments crisis set the course of the Turkish economy in subsequent decades.

The Turkish economic bureaucracy, under the leadership of Turgut Özal—first as the economy czar under Demirel government and the military regime and later as the leader of the MP—liberalized domestic markets in a gradual fashion. That being said, reforms were not carried out in a consistent manner. The liberalization process involved many mistakes, including a haphazard interest rate reform that led to the collapse of financial markets in 1982. Nevertheless, the Turkish economy grew rapidly in the 1980s.

A number of factors underlay the economic growth in this period. Wages were repressed, which ensured high profitability. Exports surged with trade liberalization. The public sector initiated an exceptional increase in infrastructure investment. However, the economic growth was not sustainable. The government financed state infrastructure investment through foreign and domestic debt. As a result, Turkish public finances deteriorated in the 1980s. The export industry utilized the excess capacity built in the previous era of import substitution industrialization, but did not invest further in productive capacity. In 1988, the rapid economic growth came to a halt and inflation doubled. Since the MP owed its political power to rapid growth, political repression, and high levels of public spending, these economic developments presented a challenge to the government. It was this conundrum that set the stage for the capital account liberalization reforms in 1989.

The MP's dominant position in Turkish politics faced significant challenges beginning in 1987, as the leaders of the previous era returned to politics. The rapid economic growth turned out to lack a solid base. The Turkish economy became increasingly unstable in 1988. The public sector borrowing, which contributed greatly to the economic growth in the 1980s, reached an unprecedented percentage of the Turkish GDP. The result was an increasing public sector borrowing requirement in an economy with high inflation and low economic dynamism. At the same time, workers and farmers began to recover from a decade-long repression. The MP government reacted to these pressures by implementing expansionary policies, which further stimulated the already high levels of inflation and debt stock. It was under these conditions that the MP and Prime Minister Özal embraced capital mobility, apparently with the hope of relaxing restrictions on external borrowing and stimulating economic growth. The political calculus of Prime Minister Özal was linked to immediate electoral risks and his future electability as the president of the republic.

The Turkish case is an example of how financial opening due to severe distributional pressures can lead to long-term adverse consequences. The comprehensive capital account liberalization in Turkey did not distinguish between different types of capital flows. The subsequent course of the Turkish economy brings to light the substantial risks that this approach entails. The Turkish economy became dependent on external capital flows—especially the short-term variety—during the 1990s. Such dependence carried costs. Within a span of 13 years, the Turkish economy experienced two massive financial crises that were directly linked to short-term capital flows. The 1990s were the lost decade of Turkey. The capital account liberalization in 1989 was an important factor that led to this outcome.

5 Conclusion

As seen in Chile, South Korea, and Turkey, financial opening—partial or complete—links these economies inexorably to the world financial markets. The free flow of finance capital empowers certain social classes, strengthens the structural power of the finance sector in the economy, and constrains the state's ability to shape economic policies.

The increasing freedom of international capital flows has some striking similarities to one of its predecessors, the Gold Standard under the orthodox liberalism of the nineteenth century. A strong commitment to currency and exchange rate stability characterized the Gold Standard (Eichengreen, 1996). Such commitment and stability were not costless; they imposed strict limitations on the use of monetary policy to affect domestic outcome and employment. The costs of this system are aptly summarized by Block (2001, xxxi):

> The reality was that the simple rules of the gold standard imposed on people economic costs that were literally unbearable. When a nation's internal price structure diverged from international price levels, the only legitimate means for that country to adjust to the drain of gold reserves was by deflation. This meant allowing its economy to contract until declining wages reduced consumption enough to restore external balance. This implied dramatic declines in wages and farm income, increases in unemployment, and a sharp rise in business and bank failures.

Similar to the Gold Standard, a commitment to financial openness in emerging economies today is also likely to increase inequality. One mechanism through which social inequality increases is the financialization of the economy. As financial openness and integration with the world rise, financial revenues become a greater source of income for those who already own finance capital. Fixed-income classes such as workers do not have access to revenues generated by financial assets (Appendix B). They are thus adversely affected by financial openness. The aftermath of the capital account liberalization in Turkey illustrates this mechanism of rising inequality.

However, financial crises caused by the imprudent opening to global capital flows create even greater social inequality. Financial crises lead to economic contractions where social classes with no accumulated wealth see sudden drops in their income. Furthermore, under such conditions, governments in emerging economies are forced to exercise fiscal discipline and austerity that have additional negative impacts on workers, farmers, and middle classes. The frequency of financial crises following capital account liberalization is a testimony to the severity of this problem. It should be observed that all three cases examined in this study experienced at least one financial crisis related to global capital flows: Chile in 1982, South Korea in 1997, and Turkey in 1994 and 2001.

In a famous article concerned with "the absence of income equalizing international capital flows" (1990, 96), the Nobel laureate economist Robert Lucas asks why capital doesn't flow from rich to poor countries, as neoclassical economic theories of trade and growth predict. The previous chapters have shown that an equally important question is what happens when capital is abundant in the world economy and is eager to flow from rich to poor countries. The problem is that when capital does flow from rich to poor countries, the effects might not be all that pleasant (Appendix C). Motivated by this concern, this book has investigated the politics of international capital flows. The main question I have examined is what are the conditions under which emerging economies embrace international capital mobility. In particular, this book sought to explain why emerging economies embraced risky capital opening by liberalizing the most volatile forms of international capital flows. Such policies—as the analysis of the first episode of Chilean as well as South Korean and Turkish capital account reforms showed—ended in disastrous economic crises.

Thus, international capital mobility warrants close scrutiny, simply because some variant of neoliberalism is, astonishingly, still the reigning paradigm of policy-making in many countries around the world. In neoclassical theories economic forces such as capital flows seem to operate according to a logic of their own, independent of the social, political, and historical context. Hence, this line of thinking presents international capital mobility as a simple issue of economic cost-benefit analysis. One of the main motivations of this book has been to show that even when neoliberalism was at work in shaping capital account reforms, there were crucial structural determinants that created the conditions conducive to institutionalizing capital mobility. The previous chapters have shown that in Chile, South Korea, and Turkey—three crucial emerging economies of the 1980s and 1990s—distributional struggles paved the road to institutional change pertaining to capital mobility. In conclusion, it is worth reexamining the analytical strategy and empirical findings. Such an analysis illuminates the patterns and the comparative conclusions regarding the politics of global capital in emerging economies. It also sheds some light on the broader issues of neoliberalism and the adoption of neoliberal policies.

Interests, ideas, and diffusion

There is no shortage of theories that attempt to explain financial liberalization and capital account opening. In the introductory chapter, I grouped the existing explanations into three broad categories according to the primary causal factors these explanations employ: domestic preferences and interests; ideas, norms, and mental models; and policy diffusion around the world. It is worth reiterating that these explanations capture important elements of capital account reform in the countries examined in this book. But they also miss quite a lot.

Interests and domestic preferences

Studies prioritizing the preferences of various domestic groups in explaining capital account reforms share a common explanatory logic. Regardless of the particular theoretical model adopted (class interests, specific-factors, open economy politics),[1] the expected benefits and losses from international capital mobility become the prime driver of reforms. In the introductory chapter, I showed that these models do not offer a convincing account of capital account reforms in Argentina, despite the fact that the large, oligarchic, and international segment of the Argentine capitalist class had an influence in Menem's neoliberal reforms. Although such influence was a factor, Menem's embrace of capital account convertibility was surprising even to the large economic groups that had the administration's ear in economic policies. In fact, this was a repeated pattern in all the cases examined in this book. Domestic preferences of powerful actors were important factors in shaping the overall neoliberal agenda, but such interests were not sufficient to explain the complex trajectories of capital account reforms in Chile, South Korea, and Turkey.

The first episode of capital account liberalization in Chile occurred between 1977 and 1980. In broad strokes, it had an undeniable class element. The Pinochet regime was anti-communist and had close links to the different segments of the capitalist class. Furthermore, a broad coalition of capitalists had direct input in *el ladrillo*, the document that outlined some of the economic reform agendas of the post-Allende regime. Nonetheless, the link between the preferences of the capitalist coalition that lent its support to the Pinochet regime and capital account reforms was not direct, as opposed to what domestic preference theories suggest. First, such arguments ignore the severe distributional conflicts in the previous decades that created the conditions for the military regime and the rise of the Chicago Boys. Second, more than catering to particular class interests, the Pinochet regime had an immediate interest in economic growth that would legitimize its authoritarian political rule. The fragile boom between 1978 and 1982, which was largely a result of surging capital inflows, provided the legitimacy-granting economic growth that the regime sought.

Among all the cases examined in this book, the Korean liberalization in the early 1990s is the one where domestic preferences and the interests of the most powerful segment of the capitalist class, *chaebols*, played the most direct role in capital account reforms. The *chaebols* had become the engine of Korean economic growth by pursuing expansion through high indebtedness. They followed the same expansionary strategy in the early 1990s and acquired merchant banks that enabled them to access international capital markets. However, putting too much causal weight to *chaebol* preferences ignores several facts. The big corporations' interest in international capital was itself determined by the exhaustion of a

1 I review some of these theories in Appendix B.

growth regime that had relied on repressing wages and domestic consumption. Furthermore, the financial policies that favored the *chaebols* at the expense of domestic savers had provided the much-desired capital for the big corporations. These particular distributional bargains were less and less feasible during the 1980s. They stopped being policy options by the early 1990s, when South Korea established a pluralistic and competitive electoral democracy.

The Turkish capital account reform, in contrast, stands out as a case where political calculations were the prime driver of embracing a comprehensive package of capital account liberalization. Again, it should be emphasized that the liberal reforms of the 1980s found strong support among the various segments of the capitalist class. Furthermore, the Motherland Party's political programme was unabashedly capitalist and globalist. However, the 1989 capital account reforms took even the most ardent supporters of the Motherland Party rule by surprise. To put it simply, a comprehensive capital account liberalization reform was not on any domestic group's agenda.

Ideas

As opposed to accounts emphasizing domestic preferences, where the interests of actors are taken as given, the approaches that emphasize ideas take a constructivist turn to policy-making. The case studies on Chile, South Korea, and Turkey illuminate the extent to which economic and political ideas shape financial opening policies. The first financial opening in Chile, between 1978 and 1982, stands as the case where a particular economic ideology played an important role. The Chicago boys, as a group, shared an unusually coherent set of ideas on how to govern the economy. Motivated by a textbook-style set of stipulations about the efficiency of capital account opening, they did not hesitate to implement a rapid opening to global capital flows. The simplicity and single-mindedness of their economic ideas were exactly what led to the disastrous 1982 financial crisis in Chile. However, the rise of the Chicago boys to power came after a long history of conflictual distribution relations in Chile. It was this long history of class polarization and warfare that created the opportunity structure favorable to the Chicago Boys' radical neoliberalism.

In Turkey too, economic and political liberalism was a contributing factor to the process of financial liberalization. However, in the case of Turkey, the role of ideology was minor compared to the first financial opening episode in Chile. It is true that, in rhetoric and broad orientation, Turgut Özal and the Motherland Party embraced the ideas of liberalism. However, in practice, their liberal ideas were inconsistent. The policies implemented under the Motherland Party governments often contradicted the basic tenets of liberalism. Rather than being shaped by a coherent ideology, these policies were the product of pragmatism, populism, and frequent recourse into political opportunism. The 1989 capital account liberalization was not an exception to this pattern. The roots of the capital account reform lay in Özal's electoral calculations in an increasingly competitive political environment and mounting distributional pressures.

In the case of South Korea, neoliberal economic ideas gained ground as a new generation of economists, trained in the United States, rose to prominence under the Chun Doo-hwan governments. Their recommendations shaped economic policy-making particularly in the early 1980s. However, the traditionalists in the Korean economic bureaucracy continued to dominate policy-making after the initial foray into economic liberalization. One of the underlying reasons for the brief and inconclusive flirtation of the Chun Do-hwan regime with liberal policies was that Chun Doo-hwan was an ally of liberalization to the extent that liberal economic reforms legitimized his highly unpopular rule. Chun Doo-hwan sought to legitimize his rule through economic reforms that would benefit the social classes that were neglected under the Park Chung Hee regime. However, even this semi-populist turn in policy-making was not sufficient for pushing a comprehensive financial liberalization agenda, as evidenced by the internal struggles within Korean economic bureaucracy and by how the *chaebols* blocked ambitious reforms of interest rate deregulation.

Policy diffusion

Policy diffusion denotes a process where "the decision to liberalize (or restrict) by some governments influences the choices made by others" (Simmons and Elkins, 2004, 171–72). The novelty in this approach lies in seeing the liberalization decisions of governments as resulting from interdependence among different countries. As a consequence, policy diffusion is distinguished from processes such as different governments responding similarly to common phenomena (Simmons and Elkins, 2004). A number of mechanisms can be identified as causes of policy diffusion. Dobbin et al. (2007) distinguish four: social construction, learning, coercion, and competition. In the cases examined in this book, there is no doubt that these mechanisms were at work in shaping the momentum toward the liberalization of cross-border flow of finance capital. Nevertheless, the shortcoming of this approach is that its objective is to explain a common trend, rather than the variation in financial opening policies. Although financial opening was a common trend, there were significant differences among the set of policies implemented in each country. It is not clear how the policy diffusion perspective can explain such variation. That being said, studies that emphasize diffusion are most powerful when they focus on the role of supranational organizations in capital account reforms. Hence, in what follows, I briefly consider the role of supranational organizations in capital account reforms in Turkey and South Korea.

Woods (2006, 5) gives a compelling argument about the power of the IMF and the World Bank over policy-making in emerging and developing economies:

> The persuasive influence of the IMF and World Bank is at its height when dealing with able and willing interlocutors in borrowing governments. Where government officials are sympathetic to the policies prescribed by the Fund and Bank, and where these officials enjoy power and authority to implement such policies, the Fund and Bank will succeed. Paradoxically, this success

becomes more and more difficult as policy-making is opened up to greater number of participants, more interest groups, and further debates.

The case studies on Turkey and South Korea confirm this argument. The Turkish economic liberalization in 1980 is a clear example of the IMF and the World Bank exercising decisive influence with the help of sympathetic policy-makers. The Turkish economy was severely depressed and in dire need of external finance in the late 1970s. Under these conditions, Turgut Özal implemented a structural adjustment program with the support of the IMF and the World Bank, which supplied the much-needed financing. The military intervention in September 1980 strengthened the IMF-supported liberalization program by abolishing political participation and repressing all political dissent. However, despite their influence on the 1980 liberalization reforms, the IMF and the World Bank did not play much of a role in the 1989 capital account liberalization.

The role of supranational organizations was strongest in the case of South Korean capital account reforms. It is the case that the U.S. pressure on capital account opening and the prospect of the OECD membership accelerated capital account liberalization reforms in Korea. However, as discussed in Chapter 3, the main impetus behind capital account liberalization was largely domestic. The exhaustion of a rapid growth regime—a growth regime that relied on particular distribution relations—prepared the stage for the Korean capital account reforms in the early 1990s. Furthermore, the domestic distributional struggles over interest rate deregulation and external financing determined the pace and style of Korean financial opening. Korean authorities resisted the particular capital account reforms prescribed by the OECD. The existing evidence indicates that the Korean economic bureaucracy (1) was fully aware of the risks created by capital account liberalization, and (2) successfully resisted the pressure by the supranational organizations for rapid liberalization. What the Korean economic bureacuracy could not contain was the pressure by the *chaebols* for tapping into international financial markets through merchant banks.

Distribution relations, neoliberalism, and institutional change

The main argument in this book has been that distribution relations play a fundamental role in shaping the trajectories of capital account reforms in emerging economies. In particular, I have suggested that a high degree of distributional conflict makes it much more likely that a country embraces international capital mobility in a comprehensive manner or in a way that prioritizes portfolio and debt flows. The comparative-historical analysis in this book has focused on three countries—Chile, South Korea, and Turkey—to test these arguments. This set of countries have been chosen to ensure that they vary in the degree of distributional conflict and in the historical patterns of distribution relations. Furthermore, the case selection aimed to avoid the evident regional clustering in the timing and type of capital account liberalization (Figure 1.5). Starting from a theoretical framework that conceptualizes economic relations and prices as distribution-laden, I argued that conflictual distribution relations erode existing institutions. I highlighted multiple mechanisms through which institutional erosion might occur (Table 1.1). I proposed that institutional erosion through distributional struggles is likely to be much more severe in contexts where economic growth is anemic. In such a context, international capital mobility becomes a much more viable option for policy reform and institutional change, simply because capital inflows and integration with global finance offer an easy way to enlarge the domestic economic pie.

The in-depth case studies in this book provide strong support for these arguments. Furthermore, the comparative-historical examination in this book reveals causal patterns that are difficult to pinpoint through cross-country quantitative and individual case studies. In all the cases that this book examines, distribution relations had a profound effect on the trajectory of capital account liberalization. In each episode investigated in this book, distribution relations set the stage for the preponderance of a different causal mechanism that shaped capital account reforms. Ideology clearly played a significant role in the first episode of Chilean liberalization, but what made the radical views of the Chicago Boys effective was a country mired in weak growth and prolonged distributional struggles. Notably, it was the redistributive agenda of the Aylwin administration and strong growth that enabled the Chilean authorities to curb capital inflows. In South Korea, the erosion of the existing growth regime, the changing balance of power between state and big corporations, and the rise of distributional demands by long-repressed groups created the conditions favorable to the liberalization of the most volatile forms of capital inflows. In Turkey, the political drive for the rapid expansion of the economy under rising distributional pressures led to a comprehensive capital account reform.

Neoliberalism is a broad ideology that sanctifies the market as a coordination mechanism (Polanyi, 1968). In its extreme versions, the optimality of the market as a coordination mechanism is taken as an article of faith (Lepage, 1978; Mudge, 2008). As such, neoliberalism is often a form of market fundamentalism, despite its variegated forms (Block and Somers, 2014; Mann, 2012; Brenner et al., 2010). A voluminous literature examines neoliberalism. However, what is often missing in the literature on neoliberalism is that its distributive power is the key to understanding its origins as well as its continuing efficacy as an ideology. A recent body of work goes a long way in addressing this lacuna in the literature on neoliberalism (Hung and Thompson, 2016; Fourcade-Gourinchas and Babb, 2002; Martin, 2008; Krippner, 2011; Prasad, 2012). For instance, Mann (2012, 129) argues that "neoliberalism has endured ... because of its distributive power, which has been exercised on behalf of powerful classes and nations over the less powerful." One of the main objectives of this book has been to show that not only the persistence but also the origins of neoliberalism lies in distribution relations.

Distribution relations are important for explaining the origins and persistence of neoliberalism because such relations link factors underlying neoliberalism to institutional change that culminates in neoliberal policies. Chorev (2010) categorizes accounts on the origins of neoliberalism with the help of two analytical dimensions: (1) domestic versus global factors, and (2) political actors versus institutional factors. The existing explanations of capital account reforms (Chapter 1) can easily be mapped to a Cartesian coordinate system where the axes are the analytical dimensions that Chorev (2010) identifies. For instance, diffusion explanations emphasizing the role of supranational organizations employ global and institutional factors in accounting for the origins of neoliberalism.

The theoretical framework I advance in this book is useful precisely because it bridges the analytical divides found in the literature on neoliberalism. The case studies in this book show that the causal efficacy of global factors such as the IMF pressure depends on domestic factors. For instance, the Korean capital account liberalization in the early 1990s is a poignant example of how the politics of distribution mediates global factors. Likewise, the dichotomy of political actors versus institutional factors can also be bridged when distribution relations are taken into account. Political actors mobilize institutional factors and become effective in steering institutional change when distributional struggles create the opportunity structures that skillful actors exploit. The Chilean capital account liberalization between 1978 and 1982, during which the Chicago Boys had the Pinochet regime's support to implement their neoliberal ideas, starkly illustrates the link between political actors and institutional change.

The key to this theoretical framework is the proposition that in a capitalist market economy all prices are distribution-laden. This is a framework inspired by a theoretical tradition that goes back to classical political economy (Roncaglia, 2006). In particular, this theoretical framework rests on the Sraffian analysis of prices as determined by power struggles and institutional factors—factors that are distinct from economic determinants such as technique of production (Sraffa, 1926, 1960; Garegnani, 1984; Roncaglia, 2009). Such a proposition is not foreign to the sociological tradition that guided this book but it contains a radical insight that receives scant attention in the current social-scientific analysis of economic transformations (cf. Beckert 2011 and Çalışkan 2010). It suggests that the causal arrow goes from distributional dynamics to prices; that struggle over prices are, just as Weber (1978) suggested, power struggles; and, that supply and demand relations scratch only the surface of economic phenomena. Distributional struggles are political struggles that take place in an institutionalized arena. As such, economic transformations and institutional change are causally related to but not determined by economic relations. Political struggles determine the nature and direction of broad economic transformations, and not the other way around.

An institutional change such as capital account reform, which has broad and lasting consequences, is likely when the existing distribution relations are conflictual. The likelihood of institutional change increases if distributional conflict takes place in the context of low or non-existing growth. However, it would be a mistake to infer that distributional conflict determines institutional change. The problem is that distributional struggles only create the structural conditions conducive to change. Political action is necessary to turn such potential into institutional change. This is the reason why this book has combined a perspective on distributional struggles with the existing explanations emphasizing ideas, interests, and diffusion. In all the cases I examined, distributional struggles were necessary conditions to produce capital account liberalization. However, by themselves, these struggles were not sufficient to bring about institutional change that culminated in capital mobility across borders.

The causal link between distribution relations and institutional change also highlights why an analytical perspective attentive to distributional dynamics is necessary to explain the origins and persistence of neoliberalism. As Polanyi (2001 [1944]) demonstrated, the market economy emerged not despite political authority but because the state played a crucial role in instituting the market economy. Such institutionalization came about only because the technological and social transformations in previous centuries created the set of actors whose interests were closely aligned with the capitalist market. The trials and tribulations of the market economy in the nineteenth century were inevitably distributional struggles (Dale, 2010, 2016; Mann, 1993). Likewise, the trials of neoliberalism in today's world revolve around distributional struggles in a political context marked by increasing inequality (Mann and Riley, 2007; Mann, 2012; Piketty, 2014). Yet such struggles do not automatically translate into institutional change. Nor is it possible to predict the outcome of distributional struggles without taking into account the complex dynamics in the political arena. In fact, all the cases examined in this book, including Argentina, reveal the complex interplay between class actors, sectoral interests, ideational carriers such as the Chicago Boys, and political calculations. Distribution relations do not determine the outcome of these complex dynamics. But they create the structural conditions that set the parameters of how these different factors interact with each other. Thus, understanding the complex dynamics of distribution relations is a must if the objective is to explain how and why neoliberalism persists and when it is likely to change.

Concluding words

The theoretical and empirical analyses in the previous pages have highlighted the severe dilemma associated with international capital mobility for developing and emerging economies. These countries embrace capital mobility, in principle, for accelerating economic growth and development. However, capital mobility carries severe risks. Ironically, countries that are most vulnerable to international capital flows often end up embracing the most reckless capital account reforms. This book has shed light on this puzzle. It has shown that distribution relations and struggles create the structural conditions that determine the timing and type of capital account reforms. By examining capital account liberalization, a crucial area of neoliberal policies, this book has also advanced a theoretical framework on the causal connection between distribution relations and institutional change. The history of international capital mobility is a sobering tale. The analysis in this book has shown that this tale is inevitably linked to the political and economic struggles between different social actors.

Appendix A
Distribution and economic growth

The theoretical perspective highlighted in Section 1 of the introductory chapter rests on a particular model of economic growth and distribution. As argued in the introduction, the distribution relations between the capitalist and working classes are taken as the most important social relations in determining the trajectory of a capitalist economy over the long run. However, the distribution relations between capitalists and workers over wages and profits do not exhaust the determination of distribution. In fact, I have argued that other distributive variables—such as interest rate, exchange rate, and inflation—can determine the trajectory of a capitalist society at particular historical moments. Nonetheless, given the difficulties of studying the distribution of income based on variables other than wage rate and profit share, the empirical chapters in this book opt to illustrate the basic contours of distributional struggles through the historical trajectories of wage share, profit rate, labor productivity, and capital productivity. In what follows, I outline the relations between these distributive variables and the dynamics of economic growth. The relations highlighted below underpin the graphical illustrations in Figures 2.1, 2.2, 2.5, 2.6, 3.1, 3.2, 4.1, 4.2, and 4.8.

The exposition in this appendix closely follows Foley and Michl (1999), who provide a framework attentive to the growth and distributional dynamics of capitalist economies with a minimal set of assumptions. Most importantly, these authors deliberately eschew assumptions such as smooth production function that are highly unrealistic and that are, unfortunately, fundamental to neoclassical economic analysis.

In what follows, X denotes the real output, N is the number of employed workers, W is the total wage bill, and K is the capital stock in any given period. Lower-case variables ($x = X/N$, $w = W/N$, and $k = K/N$) denote quantities per worker for each period. x is the output per worker, w is the average real wage, and k is the capital stock per worker. Thus, x measures the average labor productivity in a given period, and its unit is ¥/worker-period, where ¥ denotes an unspecified currency. Measurement of input productivity can be extended to capital as well (Foley and Michl, 1999). Hence, we can define $\rho = X/K = x/k$ as the quantity of output per unit of capital, which measures average capital productivity in a given period. Unlike labor productivity (x), capital productivity (ρ) is a pure number.

To illustrate distribution and growth dynamics in a compact fashion, the distributional dynamics figures in the empirical chapters use two vertical axes simultaneously. The left axis measures data series whose units are in 2005 purchasing power parity (chain index). Thus, real GDP and wage figures are illustrated based on 2005 purchasing power parity. The right axis measures, simultaneously, capital productivity (a pure number), wage share, and profit rate. Collapsing the different scales of capital productivity (a pure number that can exceed 1), wage share (a number between 0 and 1), and profit rate (by converting percentages to a number between 0 and 1) is an abuse of distinct scales. However, it is not ambiguous, and it enables the simultaneous illustration of variables that are closely related to each other.

At the most proximate level, economic growth under capitalism derives from the accumulation of a greater stock of capital. Hence, the trajectory of capitalist development is characterized by rising stock of capital, K, and thus increasing level of capital per worker, k. Because k and ρ are inversely proportional to each other, ρ decreases with economic growth. In contrast, increase in worker productivity accompanies economic growth.

The above sketch is, by necessity, highly simplified. In particular, it says little about how factors such as relative prices, technology, and population growth affect the relationships among growth, labor productivity, and capital productivity. Nonetheless, it gives an invaluable base model to analyze the trajectory of economic development in a particular country, as the association of lower capital productivity and higher labor productivity with economic development is a pattern that has been repeatedly observed across the world in the history of capitalist development (Foley and Michl, 1999, 15).[1]

Now, the economic output in a given period consists of the wage bill of employed workers and the profit that accrues to the owners of capital. Use Z for the total profit in a given period, and $v = Z/K$ for the average profit rate. Note that:

$$vk = \frac{Z}{K}\frac{K}{X} = \frac{Z}{X} \tag{A.1}$$

Thus, vk denotes the average profit per worker.

The wage share in the economy is defined as:

$$\frac{W}{X} = \frac{W}{N}\frac{N}{X} = \frac{w}{x} \tag{A.2}$$

Then, the profit share, π, is defined as:

$$\pi = 1 - \frac{w}{x} \tag{A.3}$$

1 On this point, see the historical analysis of long-term trends of technological change in relation to capital and labor productivities in Marquetti (2003).

By using these definitions, we can express the relations between wage, profit, capital stock, and output per worker as:

$$x = w + vk \tag{A.4}$$

$$w = x - vk \tag{A.5}$$

$$v = \frac{x}{k} - \frac{w}{k} \tag{A.6}$$

We also have the relationship between output, capital stock, and capital productivity:

$$k = \frac{K}{N} = \frac{K}{X}\frac{X}{N} = x\frac{1}{\rho} = \frac{x}{\rho} \tag{A.7}$$

Using Equations A.5 and A.7, we obtain:

$$w = x\left(1 - \frac{v}{\rho}\right) \tag{A.8}$$

Equation A.8 captures the distributional conflict at the heart of capitalist economies. It indicates that the average wage and profit rate are inversely related to each other. However, this inverse relationship is counter-balanced by capital and labor productivities. If we take the profit rate as a constant magnitude, an increase in either labor or capital productivity supports a concomitant increase in the wage rate.

The inherently conflictual relationship between the capitalist and working classes can be better seen by using Equations A.8 and A.6 to obtain the following set of relationships between profit rate, profit share, capital productivity, wage, and output per worker:

$$v = \left(1 - \frac{w}{x}\right)\rho = \pi\rho \tag{A.9}$$

Equation A.9 indicates that, all else being equal, a higher wage rate leads to a lower profit rate and thus a lower profit share. However, the profit share depends not only on the profit rate but also on capital and labor productivities (ρ and x, respectively). Thus, distribution relations under capitalism are not always zero-sum. For instance, a rise in labor productivity can compensate for higher wage rate, leaving average profit rate and the profit share in the economy at the same level. Similarly, rising capital productivity in periods of rapid technological change enables higher wages for a given level of profit share.

Appendix B
Capital mobility and social interests

The emphasis of the dominant interest-based approach in the literature has been to analyze the politics of capital mobility and financial internationalization primarily through the analysis of sectoral cleavages and sectoral economic interests (Frieden, 1991b). The analysis below first gives a summary of the sectoral cleavages analysis of capital mobility and of its predictions regarding the economic interests of various social groups. It then describes how a class-analytic framework can contribute to the sectoral cleavages model.

The well-known economic model underlying the sectoral cleavages analysis (i.e., the specific-sectors model) concerns sectors where the stock of capital is fixed in the short-run and not amenable to various uses (i.e., capital is specific to a certain production technique) while labor is relatively mobile among different sectors (Jones, 1971; Mayer, 1974; Mussa, 1974; Samuelson, 1971). Thus, the sectoral cleavages model finds its analytical warrant in the sector-specificity and the time-fixity of certain factors of production. As Frieden (1991b, 436) puts, "some factors of production are specific to a particular use for at least the short-run." Consequently, the emphasis on sector-specific factors of production draws attention to sectoral interests rather than class interests.

According to this approach, there are two distinct channels through which capital mobility affects economic sectors' interests. The first is the effect of capital mobility on exchange rate. A variation in exchange rate not only has consequences for the price of domestic products in world markets, but it also alters the relative prices of tradable and non-tradable goods in domestic economy. An appreciation (depreciation) of domestic currency lowers (raises) the price of tradables relative to non-tradables, since tradables are—albeit imperfectly—subject to world markets' supply and demand conditions whereas non-tradables are restricted to domestic markets.[1] Thus, an inflow of capital affects tradable goods sectors negatively and non-tradable goods sectors positively, whereas an outflow of capital brings forth the opposite outcome.

A change in the relative prices of goods induces reallocation of labor among sectors and thus raises production in certain sectors. Because of full labor mobility,

1 See Frieden (1991b).

wages equalize among sectors and the effects on workers are ambiguous.[2] However, producers in sectors whose products' prices have risen are unambiguously better off. Thus, as Frieden (1991b, 436) notes, "Changes in the relative prices of goods have their principal effect on the sector-specific producers of the goods, rather than on a whole class of factor-owners."[3]

The second channel is the cost of capital (rental price of capital)[4] in relation to capital mobility. Financial integration with the rest of the world increases the supply of finance capital to developing countries. Thus, assuming that capital is scarce in developing countries and that its price is higher than the rest of the world, the cost of sector-specific capital decreases. The decrease in the cost of capital implies expansion of production for economic sectors that gain access to cheaper finance as a result of financial integration. Which sectors have access to financial resources is not merely an economic problem; it depends on political influence and power, the organization of domestic financial markets, and state structures. However, it can be said that greater financial internalization propagates the alignment of economic interests in line with sectoral competition for increasing supply of finance capital.

It should be noted that while the sectoral cleavages model is powerful in analyzing capital account liberalization around sectoral interests, its implications derive only from two channels (i.e., changes in the relative prices of factors of production and in the real exchange rate). In developing countries, equally important are how domestic asset prices and money supply react to the transfer of foreign funds into the domestic economy. Suppose that capital inflows occur in an environment of limited sterilization policy and managed float (a realistic scenario). The effects of capital inflows in such an economic environment are manifold. First, there is an increase in money demand, due to the following chain of events. As foreign funds flow in, domestic borrowers and foreign investors exchange foreign currency for domestic currency in order to carry out transactions in the domestic economy. Since monetary authority does not sterilize all inflows, it accommodates the rising money demand by creating domestic currency (Calvo et al., 1996, 133).[5] As domestic borrowers and foreign investors acquire domestic assets, the amount of checkable deposits increase. Thus, capital inflows to a developing country raises domestic money supply in the short run (both central bank money and commercial bank money increase). Second,

2 This is because while wages rise, prices of some products rise as well. It is not possible to analyze the effects on workers' real income without knowing their spending baskets.

3 The specific-factors models becomes more accentuated in its demarcation of sectoral interests from class interests under two additional (and more realistic) assumptions: low mobility of skilled workers among sectors and underemployment of unskilled workers. Because under such assumptions economic interests take shape around the expansion or contraction of sectoral production, rather than the increase or decrease of capitalists' or workers' share. Indeed, these assumptions underlie Frieden's (1991b) use of the specific-factors model.

4 Theoretically, interest rate moves in parallel with the cost of capital under the assumption of constant depreciation rate.

5 Otherwise, the increased demand for domestic currency will put pressure on the exchange rate. It is assumed here that the monetary authority prioritizes a stable exchange rate rather than an erratic one.

Table B.1 Stylized Facts on Capital Inflows

	Select Macroeconomic Aggregates		
	Money Supply	*Asset Prices*	*Credit Supply*
Effect of Capital Inflows	Increase	Increase	Increase
Economic Environment	Limited Sterilization, Managed Float		
Mechanism	Money demand increases as a result of inflows. To avoid appreciation of currency, central bank "monetarizes" incoming finance capital.	Increase in money supply raises funds available to economic actors. Residential as well as business investment go up, which puts upward pressure on asset prices.	Economic expansion as a result of capital inflows leads to a surge in banks' liabilities. Some of this liability increase is balanced by expanding and extending credit lines.

domestic asset prices go up because of increased residential and business investment. Finally, as domestic and foreign agents deposit money into bank accounts, the liabilities of banks increase. Accordingly, domestic banks increase their assets in loans and bonds in order to balance their assets and liabilities.[6] This implies that the credit supply, as well as the willingness of domestic financial intermediaries to finance public spending, increases. These stylized facts are summarized in Table B.1.

In light of the above schema, it can be seen that capital mobility has implications not only for economic sectors but for classes as well. The primary mechanisms through which capital mobility affects economic classes' interests are changes in asset prices and credit supply. This is because (1) the distribution of assets follows an economic class pattern, and (2) social agents' endowments of skills, material resources, as well as their relations to productive activities take central stage in claiming access to bank credit.[7]

Assets in which wealth can be accumulated, such as fixed assets (e.g., equipment, land, building) and securities (e.g., common stock, bonds), are unequally distributed in capitalist economies. Propertied classes (capitalists, small and medium-scale employers, and petty-bourgeoisie) own a considerable share of assets in an economy whereas workers and farmers do not have accumulated wealth (and thus assets). On the other hand, the middle class of managers, professionals, experts, and non-manual workers accumulate wealth, even though such accumulation is not comparable to propertied classes' ownership of assets. The

6 It is assumed that the reserve requirement ratio for banks is fixed in the short run. Again, this is a realistic assumption.

7 The class schema utilized here is the one developed by Wright (1979, 1996). However, that schema is extended by employing Huber and Stephens' (2001: 17–18) definition of class-analytic framework.

unequal distribution of wealth in the form of assets implies that the wealth effects due to an increase or decrease in asset prices accrue differently to classes. Consider the case of an increase in asset prices, which reflects the experience of many emerging economies following capital account liberalization. Such increase is detrimental to workers and farmers because it raises their cost of living.[8] While the wealth effect for middle classes is somewhat ambiguous, the upper middle class of managers and professionals benefit from such increase in domestic asset prices.

The impact on propertied classes is more subtle. Capitalists' stock of assets exceeds their working capital, and they have access to a greater set of financing resources (internal and external). Accordingly, they unambiguously benefit from increases in asset prices because their net worth goes up. Small employers and petty bourgeoisie do not own all of their working capital, and they face rental costs arising from the use of equipment, machinery, and buildings. Hence, as asset prices rise, their cost of working capital surpasses the increase in their net worth. The impact on medium-scale employers depends on the balance sheet of the firm in question and is ambiguous. However, given the relative scarcity of working capital and limited venues for internal and external finance for medium-scale employers in emerging economies, the analysis here assumes that an upward movement in asset prices hurts medium-scale employers rather than benefits them.[9]

The other mechanism through which capital account liberalization affects class interests is the credit supply channel. As argued above, capital inflows lead to an increase in banks' liabilities, which in turn boosts the domestic credit supply. The shift in the domestic credit supply is not benign in terms of distributional implications. Given the imperfections in emerging economies' financial markets, domestic banks prefer to lend to economic agents with high net worth. Thus, the surge in domestic credit supply mainly benefits the propertied classes and upper middle classes of managers and professionals, who can utilize their endowments of assets and skills as financial assurance and collateral. Thus, capital inflows not only lower the cost of borrowing for investment purposes but also the cost of consumer loans. An increase in the purchasing power of social classes with access to loans feeds domestic demand and pushes prices of goods and services upward.[10] Since workers and farmers have poor access to credit markets, the upward movement in prices causes a decrease in their real income.

The above economic analysis provides a framework to analyze how capital mobility affects class interests. Table B.2 offers a stylized overview of how capital mobility impacts classes through the channels of asset value and credit supply. Each cell in this table corresponds to the levels of asset value and credit supply that yield the greatest economic benefit to a particular class. It is a fallacy to assume that the economic benefits summarized in Table B.2 would directly correspond to

8 It is assumed that wages are sticky in the short run.

9 Obviously, this assumption should be calibrated in empirical analysis.

10 Demand inflation following capital account liberalization is a frequently observed phenomenon in emerging market countries. See Calvo et al. (1996, 133) for a more detailed discussion.

Table B.2 The Impact of Capital Mobility on Social Classes

		Asset Value	
		Low	*High*
Credit Supply	*Low*	Workers, Farmers	Ø
	High	Small & Medium Scale Enterprises	Capitalists, Big Business

"policy preferences." For instance, big business was an advocate of greater capital mobility in Chile during the first episode of capital account liberalization (Chapter 2), and the policy preference of this particular class in that episode is in line with the framework presented here, given the trajectory of asset prices and credit supply in Chile between 1978 and 1982. Likewise, the *chaebols* in South Korea in the early 1990s advocated for the removal of restrictions on foreign borrowing by certain types of financial intermediaries (Chapter 3). Furthermore, the *chaebols*' desire to utilize foreign funds, either by tapping directly into international capital markets or through domestic financial intermediaries, was a significant factor in their pressure on the Korean government to liberalize certain types of capital inflows. That is again in line with the above theoretical framework. However, the large conglomerates in Turkey opposed capital account liberalization (Chapter 4). The stance of the Turkish large conglomerates was the result of a complex set of factors, some of which were peculiar to the trajectory of economic development in Turkey. For instance, the Motherland Party (MP) governments under Prime Minister Özal rarely consulted with the large conglomerates in shaping economic policies during the 1980s, although the MP rule was unabashedly beneficial to the capitalist class. Yet, another reason for the large conglomerates' opposition to capital account liberalization was their control over the export sector. The simple theoretical framework presented here cannot capture all of these complexities, but it offers a useful set of conceptual tools to simultaneously analyze overlapping—and at times contradictory—sectoral and class interests. As such, the theoretical framework presented in this Appendix forms the backbone of a significant portion of the historical analysis in the empirical chapters.

Appendix C
Perils of capital account liberalization

There are four possible adverse consequences associated with capital account liberalization. The first concerns the allocation of newly acquired funds in the domestic economy. There is now a consensus that the allocation of funds borrowed from the rest of the world has rarely been efficient in developing and emerging market countries. The second relates to monetary policy autonomy. Capital mobility brings important limitations on how domestic monetary policy is conducted. The third adverse consequence is that capital inflows act as an inherent bias against exports. Finally, the fourth deals with the issue of vulnerabilities spurred by the volatile behavior of capital inflows and outflows. This section explains each one of these negative consequences by following the schematic outline in Figure C.1.

In theory, a widening gap between domestic saving and investment—the difference being financed by foreign saving—is beneficial to a developing economy when (1) borrowed funds are channeled into investment and (2) returns on new investment surpass the cost of borrowing from the rest of the world. In other words, foreign borrowing is welfare enhancing only when it is channeled to investment that has a higher rate of return than the world interest rate, as Sachs (1989, 13) aptly remarks in reviewing the experience of developing country borrowing in the 1970s and 1980s. Otherwise, the cost of servicing existing loans should be carried either by a country's own resources or by borrowing fresh loans, which in turn increases the stock of loans and thus the cost of servicing the existing debt (Sachs, 1989, 9–14). The necessity of surpassing the cost of borrowing from the world markets imposes constraints on emerging market countries: borrowed funds should finance investment rather than consumption. This is because while increased consumption raises national income in the short run, such increase does not contribute to the productive capacity of an economy. The irony is that there is a marked tendency in developing and emerging market countries to raise consumption rather than investment following a sudden income increase.

The developing country borrowing in the 1970s and the early 1980s—which eventually led to the debt crisis—was heavily used for consumption spending (Sachs, 1989, 13). Needless to say, such use failed to meet the condition that the return on borrowed funds surpass the world interest rate. Indeed, it was even the case that debt service was performed by using new loans, creating a

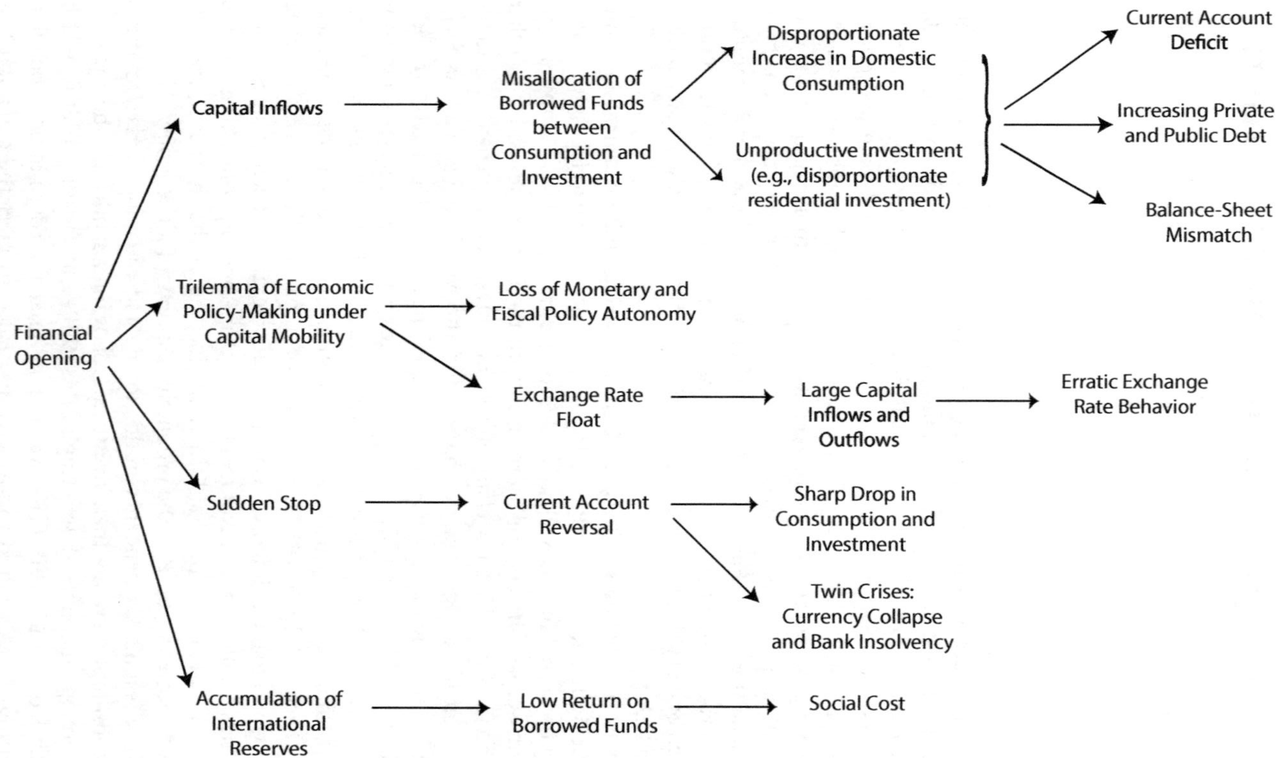

Figure C.1 Risks and Adverse Consequences Associated with Financial Opening.

vicious spiral of increasing indebtedness (Sachs, 1989). What occurred after capital account liberalization in the 1980s and the 1990s was similar to the foreign debt pattern of the 1970s and 1980s. Foreign borrowing in most developing and emerging market countries did not lead to a dramatic upswing in investment. A detailed investigation of the composition of capital inflows (i.e., the respective shares of foreign direct investment, portfolio investment, and loans) for a large panel of developing countries reveals that only foreign direct investment (FDI) was associated with a positive effect on domestic investment (Bosworth et al., 1999). Portfolio investments had no effect on investment; loans had a positive effect on consumption and no significant effect on investment (Bosworth et al., 1999). These are striking findings, considering that more than half of the capital flows to developing countries were in the form of portfolio investment and loans. Instead of being channeled into investment, large inflows to most developing countries were followed by a dramatic increase in bank lending to consumers and an ensuing boom in consumption (Bosworth et al., 1999; Calvo et al., 1994, 1996; Eatwell and Taylor, 2000; Stiglitz, 2000). Contrasting this pattern with the period before 1914 is further illuminating:

> In the earlier prewar period, when nearly 44 per cent of all international long-term lending (including foreign direct investments) went to the regions of Africa, Asia and Latin America, it found its way into the development of railways, port installations, mines and factories (Hoogvelt, 1997, 84).

In conclusion, it is no wonder that the alleged positive link between foreign capital and economic growth in developing and emerging market countries is a dubious one. In testimony to this, Prasad et al. (2007, 165), in one of the most comprehensive and robust analysis of the relationship between foreign capital and growth, reach the following conclusion: "Developing countries that have relied more on foreign finance have not grown faster in the long run, and have typically grown more slowly."[1]

The second adverse consequence of capital mobility is "the trilemma"[2] (Obstfeld and Taylor, 2004) of open economy macroeconomics (Fleming, 1962; Frenkel and Razin, 1987; Mundell, 1960, 1962, 1963; Obstfeld, 2000). A country that is open to the flow of materials, goods, and services can implement only two of the following three macro-policy alternatives: monetary autonomy, exchange rate stability, and capital mobility (Cooper, 1968; Eatwell and Taylor, 2000; Krugman and Obstfeld, 2000, 712–14). This means that if a country implements capital mobility and monetary autonomy (e.g., domestic interest differ from world interest rates), it cannot fix its exchange rate to a predetermined value. The fixed exchange rate will be undermined by investors willing to exploit interest rate differences through speculative finance capital movements. Insisting on

1 In this context, the following observation about domestic saving and investment by Tobin (2000, 1101) is important as well: "Although developing countries have increasingly benefited from inflows of capital, the investments that propelled their growth have been mainly due to their own internal savings."

2 Another term used is "the unholy trinity" (Cohen, 1996, 280).

a fixed exchange rate regime under these circumstances often results in speculative attacks on domestic currency. Similarly, a country can follow the policy of a floating exchange rate and capital mobility. Then, a country adopting these two macro-policies is free in its choice of monetary and fiscal policy. The trade-off is that the divergence between world and domestic interest rates causes capital movements that directly impact the exchange rate level. Hence, a country adopting capital mobility would live with volatile exchange rates if it wants to have maneuver room in monetary policy. Finally, take the case of fixed exchange rates with no capital mobility, which more or less characterized the world after the World War II until the early 1970s. There, the absence of capital flows allowed maintaining exchange rates and monetary and fiscal policy autonomy.

Indeed, as emphasized by Obstfeld and Taylor (2004), each international monetary regime provides a particular solution to the macro-policy trilemma of open economies. For example, under the classic Gold Standard, the value of a national currency was fixed to a certain amount of gold: economic actors could convert their currency assets into gold at a predetermined rate as long as the gold reserves of the monetary authority were sufficient. The rates of exchange among national currencies were fixed. In theory, the flow of gold among nations served as the adjustment mechanism if a currency became over- or under-appreciated. In practice, gold flows were rather rare because the central banks used other instruments to adjust the money supply (Ruggie, 1983). For example, in the case of a payments deficit, central banks increased the discount rate that led to a fall in money supply due to contraction in credit markets. A fall in money supply led to a fall in economic activity and decrease in prices, which in turn increased export competitiveness and caused adjustments in the balance of payments. Overall, countries that adhered to the Gold Standard accepted fixed exchange rates with capital mobility, which deprived them of control over fiscal and monetary policy.[3]

Thus, the policy trilemma for open economies implies that the state's capacity to maintain exchange rate stability and target macroeconomic outcomes through changes in domestic money supply or interest rates decreases proportionally with capital mobility (Andrews, 1994, 204–09). That is a heavy burden on the freedom and efficacy of monetary policy for emerging market countries. In brief, the movement toward adopting greater capital mobility implies that the state's ability to steer economic activity is severely limited for these countries (Grabel, 1996). In the words of Willett (2000, 1), the consensus view is that "high capital mobility is eroding national sovereignty."

The third negative consequence of capital mobility is the effect capital inflows and outflows exert on the volatility and level of exchange rate. Overall, high volatility in the exchange rate is detrimental to the export performance of developing and emerging economies. Furthermore, high volatility negatively affects the investment in tradable-goods sectors in these economies, since such volatility increases uncertainty in these sectors. Various studies confirm this diagnosis.[4] Similarly, the exchange rate is of primary importance in the determination

3 For further detail, see Eichengreen (1996, 25–30) and Obstfeld and Taylor (2004).

4 See Arize et al. (2008) for a review of the literature.

of export-import balance in developing and emerging economies. In this context, the effect of heavy capital inflows is particularly noticeable. These inflows adversely affect the traded/non-traded goods price ratio and lead to currency appreciation in a developing country, hurting its exports and trade balance (Eatwell and Taylor, 2000). Thus, an overvalued exchange rate is an implicit tax on exports even in the absence of tariffs and trade quotas. From the perspective of domestic business, this makes importing more advantageous vis-à-vis exporting (Sachs, 1989, 14). The consequence of a long period of overvalued exchange rate is a shift of investment and economic activity away from exporting to importing. The cumulative effect is an imbalance in the trade pattern, along with a growing trade deficit.

The fourth adverse consequence of capital account liberalization is the potential instability and volatility it creates in emerging market countries. Indeed, after minor and major financial crises beguiled a significant number of emerging economies during the 1990s, capital account liberalization has been associated more with sudden stops, currency attacks, and banking crises than its promises of capital formation and increase in income (Eichengreen and Hausmann, 2005, 3). There are several channels through which foreign borrowing contributes to increased volatility and potential instability in emerging economies. Hence, the following discussion does not aim for comprehensiveness. Rather, it covers the aspects of capital flows that caused most trouble in developing and emerging economies: sudden stops, current account reversals, and the cost of international reserve accumulation.

The most serious forms of potential instability caused by capital flows are associated with two phenomena: sudden stops and current account reversals (Eichengreen and Hausmann, 2005). As defined by Calvo et al. (2006, 405), "A Sudden Stop is a sharp fall in capital inflows relative to their past trajectory." A sudden stop is often triggered by external factors related to international financial markets. Yet, its amplification is propelled by domestic economic vulnerabilities (Calvo et al., 2006). A current account reversal is a sharp drop in the current account deficit (Edwards, 2004, 59). It implies a current account adjustment, often through a significant decrease in imports. In theory, sudden stops and current account reversals might be decoupled. However, they often go hand-in-hand: sudden stops are followed by current account reversals.

In fact, there are only two cases where a current account reversal is decoupled from a sudden stop (Edwards, 2004). One is the case of a country that has received insignificant levels of capital inflows. The other is the case of a country accumulating large foreign exchange reserves (Edwards, 2004). As is well recognized in the literature (Aizenman, 2007; Edwards, 2004; Eichengreen and Hausmann, 2005; Jeanne, 2007; Rodrik, 2006), foreign exchange reserves can act as an effective buffer in the case of a sudden stop. This is because sudden stops cause foreign exchange shortage and liquidity problems that could be alleviated with central bank interventions in the form of supplying foreign exchange to the domestic market. Furthermore, large international reserves act as a signal to domestic and foreign economic actors that the domestic currency is stable and that there is no risk of depreciation (Black et al., 2006).

Foreign exchange reserves can be accumulated through open market operations. In the case of a capital inflow, the central bank purchases foreign exchange from markets at the given exchange rate. As a result, the central bank accumulates foreign exchange reserves. However, such an operation increases the domestic money supply and might lead to inflationary pressures. The increase in the money supply can be neutralized by selling public bonds to domestic markets. This operation is called sterilization. While unsterilized open market operations involve the risk of overheating and inflationary pressures in an economy, sterilization carries the danger of increasing domestic interest rates and depressing domestic investment.

Thus, accumulating reserves is no free lunch (Jeanne, 2007; Rodrik, 2006). Furthermore, as argued by Rodrik (2006, 2), the self-insurance provided by foreign exchange reserves has a social cost that is equal to "the spread between the yield on liquid reserve assets and the external cost of funds." Since foreign exchange reserves are usually invested in short-term U.S. Treasury Bonds, this spread is of considerable magnitude (Rodrik, 2006). For developing nations, Rodrik (2006, 2) estimates the cost of large foreign exchange reserves to be around 1 percent of their GDP.[5]

A sudden stop is significant for developing and emerging market countries because it initiates a chain effect that could reduce output and growth by a considerable margin. Indeed, without measures providing liquidity to the system, a sudden stop leads to the collapse of domestic currency. The currency collapse intensifies the pressure on economic actors who hold debts in foreign currency but revenues in domestic currency. As bad loans and bankruptcy rates increase, the solvency of domestic banks comes into question. Thus, the currency collapse transforms a shock instigated by a sudden stop to twin crises involving currency markets and the banking sector (Kaminsky and Reinhart, 1999).[6] This type of full-fledged financial crisis causes a current account reversal, which might virtually bring an economy into a halt.

The possibility of twin crises following a sudden stop increases with the level of financial openness. Financial openness increases the foreign exchange exposure of financial intermediaries and other economic actors (Kaminsky and Reinhart,

5 Bosworth et al. (1999, 150) echo the same point in their analysis of developing and emerging country borrowing during the 1990s:

> Roughly a third of the inflows have been funneled into reserve assets. The need to hold reserves is a significant concern in evaluating the net benefits of financial inflows, because the return on reserves is typically very low. To offset this low return would require a high private return on the remaining inflows or substantial net externalities.

6 The causal chain between currency and banking crisis is complex, rather than unidirectional (Kaminsky and Reinhart, 1999, 474). However, as Kaminsky and Reinhart (1999, 474) argue, "The collapse of the currency deepens the banking crisis, activating a vicious spiral." Thus, although the analysis here simplifies the causal chain of events, the picture depicted with respect to the effects of sudden stop and current account reversals is accurate.

1999; Kaminsky and Schmukler, 2003). In an environment where financial markets become more complex, the catalyst of a crisis moves away from fundamentals to expectations and investor sentiment, as stressed by the literature on financial crises (Krugman, 1979; Krugman, ed, 2000; Eichengreen, 2003b).

In this context, the episodes of elevated levels of short-term capital inflows are especially relevant to understanding the vulnerabilities created by financial opening. Capital flows with short-term maturity—or no maturity at all, such as flows toward the purchase of publicly traded common stock—have a fundamentally different nature than long-term capital inflows (e.g., foreign direct investment). Instead of providing much-needed funds for domestic industries, short-term capital is seeking arbitrage profits through interest rate spreads between a country and the rest of the world or it seeks to exploit stock market booms. Thus, these types of capital flows are whimsical: they constantly move to the place where there are greater arbitrage profits and smaller risks. Even worse, short-term capital flows to the place where investors ***think*** there are greater profits and less risk. By this token, the movement of short-term capital is often self-fulfilling and self-reinforcing (Grabel, 1996; Eichengreen and Hausmann, 2005) since international investors watch each other even more intensely than they watch market fundamentals.

Yet, short-term capital movements constitute the majority of the gross volume of capital flows.[7] Furthermore, short-term capital flows are highly pro-cyclical. That is to say, they flow in when the economy is expanding and flow out when the economy is contracting. Hence, short-term capital flows amplify the magnitude of economic fluctuations and exacerbate the effects of business cycles. Thus, it is no surprise that volatility caused by financial opening is related to the speculative and pro-cyclical nature of capital flows (Stiglitz, 2000, 2004; Tobin, 2000).

7 Thus, as Tobin (2000, 1101) puts, "The gross volume of foreign capital flows dwarfs the net capital transfers."

Appendix D
Measuring capital account openness

Ideally, the measurement of capital account openness should be as precise as possible, simply because one of the warrants for the present comparative-historical study arises from the weaknesses of the existing approaches in explaining the timing and nature of capital account liberalization in various emerging economies. The problem is that measuring a compound outcome such as capital account openness creates both conceptual and empirical challenges. This appendix outlines my choices regarding the data sources on and measurement of capital account openness.

The most important issue in the empirics of capital account liberalization is concerned with whether measuring legal restrictions on international capital flows is sufficient to capture the degree of capital account openness. In general, it is rarely the case that the legal framework on international capital flows fully corresponds to the degree of actual capital account openness. Legal restrictions on capital mobility might not be enforced to the extent required by law, because state authorities might lack the capacity to enforce the existing restrictions. Furthermore, there are multiple ways through which capital account restrictions can be circumvented, which exacerbates the enforcement problem (De Gregorio et al., 2000; Dooley, 1996; Potchamanawong, 2007). As a consequence, it is customary to make a distinction between *de facto* and *de jure* measures of capital account openness (Fernández et al., 2015). Given that this book focuses primarily on institutional change pertaining to capital account mobility, *de facto* measures of openness are not suitable for examining differences in the timing and type of capital account reforms.

De jure measures of capital account openness predominantly rely on the *Annual Report on Exchange Arrangements and Exchange Restrictions* (AREAER), published by the IMF since 1950. This is not surprising given the difficulties in and the cost of collecting data on a large number of countries with different reporting procedures. Until 1996, the AREAER provided binary variables on restrictions pertaining to both current and capital account transactions. The pre-1996 AREAER data leave much to be desired. First, the AREAER reports restrictions through seven dummy variables: bilateral payment arrangements with members and nonmembers, restrictions on payments for current and capital account transactions, import surcharges, advance import deposits, and surrender or repatriation requirement for export proceeds. Although all of these dummy variables are related to capital account openness, only one of these categories (restrictions on capital account transactions) directly measures controls on capital account transactions. Second, the aggregate nature of the pre-1996 AREAER binary variables ignores the heterogeneity of capital account transactions. International capital flows comprise a vast array of debt, equity, and derivative instruments. As such, these instruments show remarkable variation in maturity, liquidity, and contractual terms they entail. The ideal measurement strategy is one that is sensitive to the heterogeneity of international capital flows (Chinn and Ito, 2008; Lane and Milesi-Ferretti, 2007; Miniane, 2004; Quinn, 1997). Third, the binary coding approach is not sensitive to the intensity and importance of capital account restrictions, as even minor restrictions are sufficient to classify a country as closed to international capital flows. Fourth, the pre-1996 reporting procedures do not make a distinction between capital inflows and outflows.

After 1996, the AREAER started reporting capital account restrictions in 13 subcategories and the new disaggregated dummy variables are sensitive to the distinction between capital inflows and outflows. Such an approach addresses some of the shortcomings of the pre-1996 AREAER data. However, even the new AREAER data do not capture the intensity and importance of different capital account restrictions. Furthermore, as the majority of developing and emerging countries liberalized their capital account in the 1980s and early 1990s, the post-1996 AREAER data are of limited use for examining the historical origins of capital account openness in most emerging economies.

There have been various attempts to develop *de jure* measures of capital account openness that address some of the shortcomings of the AREAER data.[1] Two measures stand out among the publicly available datasets that cover the period before 1996. Miniane (2004) extends the disaggregated analysis of the post-1996 AREAER data to the period before 1996 for a sample of 34 countries. In this effort, he relies on country-specific narratives of policy changes that the AREAER reports. Figure D.1 shows the average of Miniane index for a sample of 12 emerging countries. As opposed to Miniane, Chinn and Ito (2008) measure the average level of openness through a principal component analysis of four binary variables in the AREAER data: the presence of multiple exchange rates, restrictions on current account transactions, restrictions on capital account transactions, and the requirement of the surrender of export proceeds. In particular, Chinn and Ito (2008) use a five-year window in measuring restrictions on capital account transactions.[2] Figure D.2 shows the average of Chinn-Ito index for a sample of 24 emerging countries.

The strength of the Chinn-Ito index follows from "measuring the intensity of capital controls insofar as the intensity is correlated with the existence of other restrictions on international transactions" (2008, 312). A comparison of

1 See Miniane (2004), Potchamanawong (2007), Quinn et al. (2011), and Fernández et al. (2015) for comprehensive overviews of the literature on measuring capital account openness.

2 See Karcher and Steinberg (2013) for an extended discussion of the Chinn-Ito index and the drawbacks of using it for regression analysis.

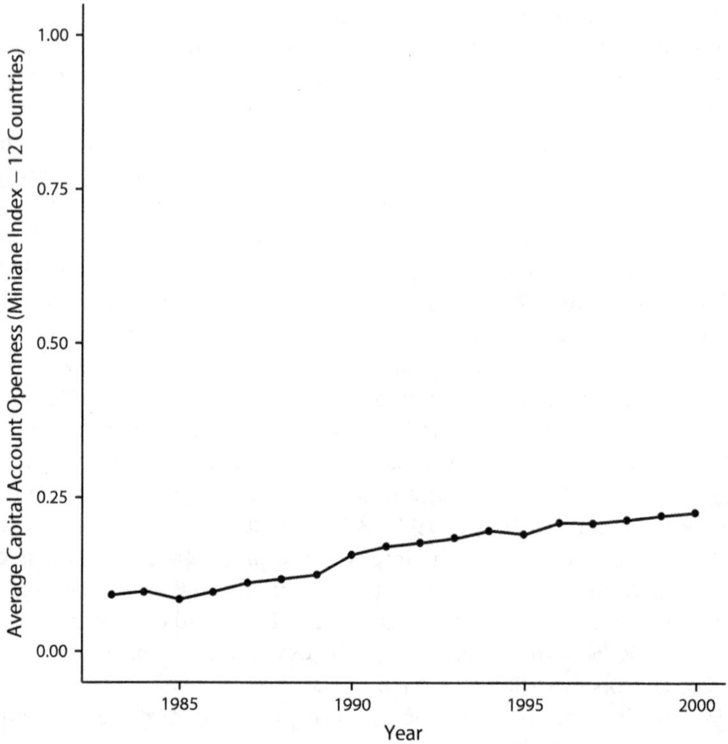

Figure D.1 Average Capital Account Openness, Miniane Index.
Source: Miniane (2004).

the Miniane and Chinn-Ito indices reveal that both of these approaches are able to capture the trend toward greater capital account openness in emerging countries. However, the Chinn-Ito index is much more sensitive to various restrictions on capital account, primarily because the authors make the reasonable assumption that restrictions on capital account transactions are likely to be highly correlated with other types of restrictions pertaining to trade and financial transactions. Such an approach enables them to partially overcome the sparseness of the AREAER data.

Nonetheless, even the Chinn-Ito index cannot fully overcome the shortcomings of the binary AREAER data. This is best seen by examining how the Miniane and Chinn-Ito indices represent the trajectory of individual countries over time. Brazil and India are two emerging countries that implemented significant capital account liberalization reforms in the 1990s. Brazil's capital account liberalization began through modest measures in the late 1980s and accelerated in the early 1990s. In this period, Brazilian authorities relaxed various measures pertaining to FDI, debt, and equity inflows (David, 2007; Goldfajn and Minella, 2005). For instance, Brazil liberalized access to international debt markets, which enabled

Figure D.2 Average Capital Account Openness, Chinn-Ito Index.
Source: Chinn and Ito (2008).

resident institutions to issue instruments such as commercial paper and American Depository Receipts (ADR). Although India's formidable *de jure* control over the capital account remained largely intact in the 1990s, Indian authorities followed a liberalization program that eased the restrictions on current account transaction, foreign exchange, and equity inflows. These reforms were cautious, but they nevertheless led to greater openness to and financial integration with the rest of the world. What is common in these countries' experiences is that some *de jure* restrictions on capital mobility remained in place, despite the fact that the partial liberalization reforms led to greater integration with the global financial system.

It is precisely this aspect of capital account liberalization, the intensity of reforms, that the AREAER data-based measures are not capable to fully capture. The Miniane index (Figure D.3) for Brazil and India either fails to capture capital account liberalization episodes or shows very modest liberalization. The Chinn-Ito index, shown in Figure D.4, is much more successful in capturing Brazil's capital account liberalization in the 1990s. However, the Chinn-Ito index barely registers other cases of capital account liberalization such as India and South Africa.

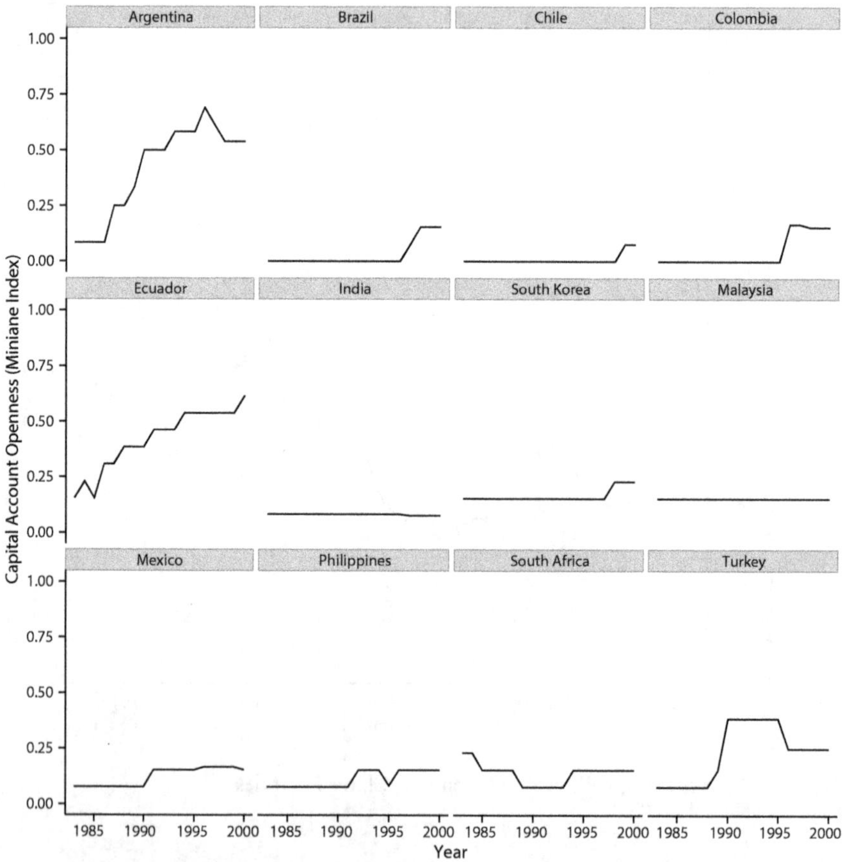

Figure D.3 Capital Account Liberalization in 12 Emerging Countries, Miniane Index.
Source: Miniane (2004).

Because of the limitations of the existing *de jure* indices based on the AREAER data, it is much more preferable to measure capital account liberalization by examining both the intensity and scope of the relevant reforms. This is precisely what Abiad et al. (2010) offer. These authors use several sources to measure the extent and timing of capital account liberalization in 91 countries between 1973 and 2005. Their measure is an aggregate of three components: whether or not the exchange rate system is unified, whether capital inflows are free and banks can borrow from abroad with minimal restrictions, and whether capital outflows are free or subject to minimal restrictions. A country is classified as fully liberalized if it scores positive on all three components, largely liberalized if it scores positive on two components, partially repressed if it scores positive on a single component, and fully repressed if it scores a zero in all three components (Abiad et al., 2010, 298).

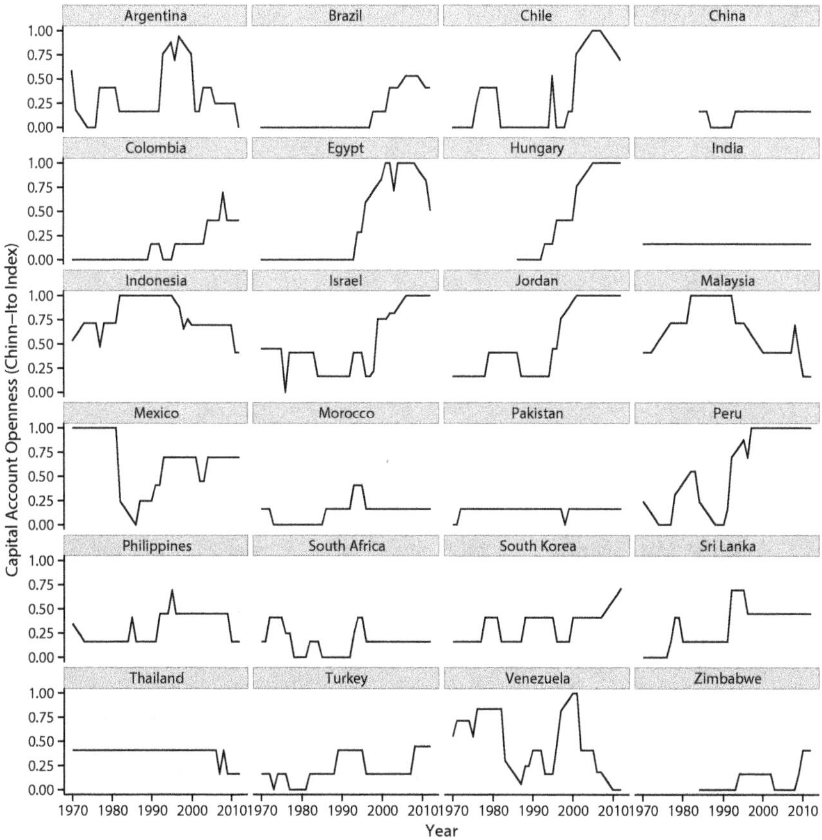

Figure D.4 Capital Account Liberalization in 24 Emerging Countries, Chinn-Ito Index. Source: Chinn and Ito (2008).

From a substantive standpoint, the Abiad et al. (2010) approach to measuring capital account liberalization is on much more solid footing. The reason is that the authors focus on aspects of capital account liberalization that are most likely to impact *de facto* integration with the rest of the world. The advantages of such measurement can be observed by comparing the Abiad et al. index (Figure 1.2) with Miniane and Chinn-Ito indices (Figures D.3 and D.4). Unlike the Miniane and Chinn-Ito indices, the Abiad et al. index captures capital account liberalization reforms in difficult cases such as India, Thailand, and Turkey. For instance, although the Chilean capital account liberalization in the second half of the 1970s led to substantial financial integration with the rest of the world, it barely registers in Miniane and Chinn-Ito indices. In contrast, the Abiad et al. index shows that Chile implemented effective capital account reforms in this period. Hence, in this book, the investigation of overall trends and the case selection procedure relies on the Abiad et al. (2010) data.

Appendix E
List of interviewees

Chile

1. De Gregorio Rebeco, José Fernando. Former Minister of Finance, Vice-President of the Central Bank.
2. Desormeaux Jiménez, Jorge. Member of the Central Bank Board.
3. Ffrench-Davis Múñoz, Ricardo. Economist, former Head of the Research Division, the Central Bank.
4. García Silva, Pablo. Head of the Financial Policy Division, the Central Bank.
5. Lagos Escobar, Ricardo Froilán. President of Chile from 2000 to 2006.
6. Le Fort Varela, Guillermo. Economist, former Member of the Research Division, the Central Bank.
7. Massad Abud, Carlos Alberto. Former Governor of the Central Bank.
8. Marfán Lewis, Manuel. Former Minister of Finance, Member of the Central Bank Board.
9. Piñera Echenique, Juan Pablo Bernardino. Former Member of the Central Bank Board.
10. Valdés Pulido, Rodrigo Osvaldo. Head of the Research Division, the Central Bank.
11. Zahler Mayanz, Roberto. Former Governor of the Central Bank.

South Korea

1. Choi Gong-Pil. Economist, Korea Institute of Finance.
2. Chung Duck-Koo. Former Minister of Finance.
3. Il SaKong. Former Minister of Finance.

4. Kang Kyong-Shik. Former Minister of Finance.
5. Kim Tae-Dong. Former Chairman of the Presidential Committee on Policy Planning, former member of the Monetary Policy Committee.
6. Kwon Tae-Kyun. Deputy Minister, Commissioner of the Financial Intelligence Unit.
7. Park Se-Il. Former Senior Secretary, the Presidential Office of the Republic of Korea.
8. You Jong-Il. Economist, Korea Development Institute.

Turkey

1. Canevi, Yavuz. Former Governor of the Central Bank, former Undersecretary of the Treasury.
2. Çakmaklı, Cemil. Economist, former Member of Parliament.
3. Çelebi, Işın. Economist, former Minister of the Treasury.
4. Demiralp, Selçuk. Former Undersecretary of the Treasury.
5. Doğan, Hüsnü. Former Minister of Agriculture and Forestry, former Minister of Defense.
6. Erçel, Gazi. Former Governor of the Central Bank.
7. Erdem, Kaya. Former Minister of Finance, former Vice Prime Minister.
8. Kılavuz, Hasan. Former CEO of Vakıfbank.
9. Oral, Sümer. Former Minister of Finance.
10. Özdemir, Biltekin. Former Undersecretary of Finance.
11. Pakdemirli, Ekrem. Former Minister of Finance.
12. Saygılıoğlu, Nevzat. Former Head of the Revenues Department of the Ministry of Finance.
13. Şıklar, Osman. Former Governor of the Central Bank.
14. Taner, Güneş. Former Minister of the Treasury.
15. Temizel, Zekeriya. Former Minister of Finance.
16. Tiğrel, Ali. Former Head of the State Planning Organization.
17. Uluğbay, Hikmet. Economist. Former Minister of the Treasury, former Vice Prime Minister.
18. Yıldırım, Zekeriya. Former Vice-President of the Central Bank, former Minister of Finance.

Bibliography

Abdelal, Rawi. 2007. *Capital Rules: The Construction of Global Finance*. Cambridge, MA: Harvard University Press.

Abiad, Abdul, Enrica Detragiache, and Thierry Tressel. 2010. "A New Database of Financial Reforms." *IMF Staff Papers* 57(2): 281–302.

Acuña, Carlos H. 1994. "Politics and Economics in the Argentina of the Nineties (Or, Why the Future No Longer Is What It Used to Be)." Pp. 31–73 in *Democracy, Markets, and Structural Reform in Latin America*, edited by William C. Smith, Carlos H. Acuña, and Eduardo A. Gamarra. New Brunswick, NJ: Transaction.

Agosin, Manuel R. 1998. "Capital Inflows and Investment Performance: Chile in the 1990s." Pp. 111–46 in *Capital Flows and Investment Performance: Lessons from Latin America*, edited by Ricardo Ffrench-Davis and Helmut Reisen. Paris, France: OECD.

———. 1999. "Trade and Growth in Chile." *CEPAL Review* 68: 79–100.

———. 2001. "Korea and Taiwan in the Financial Crisis." Pp. 38–64 in *Financial Crises in "Successful" Emerging Economies*, edited by Ricardo Ffrench-Davis. Washington, DC: Brookings Institution Press.

Ahmad, Feroz. 1977. *The Turkish Experiment in Democracy, 1950–1975*. Boulder, CO: Westview Press.

Aizenman, Joshua. 2007. "Large Hoarding of International Reserves and the Emerging Global Economic Architecture." *NBER Working Paper No. 13277*.

Akçay, Ümit. 2007. *Kapitalizmi Planlamak Türkiye'de Planlama ve DPT'nin Dönüşümü*. İstanbul, Turkey: Sosyal Araştırmalar Vakfi.

Aktan, Reşat. 1966. "Problems of Land Reform in Turkey." *Middle East Journal* 20(3): 317–34.

Akyaz, Doğan. 2002. *Askeri Müdahalelerin Orduya Etkisi*. İstanbul, Turkey: İletişim.

Akyüz, Yılmaz. 1990. "Financial System and Policies in Turkey in the 1980s." Pp. 98–131 in *The Political Economy of Turkey: Debt, Adjustment and Sustainability*, edited by Tosun Arıcanlı and Dani Rodrik. London, UK: MacMillan.

Alchian, Armen A. 1950. "Uncertainty, Evolution, and Economic Theory." *Journal of Political Economy* 58(3): 211–21.

Alderson, Arthur S. and François Nielsen. 2002. "Globalization and the Great U-Turn: Income Inequality Trends in 16 OECD Countries." *American Journal of Sociology* 107: 1244–99.

Amsden, Alice H. 1989. *Asia's Next Giant: South Korea and Late Industrialization*. New York, NY: Oxford University Press.

———. 1990a. "East Asia's Challenge to Standard Economics." *American Prospect* 1(2): 71–77.

———. 1990b. "Third World Industrialization: 'Global Fordism' or a New Model?" *New Left Review* 182: 3–31.

———. 2001. *Rise of "The Rest": Challenges to the West from Late-Industrializing*. New York, NY: Oxford University Press.

Andrews, David M. 1994. "Capital Mobility and State Autonomy: Toward a Structural Theory of International Monetary Relations." *International Studies Quarterly* 38(2): 193–218.

Angkinand, Apanard P., Wanvimol Sawangngoenyuang, and Clas Wihlborg. 2010. "Financial Liberalization and Banking Crises: A Cross-Country Analysis." *International Review of Finance* 10(2): 263–92.

Antoni, Elisabetta De. 2006. "Minsky on Financial Instability." Pp. 154–71 in *A Handbook of Alternative Monetary Economics*, edited by Philip Arestis and Malcolm Sawyer. Cheltenham, UK: Edward Elgar.

Arancibia, Patricia Clavel. 2006. *Cita con la historia*. Santiago, Chile: Editorial Biblioteca Americana.

Arize, Augustine C., Thomas Osang, and Daniel J. Slottje. 2008. "Exchange-rate Volatility in Latin America and Its Impact on Foreign Trade." *International Review of Economics and Finance* 17(1): 33–44.

Armijo, Leslie Elliott. 1999. "Balance Sheet or Ballot Box? Incentives to Privatize in Emerging Democracies." Pp. 161–202 in *Markets and Democracy in Latin America: Conflict or Convergence?*, edited by Philip Oxhorn and Pamela K. Starr. Boulder, CO: Lynne Rienner.

——— and Philippe Faucher. 2002. "'We Have A Consensus': Explaining Political Support for Market Reforms in Latin America." *Latin American Politics and Society* 44(2): 1–40.

Arnold, Caroline E. 2012. "In the Service of Industrialization: Etatism, Social Services and the Construction of Industrial Labour Forces in Turkey (1930–50)." *Middle Eastern Studies* 48(3): 363–85.

Arthur, W. Brian. 1994. *Increasing Returns and Path Dependence in the Economy*. Ann Arbor, MI: University of Michigan Press.

Arıcanlı, Tosun. 1990. "The Political Economy of Turkey's External Debt: The Bearing of Exogenous Factors." Pp. 230–53 in *The Political Economy of Turkey: Debt, Adjustment and Sustainability*, edited by Tosun Arıcanlı and Dani Rodrik. London, UK: MacMillan.

Aspromourgos, Tony. 1986. "On the Origins of the Term 'Neoclassical'." *Cambridge Journal of Economics* 10(3): 265–70.

Atılgan, Gökhan. 2015a. "Sanayi Kapitalizminin Şafağında." Pp. 521–662 in *Osmanlı'dan Günümüze Türkiye'de Siyasal Hayat*, edited by Gökhan Atılgan, Cenk Saraçoğlu, and Ateş Uslu. İstanbul, Turkey: Yordam Kitap.

———. 2015b. "Tarımsal Kapitalizmin Sancağı Altında." Pp. 393–520 in *Osmanlı'dan Günümüze Türkiye'de Siyasal Hayat*, edited by Gökhan Atılgan, Cenk Saraçoğlu, and Ateş Uslu. İstanbul, Turkey: Yordam Kitap.

Babb, Sarah. 2013. "The Washington Consensus as Transnational Policy Paradigm: Its Origins, Trajectory and Likely Successor." *Review of International Political Economy* 20(2): 268–97.

Balkan, Erol and Erinç Yeldan. 1998. "Turkey." Pp. 129–55 in *Financial Reform in Developing Countries*, edited by Jose Fanelli and Rohinton Medhora. New York, NY: St. Martin's Press.

Baltra, Alberto Cortés. 1973. *La gestión económica del gobierno de la Unidad Popular*. Santiago, Chile: Editorial Orbe.

Ban, Sung Hwan, Pal Yong Moon, and Dwight H. Perkins. 1980. *Rural Development*. Cambridge, MA: Harvard University Press.

Bank of Korea. 1996. *The Financial System in Korea*. Seoul, Korea: The Bank of Korea.

Barandiarán, Edgardo and Leonardo Hernández. 1999. "Origins and Resolution of Banking Crisis: Chile 1982–86." *Central Bank of Chile Working Papers* 57.

Barro, Robert J. and Xavier Sala-i-Martin. 2004. *Economic Growth*. Cambridge, MA: MIT Press.

Barros, Robert. 2002. *Constitutionalism and Dictatorship: Pinochet, the Junta, and the 1980 Constitution*. New York, NY: Cambridge University Press.

Bartolini, Leonardo and Allan Drazen. 1997. "Capital-Account Liberalization as a Signal." *American Economic Review* 87(1): 138–54.

Bauer, Arnold J. 1975. *Chilean Rural Society from the Spanish Conquest to 1930*. Cambridge, MA: Cambridge University Press.

Bayar, Ali H. 1996. "The Developmental State and Economic Policy in Turkey." *Third World Quarterly* 17(4): 773–86.

Becker, Gary. 1976. *The Economic Approach to Human Behavior*. Chicago, IL: University of Chicago Press.

Beckert, Jens. 2011. "Where Do Prices Come from? Sociological Approaches to Price Formation." *Socio-Economic Review* 9(4): 757–86.

Bedeski, Robert E. 1994. *The Transformation of South Korea: Reform and Reconstitution in the Sixth Republic under Roh Tae Woo, 1987–1992*. New York, NY: Routledge.

Bennett, Andrew. 2010. "Process Tracing and Causal Inference." Pp. 207–19 in *Rethinking Social Inquiry: Diverse Tools, Shared Standards*, edited by Henry E. Brady and David Collier. Plymouth, UK: Rowman & Littlefield.

Berger, Peter L. and Thomas Luckmann. 1967. *The Social Construction of Reality: A Treatise in the Sociology of Knowledge*. New York, NY: Anchor Books.

Berman, Sheri. 1998. *The Social Democratic Moment: Ideas and Politics in the Making of Interwar Europe*. Cambridge, MA: Harvard University Press.

Bernanke, Ben S. 1993. "The World on a Cross of Gold: A Review of 'Golden Fetters: The Gold Standard and the Great Depression, 1919–1939'." *Journal of Monetary Economics* 31: 251–67.

Bertocco, Giancarlo. 2008. "Finance and Development: Is Schumpeter's Analysis Still Relevant?" *Journal of Banking and Finance* 32(6): 1161–75.

Bhaduri, Amit and Stephen Marglin. 1990. "Unemployment and the Real Wage: The Economic Basis for Contesting Political Ideologies." *Cambridge Journal of Economics* 14(4): 375–93.

Bharadwaj, Krishna. 1986. *Classical Political Economy and Rise to Dominance of Supply and Demand Theories*. 2. rev. ed., London, UK: Sangam Books.

Birtek, Faruk. 1985. "The Rise and Fall of Etatism in Turkey, 1932–1950: The Uncertain Road in the Restructuring of a Semiperipheral Economy." *Review (Fernand Braudel Center)* 8(3): 407–38.

Black, Stanley, Charis Christofides, and Alex Mourmouras. 2006. "Convertibility Risk: The Precautionary Demand for Foreign Currency in a Crisis." *Annals of Finance* 2(2): 141–65.

Blaug, Mark. 1997. *Economic Theory in Retrospect*. Cambridge, UK: Cambridge University Press.

Block, Fred. 2001. "Introduction." Pp. xviii–xxxviii in *The Great Transformation: The Political and Economic Origins of Our Time by Karl Polanyi*, edited by Karl Polanyi. Boston, MA: Beacon Press.

Block, Fred L. 1977. *The Origins of International Economic Disorder: A Study of United States International Monetary Policy from World War II to the Present.* Berkeley, CA: University of California Press.

——— and Margaret R. Somers. 2014. *The Power of Market Fundamentalism: Karl Polanyi's Critique.* Cambridge, MA: Harvard University Press.

Blyth, Mark. 2002. *Great Transformations: Economic Ideas and Institutional Change in the Twentieth Century.* New York, NY: Cambridge University Press.

———. 2007. "Powering, Puzzling, or Persuading? The Mechanisms of Building Institutional Orders." *International Studies Quarterly* 51(4): 761–77.

Boix, Carles. 2003. *Democracy and Redistribution.* New York, NY: Cambridge University Press.

Boratav, Korkut. 1981. "Kemalist Economic Policies and Étatism." Pp. 165–89 in *Atatürk: Founder of a Modern State*, edited by Ali Kazancıgil and Ergun Özbudun. London, UK: Hurst.

———. 1990. "Inter-Class and Intra-Class Relations of Distribution Under 'Structural Adjustment': Turkey During the 1980s." Pp. 199–229 in *The Political Economy of Turkey: Debt, Adjustment and Sustainability*, edited by Tosun Arıcanlı and Dani Rodrik. London, UK: MacMillan.

———. 2003. *Türkiye İktisat Tarihi: 1908–2002.* Ankara, Turkey: İmge.

———, A. Erinç Yeldan, and Ahmet H. Köse. 2001. "Turkey: Globalization, Distribution and Social Policy, 1980–1998." Pp. 317–63 in *External Liberalization, Economic Performance, and Social Policy*, edited by Lance Taylor. New York, NY: Oxford University Press.

Bosworth, Barry P. 1993. *Saving and Investment in a Global Economy.* Washington, DC: The Brookings Institution.

———, Susan M. Collins, and Carmen M. Reinhart. 1999. "Capital Flows to Developing Economies: Implications for Saving and Investment." *Brookings Papers on Economic Activity* 1999: 143–80.

Boylan, Delia M. 1996. "Taxation and Transition: The Politics of the 1990 Chilean Tax Reform." *Latin American Research Review* 36(1): 7–31.

Brenner, Neil, Jamie Peck, and Nik Theodore. 2010. "Variegated Neoliberalization: Geographies, Modalities, Pathways." *Global Networks* 10(2): 182–222.

Brenner, Robert. 2002. *The Boom and the Bubble.* New York, NY: Verso.

Bridges, Brian. 2001. *Korea After the Crash: The Politics of Economic Recovery.* New York, NY: Routledge.

Brooks, Sarah M. 2004. "Explaining Capital Account Liberalization in Latin America: A Transitional Cost Approach." *World Politics* 56(3): 389–430.

——— and Marcus J. Kurtz. 2012. "Paths to Financial Policy Diffusion: Statist Legacies in Latin America's Globalization." *International Organization* 66(1): 95–128.

Brown, Jonathan C. 2010. *A Brief History of Argentina.* 2nd ed., New York, NY: Facts On File.

Bruton, Henry J. 1998. "A Reconsideration of Import Substitution." *Journal of Economic Literature* 36(2): 903–36.

Budnevich, Carlos L. and Rodrigo S. Cifuentes. 1993. "Manejo macroeconómico de los flujos de capitales de corto plazo: la experiencia de Chile." *Colección Estudios CIEPLAN* 38: 27–58.

Bulutoğlu, Kenan. 1970. *100 Soruda Türkiye'de Yabancı Sermaye.* İstanbul, Turkey: Gerçek.

Bumann, Silke, Niels Hermes, and Robert Lensink. 2013. "Financial liberalization and economic growth: A meta-analysis." *Journal of International Money and Finance* 33: 255–81.

Bussiere, Matthieu and Marcel Fratzscher. 2008. "Financial Openness and Growth: Short-run Gain, Long-run Pain?" *Review of International Economics* 16(1): 69–95.

Buzo, Adrian. 2002. *The Making of Modern Korea*. New York, NY: Routledge.

Çalışkan, Koray. 2010. *Market Threads: How Cotton Farmers and Traders Create a Global Commodity*. Princeton, NJ: Princeton University Press.

Calvo, Guillermo A., Alejandro Izquierdo, and Ernesto Talvi. 2006. "Sudden Stops and Phoenix Miracles in Emerging Markets." *American Economic Review* 96(2): 405–10.

———, Leonardo Leiderman, and Carmen M. Reinhart. 1994. "The Capital Inflows Problem: Concepts and Issues." *Contemporary Economic Policy* 12(3): 54–66.

———, ———, and ———. 1996. "Inflows of Capital to Developing Countries in the 1990s." *Journal of Economic Perspectives* 10(2): 123–39.

Campbell, John L. 1998. "Institutional Analysis and the Role of Ideas in Political Economy." *Theory and Society* 27(3): 377–409.

———. 2002. "Ideas, Politics, and Public Policy." *Annual Review of Sociology* 28: 21–38.

Carranza, Mario E. 2005. "Poster Child or Victim of Imperialist Globalization? Explaining Argentina's December 2001 Political Crisis and Economic Collapse." *Latin American Perspectives* 32(6): 65–89.

Cecco, Marcello De. 1996. "Short-Term Capital Movements Under the Gold Standard." Pp. 102–11 in *Currency Convertibility: The Gold Standard and beyond*, edited by Jorge Braga De Macedo, Barry Eichengreen, and Jaime Reis. New York, NY: Routledge.

Cha, Myung Soo and Nak Nyeon Kim. 2006. "Korea's First Industrial Revolution, 1911–40." *Naksungdae Institute of Economic Research Working Paper 2006-3.*

Chang, Ha-Joon. 1993. "The Political Economy of Industrial Policy in Korea." *Cambridge Journal of Economics* 17(2): 131–57.

Chang, Ha-Joon, Hong-Jae Park, and Chul Gyue Yoo. 1998. "Interpreting the Korean Crisis: Financial Liberalisation, Industrial Policy and Corporate Governance." *Cambridge Journal of Economics* 22: 735–46.

Cheng, Tun-jen and Yun-han Chu. 2002. "State-Business Relations in South Korea and Taiwan." Pp. 31–62 in *Emerging Market Democracies*, edited by Laurence Whitehead. Baltimore, MD: Johns Hopkins University Press.

———, Stephen Haggard, and David Kang. 1999. "Institutions and Growth in Korea and Taiwan: The Bureaucracy." Pp. 87–111 in *East Asian Development: New Perspectives*, edited by Yılmaz Akyüz. New York, NY: Routledge.

Chibber, Vivek. 1999. "Building a Developmental State: The Korean Case Reconsidered." *Politics & Society* 27(3): 309–46.

———. 2003. *Locked in Place: State-Building and Late Industrialization in India*. Princeton, NJ: Princeton University Press.

Chinn, Menzie D. and Hiro Ito. 2008. "A New Measure of Financial Openness." *Journal of Comparative Policy Analysis: Research and Practice* 10: 309–22.

Cho, Lee-Jay and Yoon Hyung Kim. 1991. "Political and Economic Antecedents to the 1960s." Pp. 3–13 in *Economic Development in the Republic of Korea: A Policy Perspective*, edited by Lee-Jay Cho and Yoon Hyung Kim. Honolulu, HI: University of Hawaii Press.

Cho, Yoon Je. 1989. "Finance and Development: The Korean Approach." *Oxford Review of Economic Policy* 5(4): 88–102.

———. 2001. “The Role of Poorly Phased Liberalization in Korea’s Financial Crisis.” Pp. 159–87 in *Financial Liberalization: How Far, How Fast?*, edited by Gerard Caprio, Patrick Honohan, and Joseph E. Stiglitz. New York, NY: Cambridge University Press.

———. 2002. “Financial Repression, Liberalization, Crisis and Restructuring: Lessons of Korea’s Financial Sector Policies.” *ADB Institute Research Paper Series No. 47.*

———. 2003. “The Political Economy of Financial Reform and the Crisis in South Korea.” Pp. 82–103 in *Financial Liberalization and the Economic Crisis in Asia*, edited by Chung H. Lee. New York, NY: Routledge.

Choe, Chongwoo and Imad A. Moosa. 1999. “Financial System and Economic Growth: The Korean Experience.” *World Development* 27(6): 1069–82.

Choi, Byung-Sun. 1993. “Financial Policy and Big Business in Korea: The Perils of Financial Regulation.” Pp. 23–54 in *The Politics of Finance in Developing Countries*, edited by Stephan Haggard, Chung H. Lee, and Sylvia Maxfield. Ithaca, NY: Cornell University Press.

Choi, Jin-Wook. 2002. “Regulatory Forbearance and Financial Crisis in South Korea.” *Asian Survey* 42(2): 251–75.

Chorev, Nitsan. 2010. “On the Origins of Neoliberalism: Political Shifts and Analytical Challenges.” Pp. 127–44 in *Handbook of Politics*, edited by Kevin T. Leicht and J. Craig Jenkins. New York, NY: Springer.

——— and Sarah Babb. 2009. “The Crisis of Neoliberalism and the Future of International Institutions: A Comparison of the IMF and the WTO.” *Theory and Society* 38(5): 459–84.

Chung, Un-Chan. 2004. “The Korean Economy Before and After the Crisis.” Pp. 25–47 in *The Korean Economy Beyond the Crisis*, edited by Duck-Koo Chung and Barry Eichengreen. Cheltenham, UK: Edward Elgar.

Chung, Young-Iob. 2006. *Korea Under Siege, 1876–1945: Capital Formation and Economic Transformation*. New York, NY: Oxford University Press.

———. 2007. *South Korea in the Fast Lane: Economic Development and Capital Formation*. New York, NY: Oxford University Press.

Chwieroth, Jeffrey M. 2007. “Neoliberal Economists and Capital Account Liberalization in Emerging Markets.” *International Organization* 61: 443–63.

———. 2008. “Normative Change from Within: The International Monetary Fund’s Approach to Capital Account Liberalization.” *International Studies Quarterly* 52(1): 129–58.

———. 2010a. *Capital Ideas: The IMF and the Rise of Financial Liberalization*. Princeton, NJ: Princeton University Press.

———. 2010b. “How Do Crises Lead to Change? Liberalizing Capital Controls in the Early Years of New Order Indonesia.” *World Politics* 62(3): 496–527.

Chwieroth, Jeffrey M. and Timothy J. Sinclair. 2013. “How You Stand Depends on How We See: International Capital Mobility as Social Fact.” *Review of International Political Economy* 20(3): 457–85.

Cizre-Sakallıoğlu, Ümit and Erinç Yeldan. 2000. “Politics, Society and Financial Liberalization: Turkey in the 1990s.” *Development and Change* 31: 481–508.

Claessens, Stijn, Simeon Djankov, and Larry Lang. 1998. “East Asian Corporates: Growth, Financing and Risks over the Last Decade.” *World Bank Policy Research Working Paper* 2017.

Cohen, Benjamin J. 1996. “Phoenix Risen: The Resurrection of Global Finance.” *World Politics* 48(2): 268–96.

Çölaşan, Emin. 1984. *12 Eylül: Özal Ekonomisinin Perde Arkası*. İstanbul, Turkey: Milliyet Yayınları.

Cole, David C. and Yung Chul Park. 1983. *Financial Development in Korea, 1945–1978*. Cambridge, MA: Harvard University Press.

Collier, Simon and William F. Sater. 2004. *A History of Chile, 1808–2002*. Cambridge, MA: Cambridge University Press.

Conde, Roberto Cortés. 2009. *The Political Economy of Argentina in the Twentieth Century*. New York, NY: Cambridge University Press.

Cooper, Richard. 1968. *The Economics of Interdependence: Economic Policy in the Atlantic Community*. New York, NY: McGraw-Hill.

Corbo, Vittorio. 1985. "Reforms and Macroeconomic Adjustments in Chile During 1974–1984." *World Development* 13(8): 893–916.

Corrales, Javier. 1998. "Coalitions and Corporate Choices in Argentina, 1976–1994: The Recent Private Sector Support of Privatization." *Studies in Comparative International Development* 32(4): 24–51.

Correa, Sofía Sutil, Consuelo Garavagno Figueroa, Alfredo Letelier Jocelyn-Holt, Claudio Cruz Rolle, and Manuel Urrutia Vicuña. 2001. *Historia del siglo XX chileno*. Santiago, Chile: Editorial Sudamericana.

Cowan, Kevin and José De Gregorio. 2007. "International Borrowing, Capital Controls, and the Exchange Rate: Lessons from Chile." Pp. 241–96 in *Capital Controls and Capital Flows in Emerging Economies: Policies, Practices, and Consequences*, edited by Sebastian Edwards. Chicago, IL: University of Chicago Press.

Cristi, Renato. 2000. *El pensamiento político de Jaime Guzmán: Autoridad y libertad*. Santiago, Chile: LOM Ediciones.

Cumings, Bruce. 1981. *The Origins of the Korean War, v. 1: Liberation and the Emergence of Separate Regimes, 1945–1947*. Princeton, NJ: Princeton University Press.

———. 1984a. "The Legacy of Japanese Colonialism in Korea." Pp. 478–96 in *The Japanese Colonial Empire, 1895–1945*, edited by Ramon H. Myers and Mark R. Peattie. Princeton, NJ: Princeton University Press.

———. 1984b. "The Origins and Development of the Northeast Asian Political Economy: Industrial Sectors, Product Cycles, and Political Consequences." *International Organization* 38(1): 1–40.

———. 1990. *The Origins of the Korean War, v. 2: The Roaring of the Cataract, 1947–1950*. Princeton, NJ: Princeton University Press.

———. 2005. *Korea's Place in the Sun: A Modern History*. New York, NY: W. W. Norton.

Dale, Gareth. 2010. *Karl Polanyi: The Limits of the Market*. Cambridge, England: Polity Press.

———. 2016. *Karl Polanyi: A Life on the Left*. New York, NY: Columbia University Press.

Dalla, Ismail. 2002. "Korea: Bond Market in Transition." Pp. 305–26 in *Restructuring the Korean Financial Market in a Global Economy*, edited by Lee-Jay Cho, Yoon Hyung Kim, and Inseok Shin. Seoul, Korea: Korea Development Institute.

——— and Deena Khatkhate. 1995. "Regulated Deregulation of the Financial System in Korea." *World Bank Discussion Paper no. 292.*

Danto, A. C. 1966. "The Historical Individual." Pp. 265–96 in *Philosophical Analysis and History*, edited by William H. Dray. New York, NY: Harper & Row.

David, Antonio C. 2007. "Revisiting Price-based Controls on Capital Inflows in a 'Sophisticated' Emerging Market." *World Development* 35(8): 1329–40.

De Gregorio, José, Sebastian Edwards, and Rodrigo O. Valdes. 2000. "Controls on Capital Inflows: Do They Work?" *Journal of Development Economics* 63(1): 59–83.

de Ramón, Armando. 2001. *Breve historia de Chile: Desde la invasión hasta nuestros días, (1500–2000)*. Buenos Aires, Argentina: Editorial Biblos.

De Vylder, Stefan. 1976. *Allende's Chile: The Political Economy of the Rise and Fall of the Unidad Popular.* New York, NY: Cambridge University Press.

Délano, Manuel and Hugo Traslaviña. 1989. *La herencia de los Chicago boys*. Santiago, Chile: Ornitorrinco.

Demerath, N. J. III. 1996. "Who Now Debates Functionalism? From 'System, Change and Conflict' to 'Culture, Choice, and Praxis'." *Sociological Forum* 11(2): 333–45.

Demetriades, Panicos O. and Kul B. Luintel. 2001. "Financial Restraints in the South Korean Miracle." *Journal of Development Economics* 64(2): 459–79.

Demir, Fırat. 2004. "A Failure Story: Politics and Financial Liberalization in Turkey, Revisiting the Revolving Door Hypothesis." *World Development* 32(5): 851–69.

Deyo, Frederic C. 1989a. *Beneath the Miracle: Labor Subordination in the New Asian Industrialism*. Berkeley, CA: University of California Press.

———. 1989b. "Labor and Development Policy in East Asia." *Annals of the American Academy of Political and Social Science* 505: 152–61.

Diaz-Alejandro, Carlos. 1985. "Good-bye Financial Repression, Hello Financial Crash." *Journal of Development Economics* 19(1): 1–24.

DiMaggio, Paul. 1988. "Interest and Agency in Institutional Theory." Pp. 3–21 in *Institutional Patterns and Organizations: Culture and Environment*, edited by Lynne G. Zucker. Cambridge, MA: Ballinger.

Dobbin, Frank, Beth A. Simmons, and Geoffrey Garrett. 2007. "Global Diffusion of Public Policies: Social Construction, Coercion, Competition, or Learning?" *Annual Review of Sociology* 33: 449–72.

Doğru, Osman. 1998. *27 Mayıs Rejimi*. İstanbul, Turkey: İmge.

Doğruel, Fatma and A. Suut Doğruel. 2005. *Türkiye'de Enflasyonun Tarihi*. Ankara, Turkey: TCMB.

Dooley, Michael P. 1996. "A Survey of Literature on Controls Over International Capital Transactions." *IMF Staff Papers* 43(4): 639–87.

——— and Inseok Shin. 2000. "Private Inflows When Crises Are Anticipated: A Case Study of Korea." *NBER Working Paper 7992.*

Dorner, Peter. 1992. *Latin American Land Reforms in Theory and Practice: A Retrospective Analysis.* Madison, WI: University of Wisconsin Press.

Douglas, Mary. 1986. *How Institutions Think*. Syracuse, NY: Syracuse University Press.

Drake, Paul W. and Iván Jaksić. 1995. "Introduction: Transformation and Transition in Chile." Pp. 1–17 in *The Struggle for Democracy in Chile*, edited by Paul W. Drake and Iván Jaksić. Lincoln, NE: University of Nebraska Press.

Eatwell, John and Lance Taylor. 2000. *Global Finance at Risk: The Case for International Regulation*. New York, NY: The New Press.

Edwards, Sebastian. 2004. "Financial Openness, Sudden Stops, and Current-Account Reversals." *American Economic Review* 94(2): 59–64.

——— and Alejandra Edwards Cox. 1987. *Monetarism and Liberalization: The Chilean Experiment*. Cambridge, MA: Ballinger.

Eğilmez, Mahfi. 2001. *Light Günlük*. İstanbul, Turkey: OM Yayınevi.

Eichengreen, Barry and Marc Flandreau. 1996. "The Geography of the Gold Standard." Pp. 113–55 in *Currency Convertibility: The Gold Standard and Beyond*, edited by Jorge Braga De Macedo, Barry Eichengreen, and Jaime Reis. New York, NY: Routledge.

Eichengreen, Barry J. 1996. *Globalizing Capital: A History of the International Monetary System*. Princeton, NJ: Princeton University Press.

———. 2003a. *Capital Flows and Crises.* Cambridge, MA: MIT Press.

———. 2003b. "Three Generations of Crises, Three Generations of Crisis Models: Regional and International Implications of the Financial Instability in Latin America." *Journal of International Money and Finance* 22(7): 1089–94.

——— and Ricardo Hausmann. 2005. "Introduction: Debt Denomination and Financial Instability in Emerging Market Economies." Pp. 3–12 in *Other People's Money: Debt Denomination and Financial Instability in Emerging Market Economies*, edited by Barry J. Eichengreen and Ricardo Hausmann. Chicago, IL: University of Chicago Press.

Eisenstadt, S. N. 1981. "The Kemalist Revolution in Comparative Perspective." Pp. 127–42 in *Atatürk: Founder of a Modern State*, edited by Ali Kazancıgil and Ergun Özbudun. London, UK: Hurst.

Ergüder, Üstün. 1991. "The Motherland Party, 1983–1989." Pp. 152–69 in *Political Parties and Democracy in Turkey*, edited by Metin Heper and Jacob M. Landau. London, UK: I. B. Tauris.

Ersel, Hasan. 1996. "The Timing of Capital Account Liberalization: The Turkish Experience." *New Perspectives on Turkey* 15: 45–64.

Ertuğrul, Ahmet and Faruk Selçuk. 2001. "A Brief Account of the Turkish Economy, 1980–2000." *Russian and East European Finance and Trade* 37(6): 6–30.

Esin, Numan. 2005. *Devrim ve Demokrasi: Bir 27 Mayısçının Anıları.* İstanbul, Turkey: Doğan.

Evans, Peter B. 1992. "The State as Problem and Solution: Predation, Embedded Autonomy, and Structural Change." Pp. 139–81 in *The Politics of Economic Adjustment: International Constraints, Distributive Conflicts, and the State*, edited by Stephan Haggard, Robert R. Kaufman, and Miles Kahler. Princeton, NJ: Princeton University Press.

———. 1995. *Embedded Autonomy: States and Industrial Transformation.* Princeton, NJ: Princeton University Press.

Evin, Ahmet. 1994. "Demilitarization and Civilianization of the Regime." Pp. 23–40 in *Politics in the Third Turkish Republic*, edited by Metin Heper and Ahmet Evin. Boulder, CO: Westview Press.

Fausten, Dietrich K. 1979. "The Humean Origin of the Contemporary Monetary Approach to the Balance of Payments." *Quarterly Journal of Economics* 93(4): 655–73.

Fernández, Andrés, Michael W. Klein, Alessandro Rebucci, Martin Schindler, and Martín Uribe. 2015. "Capital Control Measures: A New Dataset." *National Bureau of Economic Research Working Paper Series* 20970.

Ffrench-Davis, Ricardo. 1983. "The Monetarist Experiment in Chile: A Critical Survey." *World Development* 11(11): 905–26.

———. 1999. *Macroeconomía, comercio y finanzas para reformar las reformas en América Latina.* Santiago, Chile: McGraw-Hill Interamericana.

———. 2002. *Economic Reforms in Chile: From Dictatorship to Democracy.* Ann Arbor, MI: University of Michigan Press.

——— and Heriberto Tapia. 2001. "Three Varieties of Capital Surge Management in Chile." Pp. 65–106 in *Financial Crises in "Successful" Emerging Economies*, edited by Ricardo Ffrench-Davis. Washington, DC: Brookings Institution Press.

———, Manuel Agosin, and Andreas Uthoff. 1995. "Capital Movements, Export Strategy, and Macroeconomic Stability in Chile." Pp. 99–144 in *Coping with Capital Surges: The Return of Finance to Latin America*, edited by Ricardo Ffrench-Davis and Stephany Griffith-Jones. Boulder, CO: Lynne Riener.

Flandreau, Marc and Clemens Jobst. 2005. "The Ties That Divide: A Network Analysis of the International Monetary System, 1890–1910." *Journal of Economic History* 65: 977–1007.

Fleming, Marcus J. 1962. "Domestic Financial Policies under Fixed and Flexible Exchange Rates." *IMF Staff Papers* 9(3): 369–79.

Foley, Duncan K. and Thomas R. Michl. 1999. *Growth and Distribution*. Cambridge, MA: Harvard University Press.

Fontaine, Arturo Aldunate. 1988. *Los economistas y el presidente Pinochet*. Santiago, Chile: Editorial Zig-Zag.

Fontaine, Juan Andrés. 1991. "La administración de la política monetaria en Chile, 1985–1999." *Cuadernos de Economía* 83: 109–29.

Forbes, Kristin J. and Francis E. Warnock. 2012. "Capital Flow Waves: Surges, Stops, Flight, and Retrenchment." *Journal of International Economics* 88(2): 235–51.

Fortín, Carlos. 1989. "The Political Economy of Repressive Monetarism." Pp. 139–209 in *The State and Capital Accumulation in Latin America, vol. 1: Brazil, Chile, Mexico*, edited by Christian Anglade and Carlos Fortín. London, UK: Macmillan.

Fourcade-Gourinchas, Marion and Sarah L. Babb. 2002. "The Rebirth of the Liberal Creed: Paths to Neoliberalism in Four Countries." *American Journal of Sociology* 108(3): 533–79.

Foxley, Alejandro Rioseco. 1983. *Latin American Experiments in Neoconservative Economics*. Berkeley, CA: University of California Press.

———. 1993. *La economía política de la transición: El camino del dialogo*. Santiago, Chile: Ediciones Dolmen.

Frank, Volker. 2002. "The Elusive Goal in Democratic Chile: Reforming the Pinochet Labor Legislation." *Latin American Politics and Society* 44(1): 35–68.

Frenkel, Jacob A. and Assaf Razin. 1987. "The Mundell-Fleming Model A Quarter Century Later: A Unified Exposition." *IMF Staff Papers* 34(4): 567–620.

Frieden, Jeffry A. 1991a. *Debt, Development, and Democracy: Modern Political Economy and Latin America, 1965–1985*. Princeton, NJ: Princeton University Press.

———. 1991b. "Invested Interests: The Politics of National Economic Policies in a World of Global Finance." *International Organization* 45(4): 425–51.

———. 2006. *Global Capitalism: Its Fall and Rise in the Twentieth Century*. New York, NY: Norton.

Friedman, Milton. 1968. "The Role of Monetary Policy." *American Economic Review* 58(1): 1–17.

———. 1970. "The Counter-Revolution in Monetary Theory." *Institute of Economic Affairs Occasional Papers* 33: 1–14.

——— and Anna J. Schwartz. 1963. *A Monetary History of the United States, 1867–1960*. Princeton, NJ: Princeton University Press.

Fry, Maxwell J. 1972. *Finance and Development Planning in Turkey*. Leiden, Netherlands: E. J. Brill.

Garegnani, P. 1984. "Value and Distribution in the Classical Economists and Marx." *Oxford Economic Papers* 36(2): 291–325.

Garréton, Manuel Antonio M. 2001. "Popular Mobilization and the Military Regime in Chile: The Complexities of the Invisible Transition." Pp. 259–77 in *Power and Popular Protest: Latin American Social Movements*, edited by Susan Eckstein. Berkeley, CA: University of California Press.

Geddes, Barbara. 2003. *Paradigms and Sand Castles: Theory Building and Research Design in Comparative Politics*. Ann Arbor, MI: University of Michigan Press.

Geertz, Clifford. 1973. *The Interpretation of Cultures.* New York, NY: Basic Books.

Gemici, Kurtuluş. 2012. "Social Origins of Financial Crises." Pp. 25–42 in *A Tale of Two Crises*, edited by Kallidaikurichi Seetharam. New York, NY: Routledge.

———. 2015. "The Neoclassical Origins of Polanyi's Self-Regulating Market." *Sociological Theory* 33(2): 125–47.

———. 2016. "Beyond the Minsky and Polanyi Moments: Social Origins of the Foreclosure Crisis." *Politics & Society* 44(1): 15–43.

George, Alexander L. and Andrew Bennett. 2007. *Case Studies and Theory Development in the Social Sciences.* Cambridge, MA: MIT Press.

Germann, Julian. 2013. "State-Led or Capital-Driven? The Fall of Bretton Woods and the German Currency Float Reconsidered." *New Political Economy* 19(5): 769–89.

Gerschenkron, Alexander. 1962. *Economic Backwardness in Historical Perspective: A Book of Essays.* Cambridge, MA: Harvard University Press.

Giddens, Anthony. 1984. *The Constitution of Society.* Cambridge, UK: Polity.

Goldfajn, Ilan and André Minella. 2005. "Capital Flows and Controls in Brazil: What Have We Learned?" *NBER Working Paper No. 11640.*

Goldstein, Judith and Robert O. Keohane. 1993. "Ideas and Foreign Policy: An Analytical Framework." Pp. 3–30 in *Ideas and Foreign Policy: Beliefs, Institutions, and Policy Change*, edited by Judith Goldstein and Robert O. Keohane. Ithaca, NY: Cornell University Press.

Goldstone, Jack A. 2004. "Response: Reasoning about History, Sociologically..." *Sociological Methodology* 34(1): 35–61.

Grabel, Ilene. 1996. "Marketing the Third World: The Contradictions of Portfolio Investment in the Global Economy." *World Development* 24(11): 1761–76.

Gross, Neil. 2009. "A Pragmatist Theory of Social Mechanisms." *American Sociological Review* 74(3): 358–79.

Haas, Peter M. 1992. "Epistemic Communities and International Policy Coordination." *International Organization* 46(1): 1–35.

Haggard, Stephan. 1994a. "From the Heavy Industry Plan to Stabilization: Macroeconomic Policy, 1976–1980." Pp. 49–74 in *Macroeconomic Policy and Adjustment in Korea, 1970–1990*, edited by Stephan Haggard, Richard N. Cooper, Susan Collins, Chongsoo Kim, and Sung-Tae Ro. Cambridge, MA: Harvard University Press.

———. 1994b. "Macroeconomic Policy through the First Oil Shock, 1970–1975." Pp. 23–47 in *Macroeconomic Policy and Adjustment in Korea, 1970–1990*, edited by Stephan Haggard, Richard N. Cooper, Susan Collins, Chongsoo Kim, and Sung-Tae Ro. Cambridge, MA: Harvard University Press.

———. 2000. *The Political Economy of the Asian Financial Crisis.* Washington, DC: Institute for International Economics.

——— and Chung-In Moon. 1993. "The State, Politics, and Economic Development in Postwar South Korea." Pp. 51–93 in *State and Society in Contemporary Korea*, edited by Hagen Koo. Ithaca, NY: Cornell University Press.

———, Byung kook Kim, and Chung-in Moon. 1991. "The Transition to Export-led Growth in South Korea: 1954–1966." *Journal of Asian Studies* 50(4): 850–73.

———, David Kang, and Chung-In Moon. 1997. "Japanese Colonialism and Korean Development: A Critique." *World Development* 25(6): 867–81.

Hale, William M. 1980. "Ideology and Economic Development in Turkey 1930–1945." *Bulletin (British Society for Middle Eastern Studies)* 7(2): 100–17.

———. 1981. *The Political and Economic Development of Modern Turkey.* New York, NY: St. Martin's Press.

———. 1988. "Transition to Civilian Governments in Turkey: The Military Perspective." Pp. 159–75 in *State, Democracy and the Military: Turkey in the 1980s*, edited by Metin Heper and Ahmet Evin. New York, NY: Walter de Gruyter.

Hall, Peter A. 1989. "Introduction." Pp. 3–26 in *The Political Power of Economic Ideas: Keynesianism across Nations*, edited by Peter A. Hall. Princeton, NJ: Princeton University Press.

———. 1993. "Policy Paradigms, Social Learning, and the State: The Case of Economic Policymaking in Britain." *Comparative Politics* 25(3): 275–96.

Hamilton, Earl. 1934. *American Treasure and the Price Revolution in Spain, 1501–1650.* Cambridge, MA: Harvard University Press.

Harberger, Arnold C. 1985. "Observations on the Chilean Economy, 1973–1983." *Economic Development and Cultural Change* 33(3): 451–62.

Harvey, David. 2005. *A Brief History of Neoliberalism.* New York, NY: Oxford University Press.

Hedges, Jill. 2011. *Argentina: A Modern History.* London, UK: I.B. Tauris.

Held, Günther and Luis Felipe Jiménez. 2001. "Liberalización, crisis y reforma del sistema bancario: 1974–99." Pp. 133–70 in *Reformas, crecimiento y políticas sociales en Chile desde 1973*, edited by Ricardo Ffrench-Davis and Barbara Stallings. Santiago, Chile: LOM Ediciones.

Helleiner, Eric. 1994. *States and the Reemergence of Global Finance: From Bretton Woods to the 1990s.* Ithaca, NY: Cornell University Press.

Heper, Metin. 1991. "Interest Group Politics in Post-1980 Turkey: Lingering Monism." Pp. 163–76 in *Strong State and Economic Interest Groups: The Post-1980 Turkish Experience*, edited by Metin Heper. New York, NY: Walter de Gruyter.

——— and E. Fuat Keyman. 1998. "Double-Faced State: Political Patronage and the Consolidation of Democracy in Turkey." *Middle Eastern Studies* 34(4): 259–77.

Hershlag, Zvi Yehuda. 1968. *Turkey: The Challenge of Growth.* Leiden, Netherlands: E. J. Brill.

———. 1988. *The Contemporary Turkish Economy.* New York, NY: Routledge.

Hinings, C. R. and Royston Greenwood. 2015. "Missing in Action: The Further Contribution of Philip Selznick to Contemporary Institutional Theory." Pp. 121–48 in *Institutions and Ideals: Philip Selznick's Legacy for Organizational Studies*, edited by Matthew S. Kraatz. Bingley, UK: Emerald.

Hirschman, Albert O. 1968. "The Political Economy of Import-Substituting Industrialization in Latin America." *Quarterly Journal of Economics* 82(1): 1–32.

———. 1980. *National Power and the Structure of Foreign Trade.* Berkeley, CA: University of California Press.

Hoogvelt, Ankie. 1997. *Globalization and the Postcolonial World: The New Political Economy of Development.* Baltimore, MD: Johns Hopkins University Press.

Howarth, David and Tal Sadeh. 2011. "In the Vanguard of Globalization: The OECD and International Capital Liberalization." *Review of International Political Economy* 18(5): 622–45.

Huber, Evelyne and John D. Stephens. 2001. *Development and Crisis of the Welfare State: Parties and Policies in Global Markets.* Chicago, IL: University of Chicago Press.

Hundt, David. 2009. *Korea's Developmental Alliance: State, Capital and the Politics of Rapid Development.* London, UK: Routledge.

Huneeus, Carlos. 1998. "Technocrats and Politicians in the Democratic Politics of Argentina, (1983–95)." Pp. 177–95 in *The Politics of Expertise in Latin America*, edited by Miguel A. Centeno and Patricio Silva. London, UK: Palgrave Macmillan.

———. 2000. "Technocrats and Politicians in an Authoritarian Regime. The 'ODEPLAN Boys' and the 'Gremialists' in Pinochet's Chile." *Journal of Latin American Studies* 32(2): 461–501.

———. 2007. *The Pinochet Regime*. London, UK: Lynne Riener.

Hung, Ho-fung and Daniel Thompson. 2016. "Money Supply, Class Power, and Inflation: Monetarism Reassessed." *American Sociological Review* 81(3): 447–66.

Im, Hyug Baeg. 1987. "The Rise of Bureaucratic Authoritarianism in South Korea." *World Politics* 39(2): 231–57.

İstanbul Stock Exchange. 1999. *Turkish Financial History From the Ottoman Empire to the Present, vol. II: From the Foundation of the Republic to the Present*. İstanbul, Turkey: İstanbul Stock Exchange.

Jeanne, Olivier. 2007. "International Reserves in Emerging Market Countries: Too Much of a Good Thing?" *Brookings Papers on Economic Activity* 2007: 1–79.

Jeon, Jei Guk. 1994. "The Political Economy of Crisis Management in the Third World: A Comparative Study of South Korea and Taiwan (1970s)." *Pacific Affairs* 67(4): 565–85.

Jeon, Yoong-Deok and Young-Yong Kim. 2000. "Land Reform, Income Redistribution, and Agricultural Production in Korea." *Economic Development and Cultural Change* 48(2): 253–68.

Johnson, Harry G. 1977. "The Monetary Approach to Balance of Payments Theory and Policy: Explanation and Policy Implications." *Economica* 44(175): 217–29.

Johnston, Barry R., Salim M. Darbar, and Claudia Echeverria. 1997. "Sequencing Capital Account Liberalization: Lessons from the Experiences of Chile, Indonesia, Korea, and Thailand." *IMF Working Paper 97-157.*

Jones, Leroy P. and Il SaKong. 1980. *Government, Business, and Entrepreneurship in Economic Development: The Korean Case*. Cambridge, MA: Harvard University Press.

Jones, Ronald W. 1971. "A Three-Factor Model in Theory, Trade, and History." Pp. 3–21 in *Trade, Balance of Payments, and Growth: Papers in International Economics in Honor of Charles P. Kindleberger*, edited by Jagdish Bhagwati, Ronald W. Jones, Robert A. Mundell, and Jaroslav Vanek. Amsterdam, The Netherlands: North-Holland.

Jwa, Sung-Hee. 2002. *The Evolution of Large Corporations in Korea: A New Institutional Economics Perspective of the Chaebol*. Cheltenham, UK: Edward Elgar.

Kalaycıoğlu, Ersin. 2002. "Elections and Governance." Pp. 55–71 in *Politics, Parties, and Elections in Turkey*, edited by Sabri Sayarı and Yılmaz Esmer. London, UK: Lynne Rienner.

Kaminsky, Graciela L. and Carmen M. Reinhart. 1999. "The Twin Crises: The Causes of Banking and Balance-Of-Payments Problems." *American Economic Review* 89(3): 473–500.

——— and Sergio L. Schmukler. 2003. "Short-Run Pain, Long-Run Gain: The Effects of Financial Liberalization." *IMF Working Paper* 03/34.

——— and———. 2008. "Short-Run Pain, Long-Run Gain: The Effects of Financial Liberalization." *Review of Finance* 12: 253–92.

Kang, C. S. Eliot. 2000. "*Segyehwa* Reform of the South Korean Developmental State." Pp. 76–101 in *Korea's Globalization*, edited by Samuel S. Kim. New York, NY: Cambridge University Press.

Kang, David C. 2002. *Crony Capitalism: Corruption and Development in South Korea and the Philippines*. New York, NY: Cambridge University Press.

Kang, Man-gil. 2005. *A History of Contemporary Korea*. Kent, UK: Global Oriental.

Kansu, Günal. 2004. *Planlı Yıllar*. İstanbul, Turkey: İş Bankası Kültür Yayınları.

Karcher, Sebastian and David A. Steinberg. 2013. "Assessing the Causes of Capital Account Liberalization: How Measurement Matters." *International Studies Quarterly* 57(1): 128–37.

Karpat, Kemal H. 1959. *Turkey's Politics: The Transition to a Multi-Party System*. Princeton, NJ: Princeton University Press.

———. 1970. "The Military and Politics in Turkey, 1960–64: A Socio-Cultural Analysis of a Revolution." *American Historical Review* 75(6): 1654.

———. 1988. "Military Interventions: Army-Civilian Relations in Turkey Before and After 1980." Pp. 137–58 in *State, Democracy and the Military: Turkey in the 1980s*, edited by Metin Heper and Ahmet Evin. New York, NY: Walter de Gruyter.

Kaufman, Robert R. 1972. *Politics of Land Reform in Chile, 1950–1970: Public Policy, Political Institutions, and Social Change*. Cambridge, MA: Harvard University Press.

———. 1979. "Industrial Change and Authoritarian Rule in Latin America: A Concrete Review of the Bureaucratic-Authoritarian Model." Pp. 165–255 in *The New Authoritarianism in Latin America*, edited by David Collier. Princeton, NJ: Princeton University Press.

Kay, Cristóbal. 2002. "Why East Asia Overtook Latin America: Agrarian Reform, Industrialisation and Development." *Third World Quarterly* 23(6): 1073–102.

Kazdağlı, Hasan. 2001. "Özal'ın İktisadi Reformları." in *Kim Bu Özal? Siyaset, İktisat, Zihniyet*, edited by İhsan Sezal and İhsan Dağı. İstanbul, Turkey: Boyut.

Kazgan, Gülten. 2005. *Türkiye Ekonomisinde Krizler (1929–2001)*. İstanbul, Turkey: Bilgi Üniversitesi Yayınları.

Kelley, Jonathan and M.D.R. Evans. 1995. "Class and Class Conflict in Six Western Nations." *American Sociological Review* 60(2): 157–78.

Kepenek, Yakup and Nurhan Yentürk. 2000. *Türkiye Ekonomisi*. İstanbul, Turkey: Remzi Kitabevi.

Keyder, Çağlar. 1987. *State and Class in Turkey: A Study in Capitalist Development*. Guildford, UK: Verso.

Keynes, John Maynard. 1936. *The General Theory of Employment, Interest, and Money*. New York, NY: Harcourt, Inc.

Kil, Soong Hoom. 2001. "Development of Korean Politics: A Historical Profile." Pp. 33–69 in *Understanding Korean Politics: An Introduction*, edited by Soong Hoom Kil and Chung-in Moon. Albany, NY: State University of New York Press.

Kim, Byung-Kook and Hyug-Baeg Im. 2001. "'Crony Capitalism' in South Korea, Thailand and Taiwan: Myth and Reality." *Journal of East Asian Studies* 1(1): 5–52.

Kim, C. I. Eugene. 1972. "The Meaning of the 1971 Korean Elections: A Pattern of Political Development." *Asian Survey* 12(3): 213–24.

Kim, Eun Mee. 1988. "From Dominance to Symbiosis: State and Chaebol in Korea." *Pacific Focus* 3(2): 105–21.

Kim, Kwang Suk. 1991. "The 1964–65 Exchange Rate Reform, Export-Promotion Measures, and Import-Liberalization Program." Pp. 101–34 in *Economic Development in the Republic of Korea: A Policy Perspective*, edited by Lee-Jay Cho and Yoon Hyung Kim. Honolulu, HI: University of Hawaii Press.

Kim, Se Jin. 1970. "South Korea's Involvement in Vietnam and Its Economic and Political Impact." *Asian Survey* 10(6): 519–32.

Kim, Soyoung, Sunghyun H. Kim, and Yunjong Wang. 2001. *Capital Account Liberalization and Macroeconomic Performance: The Case of Korea*. Seoul, Korea: Korea Institute for International Economic Policy.

Kim, Yoon Hyung. 1994. "An Introduction to the Korean Model of Political Economy." Pp. 45–62 in *Korea's Political Economy: An Institutional Perspective*, edited by Lee-Jay Cho and Yoon Hyung Kim. Boulder, CO: Westview.

Kimball, Jeffrey. 2006. "The Nixon Doctrine: A Saga of Misunderstanding." *Presidential Studies Quarterly* 36(1): 59–74.

Kindleberger, Charles P. 2000. *Manias, Panics, and Crashes: A History of Financial Crises.* New York, NY: Wiley.

Kıray, Emine. 1990. "Turkish Debt and Conditionality in Historical Perspective: A Comparison of the 1980s with the 1860s." Pp. 254–68 in *The Political Economy of Turkey: Debt, Adjustment and Sustainability*, edited by Tosun Arıcanlı and Dani Rodrik. London, UK: MacMillan.

Kishi, Masumi. 1998. "Korean Financial System Reform: Shifts in Modes of Large-Scale Production and Related Issues." *Journal of Asian Economics* 9(1): 103–18.

Kiyota, Kozo. 2014. "Industrial Upgrading in a Multiple-cone Heckscher–Ohlin Model: The Flying Geese Patterns of Industrial Development." *Review of Development Economics* 18(1): 177–93.

Knight, Jack. 1992. *Institutions and Social Conflict.* New York, NY: Cambridge University Press.

Kogut, Bruce and J. Muir Macpherson. 2011. "The Mobility of Economists and the Diffusion of Policy Ideas: The Influence of Economics on National Policies." *Research Policy* 40(10): 1307–20.

Kohli, Atul. 1994. "Where Do High Growth Political Economies Come From? The Japanese Lineage of Korea's 'Developmental State'." *World Development* 22(9): 1269–93.

———. 1997. "Japanese Colonialism and Korean Development: A Reply." *World Development* 25(6): 883–88.

———. 2004. *State-Directed Development: Political Power and Industrialization in the Global Periphery.* New York, NY: Cambridge University Press.

Kojima, Kiyoshi. 2000. "The 'Flying Geese' Model of Asian Economic Development: Origin, Theoretical Extensions, and Regional Policy Implications." *Journal of Asian Economics* 11(4): 375–401.

Koo, Hagan. 1990. "From Farm to Factory: Proletarianization in Korea." *American Sociological Review* 55(5): 669–81.

Koo, Hagen. 2001. *Korean Workers: The Culture and Politics of Class Formation.* Ithaca, NY: Cornell University Press.

Korpi, Walter. 1980. "Social Policy and Distributional Conflict in the Capitalist Democracies: A Preliminary Comparative Framework." *West European Politics* 3(3): 296–316.

Köse, Ayhan, Eswar S. Prasad, Kenneth Rogoff, and Shang-Jin Wei. 2009. "Financial Globalization: A Reappraisal." *IMF Staff Papers* 56(1): 8–62.

Krause, Lawrence B. 1997. "The Political Economy of South Korea: Fifty Years of Macroeconomic Management, 1945–1995." Pp. 101–42 in *The Korean Economy 1945–1995: Performance and Vision for the 21st Century*, edited by Dong-Se Cha, Kwang Suk Kim, and Dwight H. Perkins. Seoul, Korea: Korea Development Institute.

Krippner, Greta R. 2005. "The Financialization of the American Economy." *Socio-Economic Review* 3: 173–208.

———. 2011. *Capitalizing on Crisis: The Political Origins of the Rise of Finance.* Cambridge, MA: Harvard University Press.

Kristal, Tali. 2010. "Good Times, Bad Times: Postwar Labor's Share of National Income in Capitalist Democracies." *American Sociological Review* 75(5): 729–63.

Krueger, Anne O. 1974. "The Political Economy of the Rent-Seeking Society." *American Economic Review* 64(3): 291–303.

———. 1979. *The Development of the Foreign Sector and Aid.* Cambridge, MA: Harvard University Press.

———. 1997. "Korean Industry and Trade over Fifty Years." Pp. 293–338 in *The Korean Economy 1945–1995: Performance and Vision for the 21st Century*, edited by Dong-Se Cha, Kwang Suk Kim, and Dwight H. Perkins. Seoul, Korea: Korea Development Institute.

Krugman, Paul R. 1979. "A Model of Balance-of-Payments Crises." *Journal of Money, Credit and Banking* 11(3): 311–25.

——— and Maurice Obstfeld. 2000. *International Economics Theory and Policy.* Reading, MA: Addison-Wesley.

———, ed. 2000. *Currency Crises.* Chicago, IL: University of Chicago Press.

Kurtz, Marcus J. 1999. "Chile's Neo-Liberal Revolution: Incremental Decisions and Structural Transformation, 1973–89." *Journal of Latin American Studies* 31(2): 399–427.

Kuznets, Paul W. 1994. *Korean Economic Development: An Interpretive Model.* London, UK: Praeger.

Labán, Raúl and Felipe B. Larraín. 1994. "The Chilean Experience with Capital Mobility." Pp. 117–63 in *The Chilean Economy: Policy Lessons and Challenges*, edited by Barry P. Bosworth, Rudiger Dornbusch, and Raúl Labán. Chicago, IL: University of Chicago Press.

——— and ———. 1995. "Continuity, Change, and the Political Economy of Transition in Chile." Pp. 115–48 in *Reform, Recovery, and Growth: Latin American and the Middle East*, edited by Rudiger Dornbusch and Sebastian Edwards. Chicago, IL: University of Chicago Press.

——— and ———. 2000. "Private Capital Flows to Chile in the 1990s: Causes, Effects, and Policy Reactions." Pp. 223–50 in *Capital Flows, Capital Controls, and Currency Crises: Latin America in the 1990s*, edited by Felipe B. Larraín. Ann Arbor, MI: University of Michigan Press.

Lake, David A. 2009. "Open Economy Politics: A Critical Review." *Review of International Organizations* 4(3): 219–44.

Landsberger, Henry A. and Tim McDaniel. 1976. "Hypermobilization in Chile, 1970–1973." *World Politics* 28(4): 502–41.

Lane, Philip R. and Gian Maria Milesi-Ferretti. 2007. "The External Wealth of Nations Mark II: Revised and Extended Estimates of Foreign Assets and Liabilities, 1970–2004." *Journal of International Economics* 73(2): 223–50.

Larraín, Felipe B. and Rodrigo M. Vergara. 2000. "Un cuarto de siglo de reformas fiscales." Pp. 71–109 in *La transformación económica de Chile*, edited by Felipe B. Larraín and Rodrigo M. Vergara. Santiago, Chile: Centro de Estudios Públicos.

Laurens, Bernard. 2000. "Chile's Experiences with Controls on Capital Inflows in the 1990s." Pp. 69–79 in *Capital Controls: Country Experiences with Their Use and Liberalization*, edited by Akira Ariyoshi. Washington, DC: IMF.

Lawson, Tony. 2013. "What Is This 'School' Called Neoclassical Economics?" *Cambridge Journal of Economics* 37(5): 947–83.

Lee, Chong-Sik. 1980. "South Korea 1979: Confrontation, Assassination, and Transition." *Asian Survey* 20(1): 63–76.

———. 1981. "South Korea in 1980: The Emergence of a New Authoritarian Order." *Asian Survey* 21(1): 125–43.

Lee, Chung H., Keun Lee, and Kangkook Lee. 2002. "Chaebols, Financial Liberalization and Economic Crisis: Transformation of Quasi-Internal Organization in Korea." *Asian Economic Journal* 16(1): 17–35.

Lee, Keun, Byung-Kook Kim, Chung H. Lee, and Jaeyeol Yee. 2005. "Visible Success and Invisible Failure in Post-Crisis Reform in the Republic of Korea: Interplay of Global Standards, Agents, and Local Specificity." *World Bank Policy Research Working Paper 3651*.

Lee, Suk-Chae. 1991. "The Heavy and Chemical Industries Promotion Plan (1973–79)." Pp. 431–71 in *Economic Development in the Republic of Korea: A Policy Perspective*, edited by Lee-Jay Cho and Yoon Hyung Kim. Honolulu, HI: University of Hawaii Press.

Lepage, Henri. 1978. *Demain le capitalisme*. Paris, France: Livre de Poche.

Lewis, Colin M. 2002. *Argentina: A Short History*. Oxford, UK: Oneworld.

Lie, John. 1998. *Han Unbound: The Political Economy of South Korea*. Stanford, CA: Stanford University Press.

Lim, Timothy C. 1999. "The Origins of Societal Power in South Korea: Understanding the Physical and Human Legacies of Japanese Colonialism." *Modern Asian Studies* 33(3): 603–33.

Loveman, Brian. 1995. "The Transition to Civilian Government in Chile, 1990–1994." Pp. 305–37 in *The Struggle for Democracy in Chile*, edited by Paul W. Drake and Iván Jaksić. Lincoln, NE: University of Nebraska Press.

Lucas, Robert E., Jr. 1990. "Why Doesn't Capital Flow from Rich to Poor Countries?" *American Economic Review* 80: 92–96.

Lukauskas, Arvid and Susan Minushkin. 2000. "Explaining Styles of Financial Market Opening in Chile, Mexico, South Korea, and Turkey." *International Studies Quarterly* 44: 695–723.

MacDonald, Scott B. and Georges A. Fauriol. 1997. *Fast Forward: Latin America on the Edge of the 21st Century*. New Brunswick, NJ: Transaction Publishers.

Mackie, John L. 1965. "Causes and Conditions." *American Philosophical Quarterly* 2(4): 245–64.

Mahner, Martin and Mario Bunge. 2001. "Function and Functionalism: A Synthetic Perspective." *Philosophy of Science* 68(1): 75–94.

Mahoney, J. 2008. "Toward a Unified Theory of Causality." *Comparative Political Studies* 41(4–5): 412–36.

Mahoney, James. 2012. "The Logic of Process Tracing Tests in the Social Sciences." *Sociological Methods & Research* 41(4): 570–97.

——— and Kathleen Thelen. 2010. "A Theory of Gradual Institutional Change." Pp. 1–37 in *Explaining Institutional Change: Ambiguity, Agency, and Power*, edited by James Mahoney and Kathleen Thelen. New York, NY: Cambridge University Press.

Mamalakis, Markos J. 1976. *The Growth and Structure of the Chilean Economy: From Independence to Allende*. New Haven, CT: Yale University Press.

Mann, Michael. 1970. "The Social Cohesion of Liberal Democracy." *American Sociological Review* 35(3): 423–39.

———. 1973. *Consciousness and Action Among the Western Working Class*. London, UK: MacMillan.

———. 1986. *The Sources of Social Power, Volume I: A History of Power from the Beginning to A.D. 1760*. New York, NY: Cambridge University Press.

———. 1993. *The Sources of Social Power, Volume II: The Rise of Classes and Nation-States, 1760–1914*. New York, NY: Cambridge University Press.

———. 2012. *The Sources of Social Power, Vol 4: Globalizations.* New York, NY: Cambridge University Press.

——— and Dylan Riley. 2007. "Explaining Macro-Regional Trends in Global Income Inequalities, 1950–2000." *Socio-Economic Review* 5(1): 81–115.

Marcel, Mario. 1997. "Políticas públicas en democracia: El caso de la reforma tributaria de 1990 en Chile." *Colección Estudios CIEPLAN* 45: 33–83.

——— and Andrés Solimano. 1994. "The Distribution of Income and Economic Adjustment." Pp. 217–55 in *The Chilean Economy: Policy Lessons and Challenges*, edited by Barry P. Bosworth, Rudiger Dornbusch, and Raúl Labán. Washington, DC: The Brookings Institution.

Marchionatti, Roberto. 2001. "Sraffa and the Criticism of Marshall in the 1920s." in *Piero Sraffa's Political Economy: A Centenary Estimate*, edited by Terenzio Cozzi and Roberto Marchionatti. London, UK: Routledge.

Marquetti, Adalmir A. 2003. "Analyzing Historical and Regional Patterns of Technical Change from a Classical-Marxian Perspective." *Journal of Economic Behavior & Organization* 52(2): 191–200.

Marshall, Alfred. 2013 [1920]. *Principles of Economics.* 8th ed., New York, NY: Palgrave Macmillan.

Marshall, Gordon, David Rose, Carolyn Vogler, and Howard Newby. 1985. "Class, Citizenship, and Distributional Conflict in Modern Britain." *British Journal of Sociology* 36: 259–84.

Martin, Isaac William. 2008. *The Permanent Tax Revolt: How the Property Tax Transformed American Politics.* Stanford, CA: Stanford University Press.

Martínez, Javier and Alvaro Díaz. 1996. *Chile: The Great Transformation.* Washington, DC: The Brookings Institution.

Marx, Karl. 1978. "The German Ideology." Pp. 146–200 in *The Marx-Engels Reader*, edited by Robert C. Tucker. New York, NY: Norton.

———. 1990 [1876]. *Capital, vol. I: A Critique of Political Economy.* Penguin.

———. 1993 [1939]. *Grundrisse: Foundations of the Critique of Political Economy.* London, UK: Penguin Books.

Mason, Edward S., Mahn Je Kim, Dwight H. Perkins, Kwang Suk Kim, and David C. Cole. 1980. *The Economic and Social Modernization of the Republic of Korea.* Cambridge, MA: Harvard University Press.

Mayer, Wolfgang. 1974. "Short-Run and Long-Run Equilibrium for a Small Open Economy." *Journal of Political Economy* 82(5): 955–67.

Mayorga, Roberto Lorca and Fernando Artaza Alvear. 1992. "La inversión extranjera en Chile: D.L. 600, Capitulo XIX." Pp. 61–68 in *La transformación económica de Chile*, edited by Julio Cordua Dittborn. Santiago, Chile: Universidad Nacional Andrés Bello.

McNamara, Dennis L. 1990. *The Colonial Origins of Korean Enterprise, 1910–1945.* New York, NY: Cambridge University Press.

Meek, Ronald L. 1956. *Studies in the Labor Theory of Value.* New York, NY: Monthly Review Press.

Meller, Patricio. 1991. "Adjustment and Social Costs in Chile During the 1980s." *World Development* 19(11): 1545–61.

———. 1996. *Un siglo de economía política chilena (1890–1990).* Santiago, Chile: Editorial Andres Bello.

Mert, Nuray. 2007. *Merkez Sağın Kısa Tarihi.* İstanbul, Turkey: Selis.

Meseguer, Covadonga. 2005. "Policy Learning, Policy Diffusion, and the Making of a New Order." *Annals of the American Academy of Political and Social Science* 598(1): 67–82.

———. 2009. *Learning, Policy Making, and Market Reforms.* New York, NY: Cambridge University Press.

——— and Fabrizio Gilardi. 2009. "What Is New in the Study of Policy Diffusion?" *Review of International Political Economy* 16(3): 527–43.

Miniane, Jacques. 2004. "A New Set of Measures on Capital Account Restrictions." *IMF Staff Papers* 52(2): 276–308.

Minsky, Hyman P. 1982. "The Financial-Instability Hypothesis: Capitalist Processes and the Behavior of the Economy." Pp. 3–47 in *Financial Crises: Theory, History, Policy*, edited by Charles P. Kindleberger and Jean-Pierre Laffargue. Cambridge, UK: Cambridge University Press.

———. 2008 [1986]. *Stabilizing an Unstable Economy.* New York, NY: McGraw-Hill.

Mitchell, C. Clyde. 1949. "Land Reform in South Korea." *Pacific Affairs* 22(2): 144–54.

Mizala, Alejandra and Pilar Romaguera. 2001. "La legislación laboral y el mercado del trabajo: 1975–2000." Pp. 201–230 in *Reformas, crecimiento y políticas sociales en Chile desde 1973*, edited by Ricardo Ffrench-Davis and Barbara Stallings. Santiago, Chile: LOM Ediciones.

Mo, Jongryn. 2001. "Political Culture and Legislative Gridlock: Politics of Economic Reform in Precrisis Korea." *Comparative Political Studies* 34(5): 467–92.

Moguillansky, Graciela. 1999. *La inversión en Chile: ¿El fin de un ciclo de expansión?* Santiago, Chile: CEPAL.

Moon, Chung-in. 1994. "Changing Patterns of Business–Government Relations in South Korea." Pp. 142–66 in *Business and Government in Industrializing Asia*, edited by Andrew MacIntyre. Ithaca, NY: Cornell University Press.

Moon, Woo-Sik and Yeong-Seop Rhee. 2000. "Foreign Exchange Market Liberalization Policies in Korea: Past Assessment and Future Options." *Journal of International and Area Studies* 7(1): 59–79.

Morandé, Felipe G. 1992. "The Dynamics of Real Asset Prices, the Real Exchange Rate, Trade Reforms and Foreign Capital Inflows: Chile, 1976–1989." *Journal of Development Economics* 39(1): 111–39.

Moschella, Manuela. 2012. "Seeing Like the IMF on Capital Account Liberalisation." *New Political Economy* 17(1): 59–76.

Moulin, Hervé. 1991. *Axioms of Cooperative Decision Making.* Cambridge, MA: Cambridge University Press.

Mudge, Stephanie Lee. 2008. "What Is Neoliberalism?" *Socio-Economic Review* 6(4): 703–31.

Mukherjee, Bumba and David Andrew Singer. 2010. "International Institutions and Domestic Compensation: The IMF and the Politics of Capital Account Liberalization." *American Journal of Political Science* 54(1): 45–60.

Mundell, Robert A. 1960. "The Monetary Dynamics of International Adjustment under Fixed and Flexible Exchange Rates." *Quarterly Journal of Economics* 74(2): 227–57.

———. 1962. "The Appropriate Use of Monetary and Fiscal Policy for Internal and External Stability." *IMF Staff Papers* 9(1): 70–77.

———. 1963. "Capital Mobility and Stabilization Policy under Fixed and Flexible Exchange Rates." *Canadian Journal of Economics and Political Science* 29(4): 475–85.

Mussa, Michael. 1974. "Tariffs and the Distribution of Income: The Importance of Factor Specificity, Substitutability, and Intensity in the Short and Long Run." *Journal of Political Economy* 82(6): 1191–203.

Myers, Ramon H. and Saburō Yamada. 1984. "Agricultural Development in the Empire." Pp. 420–51 in *The Japanese Colonial Empire, 1895–1945*, edited by Ramon H. Myers and Mark R. Peattie. Princeton, NJ: Princeton University Press.

Nam, Sang-Woo. 1994. "Korea's Financial Reform since the Early 1980s." Pp. 184–222 in *Financial Reform: Theory and Experience*, edited by Gerard Jr. Caprio, Izak Atiyas, and James A. Hanson. New York, NY: Cambridge University Press.

Noland, Marcus. 2005. "South Korea's Experience with International Capital Flows." *Institute for International Economics Working Paper 05-4.*

North, Douglass C. 1990. *Institutions, Institutional Change, and Economic Performance.* Cambridge, NY: Cambridge University Press.

Nurkse, Ragnar. 1944. *International Currency Experience: Lessons of the Inter-War Period.* Geneva, Switzerland: League of Nations.

Oatley, Thomas. 2011. "The Reductionist Gamble: Open Economy Politics in the Global Economy." *International Organization* 65(2): 311–41.

Obstfeld, Maurice. 2000. "International Macroeconomics: Beyond the Mundell-Fleming Model." *IMF Staff Papers* 47: 1–39.

Obstfeld, Maurice. 2009. "International Finance and Growth in Developing Countries: What Have We Learned?" *IMF Staff Papers* 56(1): 63–111.

Obstfeld, Maurice and Alan M. Taylor. 2004. *Global Capital Markets: Integration, Crisis, and Growth.* Cambridge, UK: Cambridge University Press.

O'Donnell, Guillermo. 1978. "State and Alliances in Argentina, 1956–1976." *Journal of Development Studies* 15(1): 3–33.

Oh, Kie-chiang John. 1999. *Korean Politics: The Quest for Democratization and Economic Development.* Ithaca, NY: Cornell University Press.

Okyar, Osman. 1965. "The Concept of Étatism." *Economic Journal* 75(297): 98–111.

———. 1979. "Development Background of the Turkish Economy, 1923–1973." *International Journal of Middle East Studies* 10(3): 325–44.

Oppenheim, Lois Hecht. 2007. *Politics in Chile: Socialism, Authoritarianism, and Market Democracy.* Boulder, CO: Westview Press.

Osborne, Martin J. and Ariel Rubinstein. 1990. *Bargaining and Markets.* New York, NY: Academic Press.

——— and ———. 1994. *A Course in Game Theory.* Cambridge, MA: MIT Press.

Oxhorn, Philip D. 1995. *Organizing Civil Society: The Popular Sectors and the Struggle for Democracy in Chile.* University Park, PA: Pennsylvania State University Press.

Oyan, Oğuz. 1989. *Dışa Açılma ve Mali Politikalar, Türkiye: 1980–1989.* Ankara, Turkey: Verso.

Ozan, Ebru Deniz. 2015. "İki Darbe Arasında Kriz Sarmalı." Pp. 663–752 in *Osmanlı'dan Günümüze Türkiye'de Siyasal Hayat*, edited by Gökhan Atılgan, Cenk Saraçoğlu, and Ateş Uslu. İstanbul, Turkey: Yordam Kitap.

Öniş, Ziya. 1986. "Stabilization and Growth in a Semi-Industrial Economy: An Evaluation of the Recent Turkish Experiment, 1977–1984." *METU Studies in Development* 12(1–2): 7–28.

———. 1991. "Political Economy of Turkey in the 1980s: Anatomy of Unorthodox Liberalism." Pp. 27–40 in *Strong State and Economic Interest Groups: The Post-1980 Turkish Experience*, edited by Metin Heper. New York, NY: Walter De Gruyter.

———. 1993. "The Dynamics of Export Oriented Growth in a Second Generation NIC: Perspectives on the Turkish Case, 1980–1990." *New Perspectives on Turkey* 9: 75–100.

Özbudun, Ergun. 1991. "The Post-1980 Legal Framework for Interest Groups Associations." Pp. 41–53 in *Strong State and Economic Interest Groups: The Post-1980 Turkish Experience*, edited by Metin Heper. New York, NY: Walter de Gruyter.

Özdağ, Ümit. 2004. *Menderes Döneminde Ordu-Siyaset İlişkileri ve 27 Mayıs İhtilali*. İstanbul, Turkey: Boyut.

Pak, Ki Hyuk. 1956. "Outcome of Land Reform in the Republic of Korea." *Journal of Farm Economics* 38(4): 1015–23.

Pamuk, Şevket. 1984. "İthal İkamesi, Döviz Darboğazları ve Türkiye, 1947–1979." Pp. 36–68 in *Krizin Gelişimi ve Türkiye'nin Alternatif Sorunu*, edited by Korkut Boratav, Çağlar Keyder, and Şevket Pamuk. Ankara, Turkey: Kaynak Yayınları.

Park, Won-Am and Gongpil Choi. 2004. "What Caused the Crisis? A *Post Mortem*." Pp. 48–71 in *The Korean Economy Beyond the Crisis*, edited by Duck-Koo Chung and Barry Eichengreen. Cheltenham, UK: Edward Elgar.

Park, Yong Soo. 2011. "Revisiting the South Korean Developmental State after the 1997 Financial Crisis." *Australian Journal of International Affairs* 65(5): 590–606.

Park, Yung Chul. 1991. "The Development of Financial Institutions and the Role of Government in Credit Allocation." Pp. 45–72 in *Economic Development in the Republic of Korea: A Policy Perspective*, edited by Lee-Jay Cho and Yoon Hyung Kim. Honolulu, HI: University of Hawaii Press.

———. 1996. "The Republic of Korea's Experience with Managing Foreign Capital Inflows." Pp. 193–220 in *The Tobin Tax: Coping with Financial Volatility*, edited by Mahbub ul Haq, Inge Kaul, and Isabelle Grunberg. New York, NY: Oxford University Press.

———. 1998. "The Financial Crisis in Korea and Its Lessons for Reform of the International Financial System." Pp. 25–64 in *Regulatory and Supervisory Challenges in a New Era of Global Finance*, edited by Jan Joost Teunissen. The Hague, The Netherlands: FONDAD.

Pierson, Paul. 2000. "Increasing Returns, Path Dependence, and the Study of Politics." *American Political Science Review* 94(2): 251–67.

Piketty, Thomas. 2014. *Capital in the Twenty-First Century*. Cambridge, MA: Harvard University Press.

Polanyi, Karl. 1968. "Our Obsolete Market Mentality." Pp. 59–77 in *Primitive, Archaic, and Modern Economies: Essays of Karl Polanyi*, edited by George Dalton. New York, NY: Anchor Books.

———. 2001 [1944]. *The Great Transformation: The Political and Economic Origins of Our Time*. Boston, MA: Beacon Press.

Potchamanawong, Pariyate. "A New Measure of Capital Controls and Its Relation to Currency Crises." Dissertation, Claremont Graduate University, Claremont, CA, 2007.

Prasad, Eswar S., Raghuram G. Rajan, and Arvind Subramanian. 2007. "Foreign Capital and Economic Growth." *Brookings Papers on Economic Activity* 2007: 153–228.

Prasad, Monica. 2006. *The Politics of Free Markets: The Rise of Neoliberal Economic Policies in Britain, France, Germany, and the United States*. Chicago, IL: University of Chicago Press.

———. 2012. *The Land of Too Much: American Abundance and the Paradox of Poverty*. Cambridge, MA: Harvard University Press.

Przeworski, Adam and Michael Wallerstein. 1982. "The Structure of Class Conflict in Democratic Capitalist Societies." *American Political Science Review* 76(2): 215–38.

Quinn, Dennis, Martin Schindler, and A. Maria Toyoda. 2011. "Assessing Measures of Financial Openness and Integration." *IMF Economic Review* 59(3): 488–522.

Quinn, Dennis P. 1997. "The Correlates of Changes in International Financial Regulation." *American Political Science Review* 91(3): 531–51.

——— and A. Maria Toyoda. 2007. "Ideology and Voter Preferences as Determinants of Financial Globalization." *American Journal of Political Science* 51(2): 344–63.

Ramos, Joseph R. 1986. *Neoconservative Economics in the Southern Cone of Latin America, 1973–1983.* Baltimore, MD: Johns Hopkins University Press.

Rhee, T. C. 1973. "South Korea's Economic Development and Its Socio-Political Impact." *Asian Survey* 13(7): 677–90.

Riesco, Manuel. 1999. "Chile, A Quarter of Century On." *New Left Review* 238: 97–125.

Rodrik, Dani. 1996. "Understanding Economic Policy Reform." *Journal of Economic Literature* 34(1): 9–41.

———. 2006. "The Social Cost of Foreign Exchange Reserves." *NBER Working Paper No. 11952.*

Rodrik, Dani and Arvind Subramanian. 2009. "Why Did Financial Globalization Disappoint?" *IMF Staff Papers* 56(1): 112–38.

Rogowski, Ronald. 1989. *Commerce and Coalitions: How Trade Affects Domestic Political Alignments.* Princeton, NJ: Princeton University Press.

Romero, Luis Alberto. 2002. *A History of Argentina in the Twentieth Century.* University Park, PA: Pennsylvania State University Press.

Roncaglia, Alessandro. 2006. *A Wealth of Ideas: A History of Economic Thought.* Cambridge, UK: Cambridge University Press.

———. 2009. *Piero Sraffa: His Life, Thought and Cultural Heritage.* Basingstoke, UK: Palgrave Macmillan.

Rosenberg, Nathan. 1960. "Capital Formation in Underdeveloped Countries." *American Economic Review* 50(4): 706–15.

Rozas, Patricio and Gustavo Marín. 1989. *1988: El "mapa de la extrema riqueza", 10 años despues.* Santiago, Chile: Ediciones ChileAmérica CESOC.

Rueschemeyer, Dietrich and Theda Skocpol, eds. 1996. *States, Social Knowledge, and the Origins of Modern Social Policies.* Princeton, NJ: Princeton University Press.

Ruggie, John G. 1983. "International Regimes, Transactions, and Change: Embedded Liberalism in the Postwar Economic Order." Pp. 195–231 in *International Regimes,* edited by Stephen D. Krasner. Ithaca: Cornell University Press.

Sabine, George Holland. 1961. *A History of Political Theory.* 3rd ed., London, UK: George G. Harrap & Co.

Sachs, Jeffrey D. 1989. "Introduction." Pp. 1–33 in *Developing Country Debt and the World Economy,* edited by Jeffrey D. Sachs. Chicago, IL: University of Chicago Press.

SaKong, Il. 1993. *Korea in the World Economy.* Washington, DC: Institute for International Economics.

Samuelson, Paul A. 1971. "Ohlin Was Right." *Swedish Journal of Economics* 73(4): 365–84.

Sayarı, Sabri. 2002. "The Changing Party System." Pp. 9–32 in *Politics, Parties, and Elections in Turkey,* edited by Sabri Sayarı and Yılmaz Esmer. London, UK: Lynne Rienner.

Schneider, Cathy Lisa. 1995. *Shantytown Protest in Pinochet's Chile.* Philadelphia, PA: Temple University Press.

Schotter, Andrew. 2008 [1981]. *The Economic Theory of Social Institutions.* Cambridge, NY: Cambridge University Press.

Schumpeter, Joseph Alois. 1983. *The Theory of Economic Development: An Inquiry into Profits, Capital, Credit, Interest, and the Business Cycle.* New Brunswick, NJ: Transaction Books.

Selznick, Philip. 1949. *TVA and the Grass Roots: A Study in the Sociology of Formal Organization*. Berkeley, CA: University of California Press.

———. 1957. *Leadership in Administration: A Sociological Interpretation*. New York, NY: Harper & Row.

Shambaugh, George E. 2004. "The Power of Money: Global Capital and Policy Choices in Developing Countries." *American Journal of Political Science* 48(2): 281–95.

Shepsle, Kenneth A. 1989. "Studying Institutions: Some Lessons from the Rational Choice Approach." *Journal of Theoretical Politics* 1(2): 131–47.

Shin, Gi-Wook. 1998. "Agrarian Conflict and the Origins of Korean Capitalism." *American Journal of Sociology* 103(5): 1309–51.

Shin, Gi-Wook. 2003. "The Paradox of Korean Globalization." *Asia Pacific Research Center Working Paper.*

Shorrocks, Anthony F. 1983. "Ranking Income Distributions." *Economica* 50: 3–17.

Shorter, Edward and Charles Tilly. 1974. *Strikes in France: 1830–1968*. London, UK: Cambridge University Press.

Sikorski, Trevor M. 1996. *Financial Liberalization in Developing Countries*. Cheltenham, UK: Edward Elgar.

Silva, Eduardo. 1996. *The State and Capital In Chile: Business Elites, Technocrats, and Market Economics*. Boulder, CO: Westview Press.

Silva, Patricio. 1991. "Technocrats and Politics in Chile: From the Chicago Boys to the CIEPLAN Monks." *Journal of Latin American Studies* 23(2): 385–410.

Silver, Beverly J. 2003. *Forces of Labor: Workers' Movements and Globalization Since 1870*. New York, NY: Cambridge University Press.

Simmons, Beth A. and Zachary Elkins. 2004. "The Globalization of Liberalization: Policy Diffusion in the International Political Economy." *American Political Science Review* 98(1): 171–89.

———, Frank Dobbin, and Geoffrey Garrett. 2006. "Introduction: The International Diffusion of Liberalism." *International Organization* 60(4): 781–810.

Singer, Morris. 1977. *Economic Development in the Context of Short-Term Public Policies: The Economic Advance of Turkey, 1938–1960*. Ankara, Turkey: Turkish Economic Society.

Skocpol, Theda. 1979. *States and Social Revolutions: A Comparative Analysis of France, Russia, and China*. New York, NY: Cambridge University Press.

Smelser, Neil J. 1976. *Comparative Methods in the Social Sciences*. Englewood Cliffs, NJ: Prentice-Hall.

Smith, William C. 1990. "Democracy, Distributional Conflicts and Macroeconomic Policymaking in Argentina, 1983–89." *Journal of Interamerican Studies and World Affairs* 32(2): 1–42.

———. 1991. "State, Market and Neoliberalism in Post-Transition Argentina: The Menem Experiment." *Journal of Interamerican Studies and World Affairs* 33(4): 45–82.

Smithin, John. 2006. "The Theory of Interest Rates." Pp. 273–90 in *A Handbook of Alternative Monetary Economics*, edited by Philip Arestis and Malcolm Sawyer. Cheltenham, UK: Edward Elgar.

Somerville, Hernán Senn. 1992. "La renegociación de la deuda externa Chilena." Pp. 107–18 in *La transformación económica de Chile*, edited by Julio Cordua Dittborn. Santiago, Chile: Universidad Nacional Andrés Bello.

Song, Byung-Nak. 1997. *The Rise of the Korean Economy*. Hong Kong: Oxford University Press.

Soysal, Mümtaz. 1969. *Dinamik Anayasa Anlayışı: Anayasa Diyalektiği Üzerine Bir Deneme*. Ankara, Turkey: A.Ü. Siyasal Bilgiler Fakültesi.

Sraffa, Piero. 1926. "The Laws of Returns under Competitive Conditions." *Economic Journal* 36(144): 535–50.

———. 1960. *Production of Commodities by Means of Commodities: Prelude to a Critique of Economic Theory*. London, UK: Cambridge University Press.

Stallings, Barbara. 1978. *Class Conflict and Economic Development in Chile, 1958–1973*. Stanford, CA: Stanford University Press.

———. 1989. "Political Economy of Democratic Transition." Pp. 181–99 in *Debt and Democracy in Latin America*, edited by Barbara Stallings and Robert Kaufman. Boulder, CO: Westview Press.

———. 2001. "Las reformas estructurales y el desempeño socioeconómico." Pp. 23–60 in *Reformas, crecimiento y políticas sociales en Chile desde 1973*, edited by Ricardo Ffrench-Davis and Barbara Stallings. Santiago, Chile: LOM Ediciones.

Starr, Pamela K. 1997. "Government Coalitions and the Viability of Currency Boards: Argentina under the Cavallo Plan." *Journal of Interamerican Studies and World Affairs* 39(2): 83–133.

Stiglitz, Joseph E. 2000. "Capital Market Liberalization, Economic Growth and Instability." *World Development* 28(6): 1075–86.

———. 2004. "Capital-Market Liberalization, Globalization, and the IMF." *Oxford Review of Economic Policy* 20(1): 57–71.

Stinchcombe, Arthur. 1997. "On the Virtues of the Old Institutionalism." *Annual Review of Sociology* 23: 1–18.

Stinchcombe, Arthur L. 1968. *Constructing Social Theories*. New York, NY: Harcourt, Brace & World.

———. 1978. *Theoretical Methods in Social History*. New York, NY: Academic Press.

Streeck, Wolfgang and Kathleen Thelen. 2005. "Introduction." Pp. 1–39 in *Beyond Continuity: Institutional Change in Advanced Political Economies*, edited by Wolfgang Streeck and Kathleen Thelen. Oxford, UK: Oxford University Press.

Stubbs, Richard. 2009. "What Ever Happened to the East Asian Developmental State? The Unfolding Debate." *Pacific Review* 22(1): 1–22.

Sunar, İlkay. 1990. "Populism and Patronage: The Demokrat Party and Its Legacy in Turkey." *Il Politico* 55(4): 745–57.

Swidler, Ann. 1993. "Foreword." Pp. ix–xvii in *The Sociology of Religion by Max Weber*, edited by J. C. B. Mohr. Boston, MA: Beacon Press.

Tachau, Frank. 2002. "The Changing Party System." Pp. 33–54 in *Politics, Parties, and Elections in Turkey*, edited by Sabri Sayarı and Yılmaz Esmer. London, UK: Lynne Rienner.

Tanör, Bülent. 1969. *Siyasi Düşünce Hürriyeti ve 1961 Türk Anayasası*. İstanbul, Turkey: Öncü.

——— and Necmi Yüzbaşıoğlu. 2001. *1982 Anayasasına Göre Türk Anayasa Hukuku*. Cogito, İstanbul, Turkey: YKY.

Taylor, Lance. 1990. "Turkish Experience: Summary and Comparative Notes." Pp. 269–75 in *The Political Economy of Turkey: Debt, Adjustment and Sustainability*, edited by Tosun Arıcanlı and Dani Rodrik. London, UK: MacMillan.

Teichman, Judith. 1997. "Mexico and Argentina: Economic Reform and Technocratic Decision Making." *Studies in Comparative International Development* 32(1): 31–55.

Tekeli, İlhan and Selim İlkin. 2003. *Kadrocuları ve Kadro'yu Anlamak*. İstanbul, Turkey: Tarih Vakfi Yurt Yayınları.

Temel, Adil. 1998. *Gelişme Sürecinde Sektörel Yapıda Değişmeler: Imalat Sanayii ve Istihdam.* Ankara, Turkey: DPT.

Teubal, Miguel. 2004. "Rise and Collapse of Neoliberalism in Argentina The Role of Economic Groups." *Journal of Developing Societies* 20(3–4): 173–88.

The World Bank. 1982. *Turkey: Industrialization and Trade Strategy.* Washington, DC: The World Bank.

Thelen, Kathleen. 2012. "Varieties of Capitalism: Trajectories of Liberalization and the New Politics of Social Solidarity." *Annual Review of Political Science* 15(1): 137–59.

——— and Sven Steinmo. 1992. "Historical Institutionalism in Comparative Politics." Pp. 1–32 in *Structuring Politics: Historical Institutionalism in Comparative Analysis,* edited by Sven Steinmo, Kathleen Thelen, and Frank Longstreth. New York, NY: Cambridge University Press.

Thurbon, Elizabeth. 2001. "Two Paths to Financial Liberalization: South Korea and Taiwan." *Pacific Review* 14(1): 241–67.

Tilly, Charles. 1984. *Big Structures, Large Processes, Huge Comparisons.* New York, NY: Russell Sage Foundation.

Tobin, James. 1978. "A Proposal for International Monetary Reform." *Eastern Economic Journal* 4: 153–59.

———. 2000. "Financial Globalization." *World Development* 28(6): 1101–04.

Tolbert, Pamela S. and Lynne G. Zucker. 1996. "The Institutionalization of Institutional Theory." Pp. 175–90 in "Handbook of Organization Studies," London, UK: SAGE.

Toprak, Zafer. 2012. *Türkiye'de Milli Iktisat, 1908–1918.* Tarih, İstanbul, Turkey: Doğan Kitap.

Torche, Arístides L. 2000. "Pobreza, necesidades básicas y desigualdad: Tres objetivos para una sola política social." Pp. 543–603 in *La transformación económica de Chile,* edited by Felipe B. Larraín and Rodrigo M. Vergara. Santiago, Chile: Centro de Estudios Públicos.

Toye, John. 2003. "Changing Perspectives in Development Economics." Pp. 21–40 in *Rethinking Development Economics,* edited by Ha-Joon Chang. London, UK: Anthem Press.

Treisman, Daniel. 2004. "Stabilization Tactics in Latin America: Menem, Cardoso, and the Politics of Low Inflation." *Comparative Politics* 36(4): 399–419.

Türkeş, Mustafa. 2001. "A Patriotic Leftist Development-Strategy Proposal in Turkey in the 1930s: The Case of the Kadro (Cadre) Movement." *International Journal of Middle East Studies* 33(1): 91–114.

Turkish Statistical Institute. 2003. *Statistical Indicators, 1923–2002.* Ankara, Turkey: Turkish Statistical Institute.

Ulagay, Osman. 1988. *Özal'ı Aşmak İçin.* İstanbul, Turkey: AFA.

Valdés, Juan Gabriel. 1995. *Pinochet's Economists: The Chicago School in Chile.* New York, NY: Cambridge University Press.

Veigel, Klaus Friedrich. 2009. *Dictatorship, Democracy, and Globalization: Argentina and the Cost of Paralysis, 1973–2001.* University Park, PA: Pennsylvania State University Press.

Vergara, Pilar. 1985. *Auge y caída del neoliberalismo en Chile.* Santiago, Chile: FLACSO.

Vernengo, Matías. 2006. "Money and Inflation." Pp. 471–89 in *A Handbook of Alternative Monetary Economics,* edited by Philip Arestis and Malcolm Sawyer. Cheltenham, UK: Edward Elgar.

Vernon, Raymond. 1966. "International Investment and International Trade in the Product Cycle." *Quarterly Journal of Economics* 80(2): 190–207.

Vial, Joaquín. 1998. "La estrategia de desarrollo: crecimiento con equidad." Pp. 183–206 in *Chile en los noventa*, edited by Cristián Toloza and Eugenio Lahera. Santiago, Chile: Ediciones Dolmen.

Vilar, Pierre. 1974. *Or et monnaie dans l'histoire, 1450–1920*. Paris, France: Flammarion.

Vogel, Steven Kent. 1996. *Freer Markets, More Rules: Regulatory Reform in Advanced Industrial Countries*. Ithaca, NY: Cornell University Press.

Wade, Robert. 1990. *Governing the Market: Economic Theory and the Role of Government in East Asian Industrialization*. Princeton, NJ: Princeton University Press.

Walton, John and David Seddon. 1994. *Free Markets and Food Riots: The Politics of Global Adjustment*. Cambridge, MA: Blackwell.

Wandschneider, Kirsten. 2008. "Review of Monetary Theory and Bretton Woods: The Construction of an International Monetary Order by Filippo Cesarano." *Journal of Economic History* 68(1): 333–34.

Weber, Max. 1978. *Economy and Society: An Outline of Interpretive Sociology, Vol. I*. Berkeley, CA: University of California Press.

Weiker, Walter F. 1963. *The Turkish Revolution, 1960–61: Aspects of Military Politics*. Washington, DC: Brookings Institution Press.

———. 1981. *The Modernization of Turkey: From Ataturk to the Present Day*. New York, NY: Holmes & Meier.

Weir, Margaret and Theda Skocpol. 1985. "State Structures and Possibilities for 'Keynesian' Responses to the Great Depression in Sweden, Britain, and the United States." Pp. 107–63 in *Bringing the State Back In*, edited by Peter B. Evans, Dietrich Rueschemeyer, and Theda Skocpol. New York, NY: Cambridge University Press.

Weiss, Linda and John M. Hobson. 1995. *States and Economic Development: A Comparative Historical Analysis*. Cambridge, UK: Polity Press.

Weyland, Kurt. 1997. ""Growth with Equity" in Chile's New Democracy?" *Latin American Research Review* 32(1): 37–67.

———. 2007. "The Political Economy of Market Reform and a Revival of Structuralism." *Latin American Research Review* 42(3): 235–50.

Whang, In-Joung. 2001. "Administration of Land Reform in Korea, 1949–1952." Pp. 3–28 in *The Korean Economy: Reflections at the New Millennium*, edited by Korean National Commission for UNESCO. Elizabeth, NJ: Hollym.

Whitman, Marina V. N. 1975. "Global Monetarism and the Monetary Approach to the Balance of Payments." *Brookings Papers on Economic Activity* 1975(3): 491–555.

Widmaier, Wesley W., Mark Blyth, and Leonard Seabrooke. 2007. "Exogenous Shocks or Endogenous Constructions? The Meanings of Wars and Crises." *International Studies Quarterly* 51(4): 747–59.

Willett, Thomas D. 2000. *International Financial Markets as Sources of Crises or Discipline: The Too Much, Too Late Hypothesis*. Princeton, NJ: International Finance Section, Princeton University.

Williams, Mark Eric. 2002. "Market Reforms, Technocrats, and Institutional Innovation." *World Development* 30(3): 395–412.

Williamson, John and Molly Mahar. 1998. *A Survey of Financial Liberalization*. Princeton, NJ: Department of Economics, Princeton University.

Williamson, John, ed. 1994. *The Political Economy of Policy Reform*. Washington, DC: Institute for International Economics.

Woo-Cumings, Meredith. 1997. "Slouching toward the Market: The Politics of Financial Liberalization in South Korea." Pp. 57–91 in *Capital Ungoverned: Liberalizing Finance in Interventionist States*, edited by Michael Loriaux, Meredith Woo-Cumings, Kent E. Calder, Sylvia Maxfield, and Sofía A. Pérez. Ithaca, NY: Cornell University Press.

Woo, Jung-en. 1991. *Race to the Swift: State and Finance in Korean Industrialization*. New York, NY: Columbia University Press.

Woods, Ngaire. 2006. *The Globalizers: The IMF, the World Bank, and Their Borrowers.* Ithaca, NY: Cornell University Press.

Wright, Erik Olin. 1979. *Class Structure and Income Determination*. New York, NY: Academic Press.

———. 1996. *Class Counts: Comparative Studies in Class Analysis.* New York, NY: Cambridge University Press.

Yang, Jonghoe. 2004. "Colonial Legacy and Modern Economic Growth in Korea: A Critical Examination of Their Relationships." *Development and Society* 33(1): 1–24.

Yeldan, Erinç A. 2001. *Küreselleşme Sürecinde Türkiye Ekonomisi: Bölüşüm, Birikim ve Büyüme*. İstanbul, Turkey: İletişim Yayınları.

Yeşilada, Birol Ali. 1988. "Problems of Political Development in the Third Turkish Republic." *Polity* 21(2): 345–72.

Yiğit, Ahu. "Celal Bayar and Political Leadership, 1937–1960." PhD dissertation, Bilkent University, Ankara, Turkey, 2013.

Yoon, Sanghyun. 1996. "South Korea's Kim Young Sam Government: Political Agendas." *Asian Survey* 36(5): 511–22.

You, Jong-Il and Ju-Ho Lee. 2001. "South Korea: Economic and Social Consequences of Globalization." Pp. 283–315 in *External Liberalization, Economic Performance, and Social Policy*, edited by Lance Taylor. New York, NY: Oxford University Press.

Zucker, Lynne G. 1977. "The Role of Institutionalization in Cultural Persistence." *American Sociological Review* 42(5): 726–43.

———. 1988. "Where Do Institutional Patterns Come From? Organizations as Actors in Social Systems." Pp. 23–49 in *Institutional Patterns and Organizations: Culture and Environment*, edited by Lynne G. Zucker. Cambridge, MA: Ballinger.

Zürcher, Erik Jan. 2017. *Turkey: A Modern History.* 4 ed., New York, NY: I.B. Tauris.

Index